WE HAVE WRITTEN,

Mary Elizabeth Raina

A TRUE STORY OF TRIUMPH OVER TRAGEDY

MARY
ELIZABETH
RAINA

PRIVATE PUBLISHING, NEPEAN, ONTARIO

Out of deference to their descendants, the following names are substitutions for the real names of people appearing in the story, although the parts they played in the case remain factual:

Normand Bourque	Royal Renaud
Napoléon Doucet	Marcel Sarazin
Mathias Poirier	Claude Thérien

CANADIAN CATALOGUING IN PUBLICATION DATA

Raina, Mary Elizabeth, 1922-
We Have Written
ISBN 0-9695013-0-7

1. Raina, Dominic. 2. Raina, Elizabeth.
3. Saint-Marc-de-Figuery (Quebec)--History.
4. Saint-Marc-de-Figuery (Quebec)--Biography.
5. Catholic Church--Quebec-Saint-Marc-de-Figuery--
History-- 20th century. I. Title.

FC2945.S228Z48 1990   971.4'13   C91-090017-5
F1054.S32R35 1990

Cover design by Miriam Raina Rodgers

Printed and bound in Canada

Privately published by Mary Elizabeth Raina

ACKNOWLEDGEMENTS

I wish to express my deep appreciation to my husband, Ronald Frank Rodgers, for his understanding of my need to publish this story, and for his encouragement and support throughout; to my children — Randall, Miriam and Karen — my greatest fans; and to all those who, either through encouragement, constructive criticism, or in any other way assisted in bringing this book to its successful completion. Special thanks to my good friends, Frank and Lorraine Emmerson, who accorded me countless hours of hospitality in their home while Frank taught me the intricacies of his computor, so that I could put my story on a disk.

Mary Elizabeth Raina

To order copies write to:
Mary Elizabeth Raina
P.O. Box No. 78041
~~Shoppers Drug Mart Outlet~~
1460 Merivale Road
Ottawa, Ontario
K2E 5P2

Price $17.95 plus $5.50 for shipping and handling charges.

Mary Elizabeth Raina - Taken in 1942.

DEDICATION

To my father, Dominic Anthony Raina, who fought the good fight, as he saw it, with admirable courage and integrity;

and

To my mother, Elizabeth Raina, the little pioneer girl who steered the family ship through the turbulent waters of my childhood, while convincing her children that life was a great and exciting adventure;

and

To my best friends, my brothers and sisters, in memory of the laughter and tears we shared.

"Love consists in this, that two solitudes protect and touch and greet each other."

Rainer Maria Rilke.

Dominic and Elizabeth Raina on their wedding day - November 4, 1919.

CONTENTS

Monsieur le Curé Jules Michaud of St. Marc de Figuery - Taken in 1943.

INTRODUCTION

This factual story is richly laden with the history — social, religious and political — of the Province of Quebec in the first half of the century, while it was experiencing its growing pains and beginning its struggle to emerge from under the domination of the Catholic clergy.

The story is held together by the experiences of the Raina family, who emigrated from Alberta during the 'thirties to take up residence at St. Marc de Figuery — a remote community in northern Quebec.

Dominic and Elizabeth Raina and their six young children discovered a life quite different in Quebec from the one they had left behind them in Alberta.

Dominic Raina hoped that, by settling in the Province of Quebec, he could give his children the benefits of a good Catholic education, as well as exposing them to the advantages of becoming thoroughly bilingual.

As Dominic Raina settled into the new community, he was appalled to discover the extent to which the Catholic clergy of Quebec were over-stepping their boundaries in controlling the flocks committed to their care, and the abuse suffered by many of the poor uneducated settlers as a consequence of the dictatorship under which they lived.

As time passed, Dominic Raina began to take an active interest in community affairs and attended the council meetings. Much to his dismay, he discovered that the principles embodied in the Municipal Act, in theory logical and fair and similar to the Municipal Act in Alberta, were completely disregarded in the new community, and that the settlers were under the power of the local priest.

Motivated by a sense of justice, and unable to tolerate in silence this abuse, Dominic Raina proceeded to protest it. His interference in the local priest's heretofore unchallenged position of authority resulted in tragedy to the Raina family. Among other things, their home was illegally confiscated.

In an attempt to obtain redress, and because of Dominic Raina's refusal to bend under pressure, the Raina case attained such magnitude that the highest religious and civil authorities in the Province of Quebec became involved.

The injustice occurred under the Taschereau administration, and continued into the Duplessis administration, both Premiers refusing to initiate appropriate action to enforce justice.

The story is of great historical value in that it depicts a true picture of rural Quebec in the 'thirties.

PROLOGUE

Funerals fall into different categories. There are those on which the sun shines benignly, casting a final benediction on the one being laid to rest and on the mourners standing by the coffin. The deceased has had a full and satisfying life, accomplished most of his goals, and enjoyed the fruits of his labours.

At a funeral of this nature can be heard remarks, such as: "It was a lovely funeral, if funerals can be called lovely," or "His family must be thankful at his peaceful passing and the fact that they had him all this time," or "I won't complain if I go that way." The natural sorrow felt at the loss of a loved one is tempered by the knowledge that the deceased had been prepared to die. His life had been good and it had followed the natural order of things.

At the other extreme, are the very sad funerals. A funeral falling into this category represents just another of the many tragedies that had befallen the deceased — a life snuffed out when there was yet much important unfinished business needing attention. The widow may be left with a large family at a time when a husband and father are still desperately needed. When the day is wet and gloomy, the sorrows seem to intensify. Comments such as: "Isn't it a tragedy!" or "I wonder how they will manage now?" or "Such a waste!" serve to cast an additional pallor upon the atmosphere.

The funeral of Dominic Raina, on the dreary day of April 22, 1952, fell into the latter category, although he had accepted his impending death with courage and resignation.

When Dominic Raina, a victim of tuberculosis, passed away in the parlour of his humble home at Kemptville, Ontario, there was a great sense of loss among his large and devoted family.

At the age of sixty-three, Dominic Raina had not accomplished his goals. He had not had the means of providing for his widow and younger dependent children, and he had not had the satisfaction of seeing any of his older children married, or any of them securely established in life.

1

To Elizabeth, his faithful and supportive wife, his death meant not only the loss of a husband but the loss of a dream — a dream that one day the two of them would recover from the Province of Quebec the home and earthly goods, which authorities there had taken from them by unjust and underhanded means.

The responsibilities inherent in finding herself at the age of fifty-two in the role of single parent to a large and boisterous family did not concern Elizabeth so much. She had always been confident that her children would land on their feet, and had conveyed that confidence to them. Inasmuch as circumstances permitted, they had never let her down.

Among the children at her side during Dominic's passing in the early hours of April 20 was twenty-seven-year-old Ralph, her eldest living son. Ralph had been her comfort during the days of Dominic's illness and had helped to nurse his father with great tenderness and expertise. Elizabeth feared that, in so doing, his own health might have been jeopardized.

After spending four years as a patient in the Royal Ottawa Sanatorium — at that time a hospital for the treatment of tuberculosis — Ralph had been discharged two years earlier. In addition to assisting extensively day and night in the care of his dying father, Ralph had been spending long hours trying to establish a business of his own since his discharge from the hospital. Because he was hard-working and ambitious, Ralph had been warned by his doctor that he would die either very young or very rich. He was cautioned to take it easier. Elizabeth feared, on contemplating the fatigue and strain so evident on her eldest son's face during that day of the funeral, that the first prophecy seemed more likely to come true than the second.

Also with her, and a witness to his father's death, was eighteen-year-old Dominic Raina Junior. He had enlisted in the Royal Canadian Air Force the previous year and was stationed at Camp Borden. He had come to spend the weekend at home and was present at his father's bedside during his final hours.

To Ralph and Nick (as Dominic Junior was called) fell the heart-breaking task of arranging for their father's wake in the family parlour – the room which had been converted into a bedroom during his illness and in which he had died.

Fourteen-year-old James Raina, the tender-hearted youngest son, had been greatly inspired by the courage with which his father had faced death. He was prepared for, and accepted, his father's passing. He had already wept copiously each time his father had hemorrhaged during his last days, and he now quite naturally expressed his sorrow in that same manner. When Jimmy sobbed it was the saddest and most woebegone sound in the world. His sobs, that day, expressed the sorrow felt by all those gathered in the room to pay their final respects.

Eight-year-old Anne Raina, the baby of the family, sat by herself in a corner and tried to make sense of everything that was happening. When Ralph had awakened her in the early hours of April 20 to tell her: "Daddy has passed away. Would you like to say some prayers at his bedside?" she dutifully complied. As she knelt beside the body of her father she patiently awaited his coming around, not understanding that he had died. Not being familiar with the term "passed away", and because no one had thought in the confusion following the death to explain it to her, she assumed that her father had merely fainted.

Nineteen-year-old George Raina had come home from Ottawa, where he was a watch repair man in a prominent Ottawa jewellery store. After several years as an invalid, he had been discharged from the Royal Ottawa Sanatorium the previous year and was getting started in his trade. His sorrow at his father's passing was clearly registered on his face.

Twenty-nine-year-old Mary Raina, the eldest living child, and twenty-five-year-old Clara Raina, arrived home together on a patient pass from the Royal Ottawa Sanatorium.

Mary had been admitted to the hospital in early January with a massive lung hemorrhage and was still bringing up blood occasionally. Consequently, she was advised to remain at the house during the funeral service, which was scheduled to take place at the Catholic Church of the Holy Cross at Kemptville.

Clara, who had passed many years as a patient at the Royal Ottawa Sanatorium and whose health was delicate, had been given similar instructions.

The two girls kept a sorrowful vigil at home while awaiting the return of the others. They felt saddened and impotent at their inability to be with their mother to offer consolation and support during those dark moments.

Twenty-one-year-old Louis Raina, who was attending an Officers' Training Course with the Royal Canadian Air Force in western Canada at the time of his father's death, was the only member of the family unable to be present. He was grateful that he had been able to say his final farewell to his father while he was still alive, on being summoned home a short time previously when the patient's condition had become critical.

When those attending the funeral eventually returned home, the Raina family drew comfort from each other, as had so often been the case in the past when faced with sorrow or adversity. Together, the children reminisced about the events that had culminated in this day.

In spite of the natural sorrow at the loss of a husband and father, the family was comforted by the knowledge that his final days had been passed among those whom he most loved, and by whom he was so greatly loved in return. They learned what was meant by dying with dignity. They were pleased that Dominic had been laid out in the parlour of his home, where the members of the family could console each other in a private and peaceful atmosphere.

All too soon, it was time for Mary and Clara to return to the sanatorium, for George to return to his boarding house in Ottawa, and for Nick to return to Camp Borden.

Elizabeth, feeling bereft, went to her bedroom upstairs. She remembered Dominic's words to her shortly before his death: "You were always so cheerful, and you could always see the pot of gold at the end of the rainbow." She tried to see it now, as she prayed for her beloved children — for those who were ill that they might recover, and for those who were well that they might succeed in their chosen careers. Also, in her thoughts and prayers, were the two sons who had predeceased their father many years ago; John Peter, her beloved first-born, and William Paul, her cherished youngest son.

Elizabeth remembered, too, that Dominic had promised shortly before his death that if there was a God in heaven he would beg him to bring his family out of adversity and into health, light and prosperity. She recalled the long road she and Dominic had travelled together and, once again, as so often in the past, she felt a renewed surge of hope!

CHAPTER I

THE NEW LAND

"To own a bit of ground, to scratch it with a hoe, to plant seeds, and watch the renewal of life — this is the commonest delight of the race, the most satisfactory thing a man can do." Charles Dudley Warner.

The young Village of St. Marc was constructed on lots forty-nine, fifty, and fifty-one of ranges three and four in the County of Figuery in the Province of Quebec. It was located ten miles south of Amos on the main road running from the town to the mines at Val d'Or. The majestic Harricana River flowed through its boundaries and down past Amos. It served as a passageway for boats taking their cargoes to and from the mines during the summer months.

Amos was the centre of administration for the Abitibi and the distribution point of supplies for the mines and lumber camps of that region. These advantages encouraged the immigration of settlers in search of new homes and promising futures.

Although the Province of Quebec had been inhabited long before western Canada had opened up to immigrants, many of its remote communities differed little from those which had sprung up with the arrival of the early settlers from France. St. Marc de Figuery was at least thirty years behind in its day-to-day style of life compared to later settlements on the Canadian prairies. In 1932, the Municipality of St. Marc de Figuery was just entering the twentieth century in many significant ways.

The political contrast was even greater! The political situation that existed in the Province of Quebec in 1932 had been created almost two hundred years earlier, when General Wolfe defeated General Montcalm and captured Quebec City in 1759. The French later confirmed this loss at the Treaty of Paris in 1763. Britain now had a new colony in Canada. What policy would she adopt towards this new-found treasure?

The policy the British adopted was a liberal one for that day and age.

5

The conquered colonists were to be allowed to keep their language, to keep their religion, and to keep their civil code. This arrangement lasted until the present day. The Quebec that Wolfe conquered was the Quebec of the *Ancien Régime*. The French Revolution had not yet occurred.

Under this old system, the citizen owed unquestioning loyalty to the King of France and the Roman Catholic Church. But now the King of France was replaced by the King of England. Consequently, the loyalty that had previously been given to king and church was transferred exclusively to the church. As a result, the church played a dual role in Quebec — political as well as religious. This was in sharp contrast to the situation in English-speaking Canada, where a separation between church and state existed and the role played by the church was principally a religious one.

When one travelled from English Canada into French Canada, during this period, there was almost a sense of moving two hundred years back in time insofar as the political situation was concerned.

The Village of St. Marc de Figuery consisted of a church, the local telephone centre, a creamery, a combination store and post-office, a few private homes, and a two-storey frame structure comprising the school and the presbytery of the parish priest, Monsieur le Curé Jules Michaud.

The people of the community of St. Marc were exclusively Catholic and French Canadian. They were a warm and friendly people who faced life with laughter and optimism. Closely bound by their family ties, they were devoted to their church and proud of their language and heritage. God was the centre of their universe and they worshipped Him, through the medium of their Catholic religion, with a devotion that was touching and unparalleled. The parish priest provided a direct link with the Almighty. The people accepted him, without question, as God's representative on earth, and accorded him the total homage deserving of such a calling.

Other parts of Canada, in most cases known only as a place where foreigners lived, held little interest for the settlers of St. Marc. They were a simple and uneducated people who looked to their priest for guidance in all personal, religious and civil matters. They were subservient to him, just as their forefathers had been to the *seigneurs* of their time.

The priest, in turn, was liberal in bestowing advice on his parishioners. The validity of his decisions on their behalf was seldom questioned. His words of wisdom were quoted with respect among the people of the community. His interpretations of biblical passages often suited his purposes and strengthened his position of authority.

While the settlers were generally possessed of high native intelligence, they were at a period of time in their history when they could ill afford the luxury of questioning any of the dogmas of their religion as taught by their clergy. It was through their faith that they drew the necessary strength required for survival under the primitive conditions of a frontier land. To question the teachings of their pastor would be tantamount to weakening the rudder so necessary in steering the course of their lives.

Winters were frigid at St. Marc de Figuery. When the snows of winter fell upon the land the settlers dressed to face the sub-zero weather. Frost-bite was a common annoyance. Warm toques and heavy scarves were donned by anyone venturing out for more than a few minutes. High rubber boots were worn by the men working in the woods and doing chores, and by the children attending school. Heavy socks or stockings, knit from crude homespun wool, were worn inside the boots. The wool, grey or an off-white in colour, was obtained from the local flocks of sheep.

For special occasions, such as when the Sacraments of Confirmation or First Holy Communion were bestowed upon the children of the parish, the little girls wore black patent leather slippers, while the little boys wore sturdy oxfords. That footwear, and any other clothing that could not be produced at home, was usually ordered from the catalogue of *Les Frères Dupuis* — a large and popular mail-order business in Quebec at the time.

After the event of the administration of the sacraments, the children were permitted to wear their new shoes to church on Sundays and on Holy Days of Obligation. They were also worn to the May devotions and to the special services held during the holy season of Lent. It was often possible to pass the footwear down to younger siblings, and much mileage could be obtained from that initial expenditure.

Much visiting took place among the neighbours during the long winter evenings. Friendly chatter was accompanied by the clicking sound of knitting needles, as women industriously produced enough of the heavy socks to last another year. They also embroidered aprons, pillow-cases, tablecloths and dresser-scarves. The floral designs were usually elaborate and beautiful and were stamped on flour and sugar bags, which had been bleached to a snowy whiteness for that purpose. Little girls wore embroidered aprons over their dresses while attending school. Scatter mats were hooked from rags salvaged from worn-out clothing. They added colour and a cheerful touch to the homes of the community.

While the women attended to their knitting and needlework, the men smoked their pipes, teased the women, and discussed the latest news from the surrounding mines, or bits of gossip gleaned on recent trips to Amos.

Socializing was conducted in the large kitchens of the homes, where the furniture was *early habitant*. It was crude and homemade, yet charming. A long table, designed to accommodate a large family, was to be found in every kitchen of the community. In the centre of the table was the dipping bowl of molasses, shared by the family at each meal. Slabs of delicious home-made bread were plentiful upon the tables. Salt pork, cured by the barrel, was one of the main staples to be found in every home. The most delicious *ragoûts* and *tourtières*, to be found anywhere in Canada, were served at the tables of St. Marc de Figuery.

Floors were generally constructed of untreated and unpainted hardwood. Saturdays were set aside by the women for the scrubbing of the floors. That chore was accomplished with strong soap, hot water, a brisk brush, and plenty of elbow grease. Restoring the floors to a snowy whiteness required several hours of labour. The quality of a woman's housekeeping could be judged by the whiteness of her floor boards.

Evidences of the Catholic faith, in the form of crucifixes, statues, and pictures of the Virgin Mary and all the favourite saints, were prominent all throughout the homes of the community. Saint Anne, the Holy Mother of Mary, held a prominent place in the hearts of the women of St. Marc. It was she they invoked, through numerous novenas, in matters relating to childbirth and female problems. The miracles she had performed on their behalf were cited frequently, and with reverence. Evenings usually ended with the recitation of the daily rosary, accompanied by either the Joyful, Sorrowful, or Glorious Mysteries, according to the religious calendar.

Much of the social life of the community was centred around the church. It was customary on Sundays and on Holy Days of Obligation for the parishioners to arrive early at the Village of St. Marc. There, they gathered at the large home of the Lemieux family so that they might socialize before the bells rang out summoning the faithful to Mass. While Georges Lemieux directed the men to his stable, where their horses were offered hospitality, his wife welcomed the women and children into her home. Madame Lemieux was a spotless housekeeper. Her floors were always scrubbed to a snowy whiteness, yet she was never bothered if wet and muddy boots invaded her kitchen on Sundays. An abundance of coffee, which had been brewed in readiness for the arrival of the company, was served with graciousness.

While the older men and women exchanged gossip and the younger children played in the Lemieux home, the young men of the parish usually congregated at the corner store of Napoléon Doucet, the Mayor of St. Marc. There, they could laugh and joke and flirt with the young girls passing by. Many romances, which later culminated in marriage, saw their birth around Napoléon Doucet's corner store before Mass on Sundays and on Holy Days of Obligation. When a young man took a young lady for a buggy ride through the community on a Sunday afternoon it was a certain sign of love in bloom, usually followed by a wedding a few months later.

Each family was assigned its own seat in the church. All ears listened attentively to Monsieur le Curé's sermons from the pulpit. After the reading of the gospel and the delivery of the homily, Monsieur le Curé customarily proceeded to instruct the members of his flock on each and every aspect of their lives. While this was not unusual in many of the rural areas of Quebec, it was perhaps more pronounced at St. Marc de Figuery, where the current priest possessed unusually strong leadership qualities and a determination to be involved with his flock as much as possible. Among other things, he advised them on who to vote for in the elections, how to spend their money wisely, what crops to plant in the spring, and how to fatten their animals. They were encouraged to never fall behind in the payment of their church dues. They were urged to go to confession regularly so that they might always remain in a state of grace.

In order to be in a state of grace it was required that a penitent free his soul of mortal sin. This could be accomplished only through the medium of the confessional. The pious people of the community were conscientious about remaining in a state of grace. Mortal sins consisted mainly in missing Mass on Sundays or on Holy Days of Obligation, eating meat on Fridays, failing to fast during the lenten season after having reached the age of majority, unfaithfulness in marriage, slander, murder, and theft. Mortal sins were of sufficiently serious a nature to condemn a soul to hell for all eternity if not absolved through the confessional. In exceptional cases, such as a sudden heart attack or a serious accident, resulting in imminent danger of death, a penitent could be absolved of his sins by saying a sincere act of contrition if a priest was not available to administer the Last Rites of the Holy Catholic Church.

Venial sins consisted of such minor infractions as disobeying one's parents, fighting with one's brothers and sisters, failing to say one's daily prayers, impure thoughts, gossiping, coveting a neighbour's wife, and telling lies. The penalty for dying with venial sins on one's soul was a sentence in purgatory, the duration of which was determined by the number and seriousness of such sins. Because the soul could expect to be transferred to heaven after having served the requisite term in purgatory venial sins were not as frightening to carry around as were mortal

9

sins. Furthermore, it was possible to buy their forgiveness through the recitation of certain prayers that carried indulgences.

What Monsieur le Curé did not already know about each and every member of his congregation he could learn through the confessional. To his credit, the priest was never known to betray the secrets confessed therein.

Meetings of the municipal council and of the school board were customarily held in the basement of the church of St. Marc after Mass on Sundays or on Holy days of Obligation. When the priest announced such a meeting from the pulpit, both the men and women of the congregation responded with enthusiasm. To the women, it meant a continuation of the visit that had been interrupted by the ringing of the church bell earlier. To the men, it meant an opportunity to contribute a few words in the interests of the community.

It was unthinkable for a woman to attend a meeting. To do so would constitute an insult to her husband, displaying a lack of confidence in his ability to contribute to the smooth running of the community without the benefit of her presence. Furthermore, the men were not eager that their women be bothered with such intellectual matters as the administration of community affairs. Their role in the community was to have babies at regular intervals, and to attend to the needs of all the members of their households.

A few of the settlers of the community earned their living exclusively through the cultivation of their land, or by selling milk to the creameries. Others worked at the gravel pits, or at the nearby mines of Siscoe or Val d'Or. Some of the men tilled their land during the summer months, and worked away from home only throughout the winter. In preparation for their absence from home, they took advantage of the warm weather to cut enough wood from their properties to feed the kitchen stoves and hungry Quebec heaters throughout the winter months.

With their husbands absent, the women took care of the family's needs and attended to the outdoor chores, assisted by the older children. Because of the status of women in Quebec at the time, which was almost equivalent to that of the children, it was not unusual for the local priest to attend to the family's financial matters when the man of the house was absent. Monsieur le Curé Jules Michaud assumed that responsibility at St. Marc de Figuery.

Teams of oxen were still prevalent in the community. These sturdy beasts provided transportation and served to haul the heavy logs from the woods. Settlers were paid bonuses to clear the bushland up to a certain acreage. The lots were long and narrow, separated by fences cleverly constructed from logs and fallen branches.

Most farmers raised cattle, pigs, poultry, and, in some cases, sheep. Occasionally, a marauding bear was known to play havoc with a flock of sheep. This was always a great loss to the farmer whose flock had been violated. Men, armed with rifles or twenty-twos, would then band together to stalk the culprit, but often to no avail. Failure to capture the bear usually resulted in another flock being attacked the following night.

Nature was wild and beautiful, and could be generous to the settlers of St. Marc de Figuery. Lac d'école was a large clean body of water located within the boundaries of the municipality. Its waters teemed with fish of many species. The settlers fished without restriction, usually by nets strung out under the water.

As impressive as the fish in the lake, were the wild berries that grew in rich abundance on the land. There were brambleberries, strawberries, raspberries, blueberries, blackberries, pincherries and chokecherries. As rapidly as the children of the community picked the berries, their mothers preserved them in the form of jams and jellies for the winter.

Bush rabbits abounded in the woods, and provided an occasional change from the customary fare served by the settlers at the evening meal.

Families were large, often as many as ten or twelve, or even fifteen children. Births customarily took place at home under the attendance of a midwife, and without the benefits of an anaesthetic. The women bore the pains of labour with admirable stoicism, and accepted this as the natural lot of women. Each new baby was greeted with love and warmth by all members of the family. Older siblings helped to care for the younger ones, resulting in the young girls being trained at an early age to become the wonderful wives and mothers for which French women are renowned.

Baptisms customarily took place shortly after the birth of the baby. To be chosen as a sponsor at the christening of an infant was considered to be a great honour. Sponsors took their responsibilities seriously as they promised, in the name of the newborn, to renounce Satan and all his works and pomps. A close relationship was always formed between the child and the godparents.

Early baptism was important because of the Catholic Church's belief that only after the administration of that sacrament could a soul enter into the Kingdom of Heaven. It was believed that if a person died prior to baptism the soul would be committed to a place called "limbo" for all eternity. In a case where a lay person perceived that an unchristened infant appeared to be in danger of death, and there was not a priest available to administer the Sacrament of Baptism, the attending lay person would automatically be empowered to christen the child. This was accomplished by making the Sign of the Cross over the child's forehead while saying: "I baptize thee in the name of the Father, of the Son, and of the Holy Ghost".

Weddings were a time of joyous celebration. After the ceremony, the young couple was feasted at the home of either the groom's or the bride's parents. The event was well attended by the neighbours. In the early hours of the following morning, after the music had stopped and much food had been consumed, the newlyweds were ceremoniously waved upstairs, where a room had been prepared for the nuptial night.

As the Christmas season drew near, the women of the community baked *tourtières* by the dozens in preparation for *Le Reveillon*, which took place in the homes after Midnight Mass. Midnight Mass was well attended by the whole community. Sleigh bells rang out everywhere on that Holy Eve as families gathered at the church. All the beautiful traditional Christmas carols resounded throughout the congregation as voices were raised in unison. After the service, there was much hugging and kissing on the steps of the church as neighbour wished neighbour a Holy and Happy Christmas. As they continued to rejoice at the birth of the Christ Child, families congregated at their homes to begin the festivities that would go on well into the morning. Christmas was first and foremost a religious celebration.

New Year's day was celebrated on a much larger scale in French Canada than was Christmas day. Families normally gathered at the home of *le grand-père*, the respected patriarch of three or four generations of family members. There, on New Year's morning, in accordance with a beautiful tradition widely spread throughout French Canada, they knelt to receive the paternal blessing and good wishes for the new year. The old patriarch would beam with pride as he looked down upon his many descendants. This was what made all the years that had passed before, when he had been so busy carving out a living in a harsh frontier land, worthwhile. It was his day to relax, smoke his pipe, and bask in the attention bestowed by the young generations surrounding him. What more could a man wish for in the twilight of his years?

As the year of 1932 was drawing to a close, an unsuspecting immigrant from far away Alberta, accompanied by his family, was preparing to settle in the little community of St. Marc de Figuery, where time had so long stood still.

The newcomer would view the situation that existed there with compassion and increasing dismay. Compelled by a sense of justice, he would disturb the placidity of the community in an attempt to catapult it into the twentieth century!

CHAPTER II

IMMIGRANTS FROM WESTERN CANADA

"Climb high, climb far, your goal the sky, your aim the star."
Anonymous.

At approximately four o'clock p.m. on November 28, 1932, the train from the west, traversing the Province of Quebec and carrying the Raina family among its passengers, neared its destination. For some miles, the Rainas had been able to view, from the window of their car, the large imposing structure of the Church of Ste. Thérèse d'Amos.

The church, a great circular building situated on a hill in the very heart of the town, stood out as a beacon — the beacon light of the Catholic faith in that remote area of Quebec.

The town of Amos (erected in 1914 and incorporated into a town in 1925) looked up respectfully, in an attitude of genuflection, to that great bulwark of the faith, and protectingly encircled it. To the south of the church, bordered by the Transcontinental Railway, lay the main business section of the town. This section consisted chiefly of the station, a convent, several schools, various stores, and government offices — the principal one of which was the Department of Colonization. To the west flowed the majestic Harricana River, the pride of the Abitibi. The main residential sections of the town lay to the north and south.

Amos was the centre of administration of the Abitibi and the distributing point of supplies for the mines and lumber camps of that region. These advantages encouraged the immigration of settlers in search of new homes and promising futures.

Dominic and Elizabeth Raina were drawn to settle in Quebec after their homestead at Hanna, Alberta, which had previously so prospered and flourished, fell victim to the elements that plagued the dry belt of Alberta. This area had been hit repeatedly by the drought during the early part of the dirty thirties. Many of the homesteaders had already given up on the parched prairies and had emigrated elsewhere in Canada. The verdant Peace River country in northern Alberta, and the neighbouring Province of British Columbia, were among the most popular choices.

There were several reasons why Dominic and Elizabeth decided to settle in the distant Province of Quebec. They were the proud parents of six young and active children, whose welfare and future education concerned them greatly. Dominic was anxious that his children have a solid grounding in their Catholic faith, and Quebec was predominantly Catholic. Furthermore, he wished his children to become fluently bilingual, and he was convinced that this could best be accomplished through total French immersion. Dominic, himself, was well versed in several languages, and he believed this to be an important factor in the rounding out of a good education. As he had repeatedly pointed out to Elizabeth while planning the education of their children: "The day will come when it will be important that the children know the two official languages of Canada." Because she had such faith in his decisions, Elizabeth agreed with him completely.

Furthermore, Dominic was aware that a wonderful opportunity for market gardening existed in northern Quebec, where many of the products could be sold to the surrounding mines.

Dominic Raina was Italian by birth, but he had become a naturalized British subject on October 30, 1915. At that time, he had taken out the patents of his homestead, twelve miles northwest of Hanna, to break the sod in the free and friendly Province of Alberta.

His wife, Elizabeth Hepp, was an Hungarian-born girl who came to Canada in 1904 at the tender age of four. She became a Canadian citizen when her father was naturalized. Happy and optimistic by nature, Elizabeth belonged to a pioneer family that had done much to tame the wilderness in the settling of the west.

Twenty-nine-year-old Dominic had been introduced to eighteen-year-old Elizabeth by a priest who was a mutual friend, and who felt that the couple was well-suited. Elizabeth was instantly enraptured with the handsome well-educated Italian, and accepted his proposal of marriage after their third meeting. In a frontier country, where women were outnumbered by men at a ratio of nearly twenty to one, Dominic could scarcely believe his good fortune at having won the heart and hand of one of the most attractive young maidens of the district.

Dominic Raina and Elizabeth Hepp were steadfast and pious Catholics. They were married in the Church of Our Lady of Grace at Castor, Alberta, on November 4, 1919, shortly after Elizabeth turned nineteen. They began their lives together on Dominic's homestead at Hanna.

At Hanna, friends were true, racial and religious discrimination was unknown, men were at peace with their neighbours and were ready to lend a helping hand when one was needed. Dominic and Elizabeth were respected and admired, and took an active part in community affairs.

While there was excitement and optimism at the challenge of planning their new lives in Quebec, Dominic and Elizabeth felt nostalgic at leaving their friends and neighbours of so many years. Consequently, it was with mixed feelings that they attended the auction of their goods on November 16, 1932. Before their departure from Hanna, they were presented with a purse and good wishes from the community for happiness and success in the Province of Quebec.

Little did Dominic and Elizabeth suspect when the train pulled out of Hanna on November 23, 1932, that they were to experience a great tragedy in their relocation, the repercussions of which would be felt within their family for many years to come.

When Dominic and Elizabeth alit from the train at Amos on November 28, 1932, they looked with interest at their new surroundings. Following closely behind their parents, the Raina children bounced enthusiastically off the train and into a confusion of passengers, buck-saws, pack-sacks and grips.

The trip from the west had been a long and arduous one, and some of the children had bad colds. Nevertheless, as the train sped across Canada, they had taken a keen interest in the passing countryside. With their noses pressed against the sooty windows of the coal-fed train, they had watched every detail of the changing landscape of their country, from the vast and empty snow-covered prairies to the dense woods of Ontario and Quebec.

Their father pointed out to them all the landmarks of importance so that they might become more familiar with their history and geography. He explained to them that travel was broadening and provided the best form of education, and that any money spent that way was never wasted.

Dominic had already seen quite a bit of the world himself. Before coming to Canada he had spent a couple of years in Uruguay, where he had bought a small banana plantation. He left Uruguay only when he was summoned home to Italy upon the death of his father. It was after the settling of his father's estate that he immigrated to North America to help to colonize the Canadian west.

At those stations at which the train stopped to take on passengers and cargo, the children were permitted to stretch their legs by running up and down the platform outside. This was always a highlight of the trip, especially when their father took them into the station to buy chocolate bars.

Added to the new adventure of their first trip by train, the children were delighted to be dressed out in new regalia for their move to a new home. Eleven-year-old Johnny and eight-year-old Ralph had new leather jackets with matching helmets. They were of a rich brown colour and the helmets sported goggles, as was the style for little boys at the time. Even though the goggles served no practical purpose, the boys liked the fact that they gave forth a rather shady appearance.

Ten-year-old Mary had a new green coat with a little brown fur collar. Her mother had ordered it from the Eaton Catalogue in the fall. More than anything in the world, Mary had wanted a red cape coat and long hair. But Mary accepted that her mother knew best, and that she was probably right when she said that Mary looked prettier with short hair, and that she would get more wear out of the green coat.

Six-year-old Clara had a baby-blue coat to match her baby-blue eyes and delicate appearance. Clara had the worst cold of all the children and she coughed continually on the trip. A kind lady eventually took pity on her and gave her a bag of peppermints, which Clara proceeded to suck with relish. The other children immediately put on a great performance of coughing as loudly as they could, but the kind lady did not take pity on them as she had on Clara. So little Clara enjoyed her peppermints while the other children ate stale sandwiches, which had been prepared for the family by relatives and friends before their departure from the west.

Two-year-old Louis was the greatest hit during the trip. He was passed back and forth among the ladies on the train, who made a great fuss over him. Six-months-old George, the adorable baby, was suffering from eczema on his face, and his hands were kept wrapped most of the time so that he could not scratch himself. He expressed his resentment at this confinement in no uncertain terms, and the older children had to take turns relieving their mother of the burden of trying to keep him quiet. They felt sorry for their little brother who was so confined, and sometimes sneaked his bandages off when their mother wasn't looking.

As the children stood with their parents on the platform before the station at Amos they felt that they had arrived just in time to witness a celebration, judging by the mass of humanity gathered at the little station. A general air of expectancy transferred itself to all members of the family, as they found themselves eagerly anticipating the arrival of a celebrity on the scene. Much to their disappointment, the crowd began to disperse rapidly as soon as the last passenger had alighted from the train. The family learned, later, that the population of Amos had the habit, as is common in small towns where life can become dull and routine, of frequenting the station at train time. A stranger, arriving by train at Amos, could rest assured that the town had sent forth numerous representatives. The general disorder, the pushing and shoving, and the speaking of a language — at that time strange and incoherent to all except Dominic (who was fluent in French) — was merely a routine occurrence.

It was amid that tumult of priests dressed in soutanes and stiff white collars, bewhiskered miners and lumberjacks, warmly bundled farmers from surrounding districts, boisterous school children, and people from other walks of life, that the Raina family observed with interest, for the first time, the almost one-hundred-percent Catholic French Canadian population of Amos.

Dominic Raina had had a previous welcome to Amos from the Department of Colonization and had been given to understand, through correspondence with the department, that one of their representatives would meet the train. Due to a misunderstanding, no one showed up. The family found themselves alone in a strange town. Nevertheless, neither the long trip nor the sub-zero weather could dispel the enthusiasm the children experienced at this new adventure.

While Dominic went to locate the office of the Department of Colonization, Elizabeth and her large hungry brood waited anxiously at the station for his return. After considerable time had elapsed, Dominic reappeared in a truck supplied by the Department of Colonization. Family and baggage were then driven to Albert's Boarding House near the west bank of the Harricana River.

The other lodgers at the boarding house consisted mainly of lumberjacks and men passing through town on their way to the mines at Val d'Or or Siscoe. The Raina family had their breakfast at long tables shared by the other guests. Pancakes were always served at breakfast. The batter for the pancakes was mixed in large bowls and, whereas Elizabeth always used milk to mix her batter, the cooks in the boarding house used only water. Although the pancakes themselves were rather tasteless, when served with pure Quebec maple syrup they became delicious. The Raina children attempted to impress the lodgers at the table by displaying their limited knowledge of French. *Oui, oui,* or *mais non,* were to be heard over and over again at the table, until the lodgers were obviously weary of listening to those seemingly illiterate children show off.

Within a few days of their arrival at Amos, Dominic succeeded in renting a house to accommodate his family pending the acquisition of a permanent home.

Those were exciting carefree days for the Raina children. With Johnny as the ringleader, they daily set forth on numerous investigative excursions and explored the town of Amos through all its length and width. They were the proud possessors of tidy little sums of pin money given them by doting aunts and uncles on their departure from the west. With this loot, they purchased the popular delicacies "Red Jacket" and "Black Jacket" gum in great quantities, until they had finally chewed up their fortunes. One of their favourite pastimes was to watch the local children sliding down the hill on their sleds and hoping that they would be invited to join them. Although they attempted to impress and befriend the children, by again displaying their limited knowledge of French, they succeeded only in drawing puzzled stares.

Following their mother's instructions, the children attended Mass in the Church of Ste. Thérèse each day to pray that God would guide their father in the selection of a suitable home for the family.

When the children returned to the house after their travels Elizabeth always met them at the door to hear about their exploits. Elizabeth could not speak a word of French, and none of the people whom she had met could speak any English. Warm and friendly by nature, she was becoming very lonely and would sometimes weep.

Dominic was gone most of the day to look at properties around Amos. He and Elizabeth were anxious to get established in a home of their own. They felt it was high time that the children return to school and become occupied with something more constructive than running loose all over town. Dominic was a strict disciplinarian who did not believe in idle hands. He was convinced that children should be given a good dose of responsibility to keep them out of mischief.

The children had great respect for their father and always strived to live up to his expectations. They also had great respect for their mother. Their father reminded them, repeatedly, that he wanted them to always be good to their mother, and that if they acted disrespectfully to her they would have to deal with him. Sometimes the children managed to manipulate their easy-going mother, but never in their father's presence. Dominic had never been heard to raise his voice to Elizabeth, but always treated her with great tenderness. For her part, Elizabeth accepted him as the undisputed head of the family and followed his leadership without question.

On December 6, 1932, Dominic contracted to buy lot thirty-nine, range three, through the Department of Colonization of Amos. The property consisted of eighty-two acres of first-class land, a fair house, and a large barn. It was located at St. Marc de Figuery, approximately ten miles south of Amos. Dominic purchased the land for the price of seven hundred dollars clear of back taxes. Five hundred dollars of that sum was paid in cash, while long-term payments were arranged to cover the balance. In 1932, this amount was an impressive sum of money.

CHAPTER III

SETTLING IN ST. MARC

"Oh God, give us serenity to accept what cannot be changed, courage to change what should be changed, and wisdom to distinguish one from the other." Reinhold Niebuhr.

On the frigid afternoon of December 14, 1932, Elizabeth herded her brood aboard the snowmobile which had been hired to drive them from Amos to their new home at St. Marc de Figuery. Dominic followed in a sleigh with a new neighbour he had met while taking a tour of the land prior to its purchase. He and the neighbour were bringing out the family's belongings. The trip from Amos to St. Marc proved to be a novel and exciting experience for the children, who had never before seen or ridden on a snowmobile.

The Raina property was located two miles west of the Village of St. Marc. The property's southern end formed a bank of the same beautiful Harricana River that flowed through Amos. Across the road, and within a stone's throw of their house, stood l'Ecole du lac. It was topped off with a cross, as was customary on all schools in that part of Catholic Quebec. The property of Joseph Lantagne Junior, their nearest residential neighbour, marked the eastern boundary of their home: one of the properties owned by Georges Lemieux drew the line on the western side.

The first visitor to greet the family shortly after they had crossed the threshold of their new home, before they were unpacked, was a man who introduced himself as being one of their new neighbours. News of the rich settlers from the west had preceded the family to St. Marc. The man came to borrow a sum of money from Dominic. He explained that he had just purchased a new stove and did not have the cash to meet his payments. That gesture led Dominic to believe that he would not be ignored in the new community, and he obligingly loaned the sum of money.

After the neighbour had departed, satisfied at the outcome of his visit, the family explored their new house. The downstairs consisted of only two finished bedrooms and a large long room, which combined the kitchen and living-room. The upstairs was as yet unfinished, but presented the inviting possibility of eventually being turned into two large bedrooms. In the meantime, the family would be living in cramped quarters.

Dominic and Elizabeth chose the largest bedroom so that baby George's crib could be placed in their room. The second bedroom was assigned to Johnny, Ralph and Louis. Mary and Clara slept in a big double bed at one end of the living-room. At that location, the coal-oil lamp on the nearby family table cast its glow right upon their faces when they wanted to sleep. An added annoyance was that they did not have much privacy to giggle and gossip. This latter drawback was partly compensated for by the fact that, from that location, they could pretend to be asleep while listening to everything their parents discussed. Though the discussions centered mainly around what crops they would plant and how many cattle they would buy, topics about which Mary and Clara couldn't care less, occasionally they would hear something more interesting. The prospect of passing on the latest juicy news to their siblings the next day was sufficient to help them forget all about the disadvantages of sleeping in the living-room.

During the following days, the Rainas met several of their new neighbours. They were charmed with the warm overtures and friendliness of the people. They were touched by the apparent simplicity of their lives, and bewildered by the primitive conditions under which they survived. The people of the community spoke a regional French, which was quite different from the parisian French that Dominic had learned in Europe.

Devotion to the Catholic faith appeared to be total. Dominic felt that his children would benefit greatly through this deep exposure to their religion. He resolved to become part of the community and to adjust to its culture, which appeared to be vastly different to that which he had been accustomed to at Hanna, Alberta. He resolved that, on his own land, he would continue to practice what he considered to be more efficient methods of agriculture than those being practiced at St. Marc de Figuery.

Due to a shortage of pupils, l'Ecole du lac, across the road from the Raina home, was closed when the family first moved to St. Marc. Consequently, the children were initiated into the study of the French language at the village school.

Although Clara had recently turned six years of age and had started school before leaving Alberta, Dominic and Elizabeth decided to teach her at home during that first school year in Quebec. Their decision was motivated by the fact that Clara's persistent cough had been diagnosed as whooping cough. Northern Quebec was extremely cold at that time of the year and the school was a two-mile walk from home. The older children left for school each day well bundled up against the elements, usually wearing two pairs of woolen socks and two pairs of heavy mitts.

They soon had many little friends, who delighted in watching their progress in the study of their language. The Raina children were absorbing and comparing with great interest the differences in culture between their new school-mates and themselves. While their little *habitant* friends admired their new leather shoes and overshoes, the Raina children longed for the heavy laced rubber boots worn by the local children. Each evening, the boots were removed and lined up to dry beside the Quebec heaters or kitchen stoves of St. Marc, where they exuded clouds of steam. Although that footwear was considered to be most unhealthy by their parents, the Raina children dreamed of the day when they would be permitted to encase their feet in moist, foul-smelling rubber. They were also fascinated to discover that slates were used by the pupils more often than was paper. Each child had a little slate that was cleaned regularly with spittle, and then wiped dry with a rag brought from home. The children could barely wait to tell their parents about the slates and to possess one of their own.

During the family's first winter at St. Marc de Figuery Dominic became well acquainted with Monsieur le Curé Jules Michaud and spent many a pleasant evening visiting the priest in his presbytery at St. Marc. Monsieur le Curé was possessed of a keen mind and was a man of many interests. His activities were arranged into neat little segments of time and methodically compartmentalized. By this system, he was able to accomplish a great deal, and was able to keep abreast of every single thing that transpired among all members of his flock.

Next to the priest's interest in his parishioners was his tendency to gamble heavily in the surrounding gold mines. He possessed many shares and calculated their values regularly. Dominic considered a visit with Monsieur le Curé to be a mutually interesting and intellectually stimulating event. They possessed the common bond of being the only two men in the parish who had received a higher education. Dominic had entered the priesthood in Italy during his youth. While he had not completed his studies at the seminary and was not ordained, he was familiar with Canon Law.

During their visits together, Dominic confided to Monsieur le Curé his plans to sow a large market garden in the spring. He expressed his confidence in the success of such a venture. He pointed out that he was not anxious to leave home to work in the mines, as was so common among many of the men of the parish, who chose that method to support their families. Dominic was a home-oriented man who wished to be a continuing influence on the lives of his children, and he felt that that could best be accomplished by working his land. He told Monsieur le Curé that he hoped, eventually, to ship garden produce to the surrounding mines, where he was convinced a great potential market existed.

Invariably, their conversations turned to politics — a subject in which both men were passionately interested. Dominic had a great deal of experience in local politics because of his involvement in the municipal council, the school board, and the Alberta Wheat Pool in the Province of Alberta. He had also served as the local crop correspondent for *The Calgary Herald*. He hoped that his experience could eventually be put to good use in the service of the community of St. Marc. Monsieur le Curé listened with attentiveness to Dominic's observations.

In addition to local politics, both men were following with great interest the changes the Taschereau administration was exerting on the province. Neither man was overly-impressed with Premier Taschereau, but they were adopting a wait and see attitude.

During their first winter in Quebec, before the Raina children had mastered French sufficiently well to converse fluently with the local children, they came to enjoy each other's company more and more. Each evening, after homework was completed, their parents turned the children loose outside to let off steam and to enjoy the biting cold sub-zero weather.

Inventive Johnny had salvaged the wooden packing crates from their move. He had tied sturdy roping to the crates in order to turn them into make-believe trains. He then tested their durability by loading them with heavy weights and pulling them through the snow-drifts. When he was convinced that they were sufficiently well constructed he set up stations at various points around the yard, where the younger children, acting as passengers, awaited the arrival of the train. Tooting and snorting, and generally giving a good imitation of an engine, Johnny pulled the train into the various stations. "All aboard for Regina," or "All aboard for Winnipeg," or "All aboard for Cochrane" (or whatever the destination), shouted Johnny. After issuing a ticket to the passenger, off went Johnny puffing and tugging to get his fare to its destination on time. The Raina children did much happy travelling during that first winter in Quebec.

Dominic and Elizabeth had got into the habit of exchanging visits with their neighbours during the long winter evenings. Friendships developed and solidified. Elizabeth was now knitting the same heavy socks for her family as the neighbour women did for theirs, and her knitting always accompanied her on the visits.

Elizabeth was learning a few sentences in French, with much encouragement from her new friends, who were charmed by *la belle jeune femme de Monsieur Raina* (Dominic Raina's attractive young wife).

As the year of 1932 passed rapidly into 1933, the Raina children were learning French at an equally rapid pace. Thrown into total French immersion, and encouraged by parents who had a high respect for education, learning a new language presented an exciting challenge. It also helped in the acquisition of new friends among the local children.

The days on which Monsieur le Curé visited the school were particularly exciting. Monsieur le Curé was an energetic wiry man with lively eyes, and he exuded an aura of unrestrained motion. As he walked rapidly into the classroom, his soutane swirling around his legs, the children rose in unison. In voices loud, clear, and well rehearsed, they respectfully acknowledged his presence with, *Bon jour Monsieur le Curé*, while the teacher beamed proudly.

With a nod of his head, Monsieur le Curé would motion with his hands that the children be seated. To the unfailing delight of the class, he would then proceed to deliver a few words of religious wisdom accompanied by a little touch of humour. He always reminded the children to say their prayers each night, and stressed the importance of regular confession. He blessed them, "In the name of the Father, the Son, and the Holy Ghost," and departed as rapidly as he had come.

During his first winter in Quebec Dominic bought a second property, again through the Department of Colonization of Amos. Lot fifty-eight, range one, of the County of Figuery, consisted of ninety-one acres of timber. From a local farmer, he also bought several heads of cattle, a horse and some poultry.

When the snows of the long winter of 1932-33 finally melted and gave way to spring Dominic and Elizabeth were able to see, for the first time, the rich loamy soil of their property. They were confident that their decision to go into market gardening was a wise one. They sowed a large garden as soon as the ground was dry enough to till. Every available hand in the family was assigned to pulling the weeds, which seemed to compete determinedly with the vegetables for their place in the sun.

The Raina children found that, since intellectual achievement was placed at such a low level at St. Marc, they had little difficulty in all placing first in their respective classes at the end of their first school year in Quebec. Dominic and Elizabeth had always stressed the importance of a good education and accepted nothing less than the best from their children.

When the bell signalling the end of class rang out one final time, at the end of that school year of 1933, the Raina children raced for home. They were eager to show their parents the impressive assortment of holy pictures they were clutching in their hands. They had so much to tell their parents, and the holy pictures were as great a proof of their achievements as were their excellent report cards. On hearing the good news, Elizabeth hugged and kissed each child in turn, while Dominic beamed on proudly. Then, looking fondly at Dominic, as she always did when the children brought home good reports, Elizabeth reminded her children that, ''You got your brains from your father.'' He responded by looking at Elizabeth with great admiration at her insight.

The children went about the pleasant task of finding places to display their holy pictures. Mary decided to put one of hers inside her prayer book at the spot that marked the beginning of the marriage ceremony. Mary found that part of her prayer book to be the most interesting, and she always read it during Mass when her father wasn't looking. Dominic believed that the Mass should be followed scrupulously, and that the children should listen carefully to Monsieur le Curé's sermons from the pulpit.

Mary was not interested in Monsieur le Curé's talks on politics or on general farming, which were so often the topics of his sermons. She didn't care who the people voted for. The part of the marriage ceremony that particularly appealed to Mary was the sentence, ''Whom God has joined together let no man put asunder.'' She was fascinated with the word ''asunder'' and planned to use it in her story. She was entering a short story into a contest sponsored by *The Family Herald and Weekly Star* for children in her age group. Her father had always been a regular subscriber to that newspaper in Alberta, and had continued to receive it in Quebec. It was one of Mary's favourite papers because it had an interesting children's section.

As Dominic's regular visits with the priest continued, he noticed that Monsieur le Curé appeared to be little concerned in bringing enlightenment to his flock. In their ignorance, they were under his domination. With the exception of a few chosen young people, who were carefully selected at a tender age to become lawyers or priests, higher education did not appear to be encouraged. A new settler, entering the community and possessing more than the generally accepted degree of knowledge, was not always kindly received. His ability to question the administration of the community and the complete authority of the priest was viewed with apprehension.

There was much activity in the Raina family during that first summer in Quebec. Now that school was over Dominic had assigned a healthy amount of responsibility to each of the four eldest children. The garden which Dominic and Elizabeth had planted in the late spring was producing beyond their wildest expectations. There were many vegetables to be sold at the market in Amos each Saturday. Friday always marked the busiest day of the week, as it was the day during which the vegetables were prepared for marketing. From early morning until late in the evening Dominic and Elizabeth, assisted by their children, dug, washed and bunched vegetables. They were loaded into the transport before the family retired for the night so that Dominic would be prepared to leave early for the market on Saturday. This ensured securing a good spot at the market place, which was located two blocks from the church of Ste. Thérèse. Dominic always took one of the children with him to Amos so that he would have assistance in delivering the vegetables to his customers. Each week the children hoped and prayed for the privilege of being chosen to accompany their father on that exciting excursion.

Dominic soon gained the confidence of the householders of Amos, and usually had little trouble disposing of all his vegetables. On the rare occasions when a few bunches remained unsold he delivered them to the nuns at the nearby convent. The good sisters were always grateful, and promised to remember Dominic and Elizabeth and their children in their prayers.

As the summer wore on, Dominic and Elizabeth decided to extend the variety of their goods to the production of cheese and home baking. That decision proved to be profitable, and the demand for Elizabeth's baking far exceeded the rate at which she was able to supply it.

During that first summer in Quebec, the Raina children became familiar with every acre of the property, from the cleared land to the dense woods. They walked for miles around the edge of Lac d'école, and discovered that it was generously inhabited by various species of fish.

They were true children of nature. The pioneer blood of their ancestors flowed freely in their veins, and Elizabeth nurtured their love of the outdoors at every opportunity. On special nights, back in Alberta, the northern lights had danced across the skies. At such times, Elizabeth had awakened her sleeping children and carried them to the window, one by one, to show them that marvel of nature. As she held them in her arms, she whispered, "Be very quiet, and you'll be able to hear them as well as to see them." The children thrilled to the swish-swish sound of that wonder of the universe sweeping across the skies.

Here, in Quebec, their discoveries were different, but equally exciting.

Coincidentally, around the same time as the discovery of the fish, a kind neighbour offered Dominic the use of his rowboat and invited him to help himself to as many fish as he could use, from the nets he had strung out in the water of Lac d'école. Johnny was put in charge of taking the leaky rowboat out whenever Elizabeth wanted fish for supper. The other children were allowed to take turns going out in the boat with Johnny on the condition that they always obeyed his instructions. The lake was large, and squalls came up without warning, sometimes making it difficult to get the boat to shore. While Johnny pulled the fish from the nets, the second in charge was assigned the task of bailing out the water as it poured into the leaky boat. Nothing tasted better than the fish of St. Marc de Figuery, unless it was the wild berries that grew in rich abundance on the land.

Much to their delight, the children discovered a great assortment of such berries growing along most of the fences, and in patches throughout the fields. Elizabeth had taught them to always give the first ripe berries of the season to their father. The children each competed to be first to surprise their father with that special treat.

Elizabeth preserved most of the berries in juice to serve as fruit, but she also made jams and jellies. From the overflow of blueberries, she made bottles of delicious wine. Occasionally, during the night, the family was awakened by a great blast which sounded like a gun going off. It was a bottle of blueberry wine popping its cork. That always delighted the children.

While most of the berries were picked right on home land, the blueberries were picked on Dominic's second property. Johnny was in charge of the blueberry picking expedition, which consisted of the four eldest children. Early in the morning of that exciting day, Johnny, Mary, Ralph and Clara gathered every available milk pail and large container they could find. They packed lunches for themselves and oats for the horse. With great jubilation, they donned their straw hats and kissed their parents good-bye, as was customary before leaving the house. As their father waved them off he reminded them again to obey Johnny. Since Johnny was a great deal of fun, and never took advantage of his superior position, the children did not resent those instructions. They felt secure with Johnny, whom their father had always said was very responsible.

The lot where the children picked the blueberries was an isolated location. It was timberland, rather than farmland. The children knew that bears lurked in the woods behind them. Johnny told his siblings to pick near the road and to rattle their pails occasionally to scare away wild animals. Such a minor annoyance as bears in the woods could not dampen

the enthusiasm of the children as they delved into the blueberrie
the time they took a late break for lunch their pails were almosi
When they reached home in the late afternoon, tired but happy, Eliza. (th
had her jars all ready for the canning process.

That evening, the children were given the not so interesting task of
cleaning the blueberries. Dominic and Elizabeth left on their customary
evening stroll through their market garden and ripening grain, while
enthusiastically making plans for the expansion of their crops the following year. With their parents safely out of earshot the children attended
to the berries amid much mumbling and grumbling. They questioned the
wisdom of having been so industrious in the berry patch during the day.
They had planned to spend the evening in the hayloft in the barn jumping
in the hay. By the time they finished cleaning the berries they knew it
would be time to jump into bed.

Having now resided at St. Marc for several months, Dominic and
Elizabeth had become well acquainted with their neighbours and were
starting to take an active interest in the community and local
administration.

Because Dominic had served for four years previously as a municipal
councillor in Alberta, he fully understood the purposes and responsibilities of a municipal council. He had also served as Secretary of the Public
School Board, and was well aware of the obligations which belonged
solely under its jurisdiction. He was perplexed to discover that the responsibilities of the municipal council, versus those of the school board, were
not always clearly defined at St. Marc de Figuery.

As he became a regular attendant at the meetings, Dominic became
increasingly appalled at the manner in which they were conducted. He
noticed that most of the members of the council were controlled to a great
extent by Monsieur le Curé, who appeared able to manipulate them like
puppets on a string. Although the priest always permitted the men to
express their views, he usually influenced them to adopt his own final
decisions on any matters they brought forward.

At St. Marc, as elsewhere, the municipal council consisted of a mayor,
a secretary-treasurer, an assistant-secretary and six councillors. Dominic
was aware that a municipal council, represented by the mayor, was
appointed by the people to fulfill the wishes of the people.

At St. Marc, the principles embodied in the Municipal Act, which were
supposed to be the guide of the local council, were logical and fair in
theory, and similar to those of the Municipal Act of Alberta. In practice,
they appeared to be completely disregarded at St. Marc. Dominic had

always understood that the secretary-treasurer was the servant of the municipal council, simply receiving a compensation for his work done as instructed.

The reverse prevailed at St. Marc de Figuery!

The secretary-treasurer, as permitted by the Municipal Act, appointed himself an assistant-secretary. Monsieur le Curé Jules Michaud instructed the secretary-treasurer to appoint him to the role of assistant-secretary.

It was unthinkable in the community of St. Marc to act against the instructions of a priest, so his wishes were carried out. The priest was not permitted by Canon Law to hold the office of secretary. By occupying the role of assistant-secretary he managed to take charge of all books and records. He drew the salary of secretary. He gave orders and instructions to the secretary, to the councillors, as well as to the mayor. He obtained all the credit for favourable accomplishments, and transferred the blame for any mistakes to other members of the council.

The secretary did not draw any wages because he was secretary in name only and did not do any work on the council. In common with most of the settlers of the municipality, he was rather uneducated and unable to distinguish a religious matter from a strictly political one.

Under that system of administration, it appeared to Dominic that the community of St. Marc was under an absolute dictatorship. Dominic expressed his concerns to Elizabeth. He was bewildered and pensive, as he meditated on the unusual way in which the community was run. Nevertheless, he decided to withhold judgment for the time being.

All too soon, the Raina family's first summer in Quebec drew to an end!

After having been closed the previous year, l'Ecole du lac, across the road from the family home, was reopening for the new school term. The requisite number of pupils to justify this move was reached when the Raina family arrived in the community.

L'Ecole du lac was constructed in such a way as to provide living quarters for the teacher, and one large classroom to accommodate all the pupils from grades one to eight.

With great excitement and curiosity, the Raina children watched Rachel Allard, the pretty young school teacher, moving in across the road. The children were also making preparations to return to school.

Tearfully, Elizabeth went about her many duties, dreading the long hours of daily separation from her children. Elizabeth thoroughly enjoyed every one of them. She shared in all their activities, inasmuch as her busy schedule permitted. In a community where she could not yet converse freely with her neighbours, because of the language barrier, an unusually strong friendship developed between her and the children.

Mary, her eldest daughter, became her confidant. She felt privileged when her mother confided to her that she was expecting a baby in February. Because she had so many younger siblings to help care for, Mary's mother always referred to her as "my big girl." Sometimes Mary craved more personal attention than being referred to as her mother's big girl or having her mother confide in her. One evening she found another way of making her mother sit up and take notice. Mary had become fascinated by the discovery that she had hairy arms. Pulling one hair up to its full length, she showed it to her mother. Her mother's reaction surprised and delighted Mary.

"You poor girl. You will always have to wear long sleeves when you grow up," sadly commented her mother. She told Mary to show her arms to her father. "Just look at that hair, Dominic," said Elizabeth. "I told Mary that she would always have to wear long sleeves when she grows up." Glancing up from his ledger, where he was calculating figures, Mary's father nonchalantly said, "It's not what she has on her arms, but what she has in her head that will be important when she grows up." Mary was not worried about the hair on her arms. She was delighted to remind her mother from time to time of her tragedy. She and her mother would then look at each other with mutual expressions of sadness and womanly understanding.

CHAPTER IV
QUESTIONING THE SYSTEM

"There is nothing more difficult to take in hand, more perilous to conduct, or more uncertain in its success, than to take the lead in the introduction of a new order of things." Niccolo Machiavelli.

At the beginning of September, 1933, the Raina home was visited by l'Abbé Charles Minette, an official of the Department of Colonization of Amos. He was accompanied by a reporter from the newspaper, *Le bulletin des agriculteurs* — a widely-read newspaper in that area of Quebec. The reporter called for the purpose of gathering from the farmers their views on the subject of farm loans. The Department of Colonization took a deep interest in encouraging settlers into the Abitibi, and it was common to visit them periodically in order to assess their feelings on farm matters.

In the latter part of that same month an agricultural fair and exhibition of the Agricultural Society was held at St. Marc de Figuery. Dominic displayed fifteen entries and obtained fifteen prizes.

During that fall, wishing to further enlarge his little herd of cattle, Dominic bought another cow from a local farmer, for the sum of twenty-five dollars. While there was nothing unusual about the purchase of a cow, the manner in which the transaction took place was by no means commonplace. Dominic was instructed to pay the money directly to Monsieur le Curé Michaud. He learned, to his amazement, that the priest acted as the go-between in most financial matters connected with his parishioners, and that he would finalize the deal with the vendor. While Dominic went along with that strange way of conducting business on this particular occasion, he was convinced that he could not continue such a practice.

As a newcomer, he did not wish to criticize too strongly long-established customs. On the other hand, it became progressively more impossible to maintain silence in the face of such an unusual way of running a community in which he hoped to become permanently established and where he planned to raise his children. He felt convinced that life must move ahead, and he wanted to be part of that movement. At St. Marc de Figuery, he was beginning to feel as if he might sink into a quagmire.

Dominic began to discuss the situation with his neighbours. He asked them how they felt about the dictatorship under which they lived. He suggested that they give some thought to exerting more control over the direction of their lives. The settlers appeared to be interested in Dominic's views, but they were reluctant to put forth any of their own, or to rock the boat of their existence. They adopted a *laissez-faire* attitude, as being the safe way to exist at St. Marc de Figuery. The children enjoyed school. Mary and Clara each had a special friend with whom to link arms and share secrets as they walked around during recess, as was customary among the little girls. The children had become fluently bilingual and were able to participate in all discussions at school and to converse freely with their friends.

At home, they were immersed in their studies and many other interests. Each evening, after the supper dishes had been washed and put away, the children were required to do their homework. When their parents were satisfied that they had completed their assignments to the best of their ability they were allowed to play outdoors, or to pursue other personal interests, in whatever time was left before evening prayers and bed.

Johnny had learned to knit his own socks. He always hurried through his homework so that he could get at his knitting and his many other projects. He was keenly interested in airplanes, and he conscientiously kept an impressive record of the many bush planes that flew through the area on their way to the mines.

Mary was engrossed in drawing embroidery patterns. She had learned, through *The Family Herald and Weekly Star*, of a method whereby a pattern could be drawn on brown wrapping paper and then outlined with a pen-nib dipped into a mixture of blueing and sugar. When this mixture had dried well onto the paper, the pattern could be transferred to the prepared material by means of a hot iron. Mary was busy creating patterns for aprons, dresser-scarves and pillow-cases. She sold her patterns to the local women and young girls for ten cents apiece.

During his first year in the Abitibi, Dominic joined *l'Union catholique des cultivateurs de la province de Québec* and attended the local meetings. He further became a member of the local *Societé d'agriculture*, and was elected vice-president of that association for the year of 1934.

Dominic felt that only by taking an active part in the politics of the community could he become fully conversant with its people and their habits, and thereby integrate more easily into their lives. He was faced with one of two choices — to leave the Province of Quebec, or to remain and help create a situation which he could tolerate. Inasmuch as possible, he attempted to accept those conditions at St. Marc which did not compromise his principles, and to work at improving those which did.

The big event in the lives of the Raina family during the winter was the birth of Dominic Anthony Raina, Junior, on February 15, 1934.

Because it was customary for the local women to give birth to their babies at home, a mid-wife from St. Marc was summoned to the house when Elizabeth went into labour in the morning. Although Elizabeth had experienced great difficulty during the birth of each of her children, she had always been reassured by the presence of a doctor at her bedside. But Elizabeth felt it was important to follow the established tradition of the community, and because she did not wish to draw attention to herself, she elected for the home confinement. It was with great difficulty, and at a serious risk to her life, that she gave birth to the largest of her babies. Nicky, as the new baby was called, delighted his brothers and sisters and was welcomed with great enthusiasm. He was a happy baby, and the older children vied with each other for the privilege of holding him.

Dominic passed the cold winter days of the family's second year in Quebec by cutting fuel and doing daily chores. Evenings were often passed in again socializing with the neighbours.

In the community of St. Marc de Figuery it was common for many of the local farmers to ship their milk to the creameries as a means of livelihood, but the method of payment for their milk appeared to be unique. Rather than the farmers receiving their milk cheques directly, they were customarily forwarded to Monsieur le Curé, who endorsed and cashed them. He retained the amount which he calculated should constitute the church dues of the parishioners in question. Being ignorant as to how business was conducted in other parts of Canada, the settlers involved expressed gratitude to the priest for what they considered to be his generosity, when he delivered the remainder of the money to them.

Dominic could not silently tolerate witnessing this exploitation of less educated and uninformed people. For that reason, he verbally opposed this method of conducting business. It was the first of many similar protests. Dominic again seriously considered leaving the province but, after much consideration, he resolved not to give up so easily. He had exhausted most of his resources towards resettling his family in their new home at St. Marc de Figuery, and to move again so soon would be disruptive.

With the coming of the spring of 1934, Dominic and Elizabeth planted a much larger market garden than in the previous year. The weekly trips to the market at Amos were resumed. Their efforts were proving to be profitable, as the demand for their vegetables, home-made cheese, and freshly-baked rolls and buns escalated.

In order to help the settlers financially, the provincial government had introduced a system whereby all families, both rich and poor, were given a ten-dollar *piton* each month. The piton had quite a story among the settlers of the Abitibi. Contrary to most cheques, pitons were redeemable only at certain stores appointed by the Government. They were exchangeable for settlers' effects, generally at exhorbitant prices far above value.

The provincial government, for the purpose of creating new homes and developing the northwestern region of Quebec as rapidly as possible, had offered several inducements to attract settlers to that region. On his arrival in the Abitibi, Dominic had been presented with the customary pamphlet, *Le guide du colon*, by Hermidas Magnan. That booklet, issued by the Department of Colonization, embodied the duties and rights of settlers, and included an article outlining premiums which were to be given them for the clearing of their land up to a certain acreage.

During August of 1934, Dominic had a misunderstanding with the Department of Colonization of Amos in connection with that particular matter. Dominic had done considerable work on his property and submitted his claim for the extra acreage. After the officials of the Department of Colonization had inspected the work, he was notified that he would receive a sum of cash. However, he was later offered grass seed as a substitute for the cash.

Wishing to be as cooperative as possible, Dominic agreed to accept the seed, on the understanding that this would not be considered a donation. It was customary to give gifts of grass seed to needy settlers, and he wished to be viewed as self-supporting. On the termination of the transaction, he was requested by the Department of Colonization to sign a statement to the effect that he had received a charitable donation from them. Dominic refused to do this. In the community of St. Marc de Figuery it was not uncommon to use bribery, in the form of grass seed or floor linoleum, to secure votes during elections, and he did not wish to be under such an unsavoury form of obligation.

During that summer, a mission was held in the local parish church. Accompanied by a group of friends, Mary skipped up the walk leading to the church to attend the evening service on the first day of the mission. Before entering the door, she was stopped by the missionary. He addressed himself to her, and told her that she had been chosen by God to be a nun, although the basis for this claim was not explained. He asked her to visit him in the rectory after the service in order to discuss the matter further. The outcome of the discussions between the missionary, her parents and herself, was that she would enter the convent of Our Lady of Lourdes at Sturgeon Falls, Ontario. The order was under the guidance of the Sisters of Wisdom. Mary was given a list of the clothes she would need to wear as a postulant. Everything visible was required to be black. The sombreness of her wardrobe symbolized the life of discipline and self-denial that she was about to enter in exchange for a privilege which she did not understand.

Early in the morning of August 20, amid hugs and tears from her family, Mary awaited the transportation arranged for her by the missionary for her journey to her new life. On her departure, she was accompanied by two other little ''chosen'' girls from St. Mathieu de Figuery — a community across the river from St. Marc de Figuery.

Although the three young girls were apprehensive in the face of the unknown, they were comforted by the knowledge that they were about to dedicate their lives to God. In their innocence, they were unaware that they were not following a path of their own choosing, nor were they mature enough to make such a serious choice. Rather, they were following the will of the clergy of their church, and it was debatable whether it was also the will of God.

But Mary was not unfamiliar with the order of the Sisters of Wisdom. Coincidentally, among all the different religious orders of nuns in the Province of Quebec, it seemed fatalistic that Mary was being recruited to join the order of the Sisters of Wisdom in the Province of Ontario.

Mary was born in the Catholic hospital of Our Lady of Grace at Castor, Alberta, which was run by the Sisters of Wisdom. When Elizabeth confided to her favourite nun that she was unsure about a first name for her child, the nun suggested, ''Why don't you call her Mary and put her under the protection of the Blessed Virgin Mary?'' Elizabeth considered that to be a beautiful suggestion.

When Mary was a little girl she enjoyed hearing how she got her name, and asked her mother to tell her the story over and over again. Mary was proud that she had been named by a nun, and felt secure to be walking around under the protection of the Blessed Virgin Mary.

Mary's second experience with the Sisters of Wisdom was when she was five years old and Johnny was six. It was the year in which both children would receive the Sacraments of Penance and Holy Eucharist. Although Dominic had already taught them their catechism and their junior

Bible from cover to cover, he wished them to have a still better grounding in their Catholic faith prior to the reception of the sacraments. Having come from Italy, where it was customary for the more affluent families to have their children educated in boarding schools, Dominic chose to enroll Johnny and Mary at the convent school of Our Lady of Grace, which was under the direction of the Sisters of Wisdom. It was adjacent to the hospital where both children had been born, and it was located forty miles from their home at Hanna.

Dominic was not averse to Mary entering the convent, where both English and French were taught, and he did not attempt to sway her from her decision.

Elizabeth, on the other hand, felt that Mary was much too young to become a nun, and she did not really approve of her going so far away. Nevertheless, as was her custom, she supported Dominic in his view that it would undoubtedly be a good experience for their daughter. Dominic was confident that, by learning first-hand what was involved in joining a religious order, Mary would be better prepared to reach a decision before taking her final vows.

In addition to already being well grounded in the Catholic faith, the older Raina children were not strangers to the Protestant denominations. In Alberta, most of their friends were Protestant, and each faith accepted the other without question. At that point in their lives, the children had never encountered bigotry of any kind, either in race or in religion.

As time went on at St. Marc de Figuery, the men of the community became more and more interested in Dominic's views of what was wrong with life in some of the rural areas of Quebec. Under his influence, they were taking a fresh look at their community and were beginning to question some of Monsieur le Curé's practices.

Dominic continued to visit the priest at regular intervals. He attempted to maintain a good relationship by means of what he considered to be constructive discussions. He expressed a hope that the settlers could be encouraged to become more independent in conducting their personal affairs. Monsieur le Curé was not receptive to Dominic's suggestions regarding the advancement and self-sufficiency of the settlers. The differences in opinion between the two men multiplied. When Dominic became more impatient and vocal at the priest's resistance to loosen control over his flock, Monsieur le Curé responded by producing his Code Book — a volume constantly used by him for the purpose of intimidating his parishioners.

Dominic carefully studied, and often disagreed, with the priest interpretation of a particular code. Monsieur le Curé was not accustomed to being questioned on his system of running the community, and was becoming antagonistic towards Dominic's interference and his refusal to accept the code at face value at all times.

One evening, in late August, Dominic confided to Elizabeth that he did not feel completely welcome or at ease in Quebec. He felt accepted and respected by his neighbours, who were interested in listening to his views and who had begun to seek his advice. But he no longer felt at ease with some of the officials of the Department of Colonization, or with Monsieur le Curé Michaud. The easy friendship he had shared with the priest had become progressively more strained, although their visits together continued. He sensed that the priest felt threatened by his presence in the community, and by the influence he had begun to exert among the parishioners.

The priest's new changing attitude towards him, combined with the incident of the bonus by the Department of Colonization earlier in the spring, did not strengthen Dominic's sense of security.

Elizabeth would have welcomed a return to Alberta. She felt far removed from all her relatives at Castor. She missed the dear friends who had chosen to remain at Hanna in a bid to survive the drought and hope for better days. She assured Dominic that if he felt it wiser to emigrate from the province she would be delighted.

Shortly after expressing his feelings to Elizabeth, Dominic visited the office of the Department of Colonization at Amos, where he told l'Abbé Charles Minette that he did not feel welcome in the Abitibi. He asked the priest for assistance in selling the property that he had bought through the department, so that he could move his family out of the Province of Quebec. L'Abbé Minette assured him that he was considered to be an excellent settler and that he should not think of leaving. The assurances, though given in a flattering manner by one of the senior officials of the Land Office, failed to reassure Dominic.

During the following week, Dominic experienced a strange incident at the market-place at Amos. While winding up with the sale of his products he noticed a smartly-dressed man alight from a car, which had drawn up and stopped just across the road from his stand. The man approached Dominic and entered into a short and rather puzzling conversation. Among other things, he asked: "Are you Catholic? Are you Canadian?" He then mentioned a nice Italian whom he had known in the Temiscouata — a region situated on the south bank of the St. Lawrence River, southeast of Quebec City.

The conversation apparently having terminated to his satisfaction, the stranger crossed the road and entered his car, where several other gentlemen were awaiting him. From the attitude they adopted, Dominic received the strange impression that he had been under an informal investigation, the reasons for which he could not imagine.

Turning to the man who occupied the stand next to his — an old-timer who was familiar with people and conditions in the area — Dominic enquired, "Who is that man?" His neighbour replied that he was a spotter.

Spotting what? Dominic was not to know the answer to that question until some time later, when all the pieces of the puzzle would fall clearly into place. After relating the events of the day to Elizabeth that evening, Dominic remarked that in future he would feel rather uncomfortable going to Amos alone.

Shortly afterwards, Dominic was scheduled to give a speech on the subject of cooperation to the United Farmers of Amos. With the puzzling incidents taking place, he felt it inadvisable to attend the meeting. Furthermore, he began thinking seriously about removing his family from the Abitibi.

To witness, in silence, the unjust system of administration under which he found himself was intolerable to him. His vocal protests were serving to enlighten the other settlers as to their rights as citizens. Since they had previously been kept in ignorance, Dominic felt that his interference might prove unacceptable to the authorities and dangerous to himself.

Before Dominic had a chance to follow through with his plans to leave St. Marc, events followed in brisk succession — the terrible and the tragic mixed with the ridiculous!

The cattle of the community of St. Marc were injected for tuberculosis testing on October 23 by an inspector from the Department of Agriculture. A few days later, when Johnny examined the neighbouring cattle to see how they had reacted to the injections, he noticed that their symptoms were identical to those of his father's cattle. He rushed home to cheerfully announce, "If ours go, they all go." Since Dominic's herd had been bought locally, and was often pastured with neighbouring cattle, it was a shock to learn that it was the only one in the entire neighbourhood condemned to be slaughtered. Dominic was instructed to dispose of his animals and to be responsible for the burning of their carcasses. One morning, as the cattle were friskily cavorting through the pasture, he shot them, one by one, and disposed of their remains, as instructed by authorities.

The misfortune came as a great a blow to the Raina family, where expenses had been heavy during the preceding two months. Just three days previously, Dominic had paid the balance of the third payment due on Elizabeth's life insurance policy. Ralph had been operated on for appendicitis a short time before. The cost of his hospitalization, in addition to the expenses of Mary's departure for Sturgeon Falls in August, had dug deeply into the family funds.

During those worrisome days, Elizabeth sought comfort by taking long walks in the woods by herself. From her pioneer parents she had inherited a great love of nature, and that was where she found her greatest comfort when faced with adversity. She missed Mary greatly. When her loneliness for her eldest daughter threatened to engulf her, she took refuge in the woods. There she walked and prayed. Although the letters she received from Sturgeon Falls were cheerful and descriptive of Mary's new life, Elizabeth felt that her daughter belonged at home with the rest of the family.

One Sunday morning before Mass, shortly after the slaughter of the cattle, Dominic called at the presbytery at St. Marc to discuss farming with Monsieur le Curé Michaud. He still hoped to re-establish a comfortable relationship with the priest.

He confided to Monsieur le Curé his bewilderment at the loss of his cattle, and he questioned how they could possibly have been the only ones condemned to be slaughtered when they were in fact part of the local herds. The priest merely shrugged his shoulders. Dominic commented that this loss would constitute a serious setback in his plans. Monsieur le Curé expressed surprise to learn that Dominic was determined to continue farming his land in preference to working at the mines, where a steady income would be assured. Dominic explained that he had great faith in the fertility of his land and was convinced that any time he spent in cultivating it would be returned a hundredfold.

Although the conversation passed off pleasantly enough, Dominic felt that his presence at St. Marc was a thorn in the priest's side. As he sat in church before Mass, he continued to puzzle over the slaughter of his cattle. He wondered if something underhanded was going on in a bid to rid the community of his presence. If so, to what lengths would this be pursued?

Dominic felt even more uneasy when the priest stated from the pulpit, during Mass, that the men of the parish should not attempt to feed their families by cultivating their land. He announced that there was plenty of work to be had at LaCorne — a mine situated about ten miles south of St. Marc — for both Canadians and foreigners. All of the people present, with the exception of Dominic and his family, were considered to be Canadians because they were French-speaking. The Raina family was the only one in the parish considered, and referred to, as foreigners because they had immigrated to the community from a Canadian province other than Quebec, and because they spoke English. Dominic was convinced that the priest's remarks had been directed at him, and he resented being struck at from the pulpit with no chance to defend himself.

One Sunday in November, at a well-attended public meeting held in the basement of the church of St. Marc, Dominic pointed out to Monsieur le Curé that he was not a foreigner. He stated: "I am a naturalized British subject, and as such I have the full rights of a British subject, from the Atlantic to the Pacific, from the American boundary to the Arctic Ocean." Monsieur le Curé replied that he did not have to believe that Dominic was naturalized.

Dominic considered the priest's remark to be antagonistic, and he experienced even greater feelings of insecurity at St. Marc. Although he got along splendidly with his neighbours, he had become convinced that his perception and questioning, of what he considered to be unethical practices by some of the authorities, were resented.

Dominic resolved to take all possible steps for the protection of his family. He had been planning to draw up a Will, but had not considered it to be an urgent matter. While he expected to live for many years, he felt it prudent to be prepared for any eventuality. That resolve was prompted by the nature of the provincial laws of Quebec: in most cases, they accorded to married women merely the rights of a minor.

Because there was not a lawyer available at St. Marc, Monsieur le Curé customarily attended to all legal matters involving his parishioners. Dominic invited the priest to his home so that they could attend to the matter of the Will. He expressed an explicit wish that a certain neighbour, who was a brother Knight of Columbus, be one of the witnesses and that he act as administrator. In view of the status of women in Quebec at the time, Dominic considered it inadvisable to appoint Elizabeth to the role. He was convinced that, in the event of his death, Monsieur le Curé would immediately take control — a situation he wished to avoid.

Monsieur le Curé failed, repeatedly, to cooperate in the matter of the Will, although he had promised to do so. After he had cancelled several appointments, when he was usually curious about such matters and eager to be consulted, Dominic concluded that for some strange reason he did not wish to be involved in his particular case. He eventually decided to go to Amos to consult one of the priests there.

This decision proved to be tragically unfortunate!

CHAPTER V

THE ABDUCTION

"Opinions cannot survive if one has no chance to fight for them." Thomas Mann.

The beginning of the censured lives of the Raina family took place on November 23, 1934, the second anniversary of their departure from Alberta.

On that day, while walking alone on the sidewalk west of Bigué's Drugstore in Amos, Dominic was approached and arrested by the town constable. Recognizing the man as a representative of law and order, Dominic did not resist. He knew himself to be innocent of any crime and assumed that he had been mistaken for another man. He asked the constable to take him to the Continental Hotel, two blocks away, so that he could be identified and released. The manager of the hotel knew Dominic well, having often bought his produce at the market.

After some deliberation, the constable reluctantly took his captive to the fire station, which served as the town jail and harboured a cell in one corner. He then ordered Dominic to remove the contents from his pockets. The constable took possession of a small jackknife, some matches, and cigarette tobacco. He instructed Dominic to retain the rest of the articles, consisting of valuable documents, papers, and a few miscellaneous items. He then locked his prisoner in a cell.

Meanwhile, much activity was taking place at St. Marc!

When Dominic had failed to return home at the expected time Elizabeth began to feel uneasy, as it was not his custom to be late. When he had not returned by early morning her uneasiness turned to panic. She resolved to go to Amos in an effort to locate him.

On reaching that decision, Elizabeth bundled up the children. She gave them hot cocoa, checked the fires and locked the door, while Johnny hitched up the horse. Holding nine-months-old Nicky on her lap, Elizabeth sat beside Johnny on the front seat of the wagon. Ralph, Clara, Louis and George were well wrapped up in a makeshift bed in the rear. The family then set out for Amos on that cold November morning.

Bells were ringing from the Church of Ste. Thérèse when the little group reached town. Those chimes convinced Elizabeth that she would find Dominic in church. It was customary for him to attend Mass whenever the opportunity presented itself. While she waited in the wagon, Johnny went to the church to seek his father. He returned with the report that he was nowhere to be found.

Being rather unfamiliar with Amos, and having as yet little knowledge of the French language, Elizabeth was undecided as to what to do next. She suddenly recalled that Dominic had occasionally dined at Blais' Restaurant on his weekly trips to the market. She hoped that he might be there. An errand of investigation again proved futile. There appeared to be no alternative but to return home with the children, who were hungry and cold.

After having progressed approximately one half-mile past the outskirts of the town, Elizabeth asked Johnny to stop the horse so that she might think matters over more carefully. Realizing that she had not accomplished a thing, she knew that positive action must be taken. Because of the many puzzling incidents of the recent past, she was fearful that harm had befallen Dominic.

After careful thought, Elizabeth instructed Johnny to return to Amos to enquire of l'Abbé Charles Minette of the Department of Colonization if he had seen his father. While Elizabeth proceeded on the homeward route with the younger children, Johnny returned on foot to Amos to do as his mother had asked.

On reaching home, Elizabeth was informed by some of her nearest neighbours that her husband had been picked up by the police. That news had preceded her to St. Marc. Was it possible that someone at St. Marc had instigated the arrest? Or was the town of Amos responsible? As is so often the case in matters of this nature, the ones most concerned were not told. Because Dominic had always been a scrupulously honest man, and because his integrity had never been questioned, Elizabeth was completely bewildered. She could not imagine where to turn for an explanation. She could only weep.

Hungry children soon inspired her to dry those futile tears and to set about the preparation of a meal. While so doing, she discovered that the house had been ransacked during her absence. Elizabeth could not fathom what had prompted such an action.

A short time later, Elizabeth was visited by four women of the parish, whom she believed had been sent to call on her. With some difficulty, because of the language barrier, she managed to carry on a conversation with them. They were the first informants of the news that Dominic was scheduled to be taken to Quebec City that very day. Bewildered and humiliated, Elizabeth resisted her desire to ask any questions or to demand an explanation, fearing the answers she might get. Being unaware as to why Dominic had been arrested, she could only wonder if he was being transferred to a jail in Quebec City. She could not imagine what the charges might be.

In the meantime, Johnny arrived home. He had made the ten-mile trip from Amos to St. Marc on foot, and was tired and hungry. As instructed by his mother, he had gone to the Department of Colonization to ask the officials there whether they had seen his father. They assured him that his father was being well cared for, although they did not specify the nature of the care. Furthermore, instead of permitting Johnny to see his father, they offered him a ten-dollar piton.

On his way home from Amos Johnny had encountered two men from St. Marc, who chatted with him and told him that his father was in the hospital. Seemingly, with the exception of the Raina family themselves, the whole community of St. Marc was aware of what had happened to Dominic.

While Johnny was giving an account of his activities, the assembled ladies were obviously attempting to translate the conversation. They were eager to know what Johnny had discovered. Before he had an opportunity to tell them, in their language, Johnny was distracted by an insistent knock on the door.

An unexpected visitor, in the person of Monsieur le Curé Jules Michaud, arrived at the house on a never-to-be-forgotten errand. He appeared to be in a great hurry as he opened the door and entered the room. With an air of authority, his first words to Elizabeth were, "Give me the number of your husband's life insurance policies."

Believing that Dominic had sent the priest, and having been taught always to recognize the clergy as representative of God, Elizabeth complied with his request. After the priest had marked the number of the policies down on a slip of paper, he instructed Elizabeth to append her signature. Fearing that Dominic might be very ill, and assuming that the priest had come in connection with his Will, Elizabeth again complied. Then, picking up the policies, she handed them to the priest, and asked, "Will you take care of them for me, Father?"

Elizabeth had never had to deal with business matters. She was in a community where she was unfamiliar with the language, and in a terrifying situation. She still trusted Monsieur le Curé, and depended on him for guidance at this crucial time. Elizabeth's naivety and trust had served the priest well: she was unaware that she had just signed over to him power of attorney over the policies.

For the second time, Monsieur le Curé produced a document, to which Elizabeth again affixed her signature. As she did so, she remarked, "Father, I am so nervous and upset, I can hardly sign my name."

When she asked the priest as to exactly what time the train was scheduled to leave for Quebec City, he replied abruptly, "four o'clock." It was then nearing three o'clock. The station was ten miles away, and there was no immediate means of transportation. It would be impossible to reach Amos by four o'clock, were she to take the horse and wagon.

Elizabeth pleaded, "Could I not see my husband before he is taken away?"

Madame Napoléon Doucet, wife of the Mayor of St. Marc and one of the four ladies present, asked, "Does she wish to see her husband?"

"Yes," affirmed a second lady, "She does."

After some contemplation, Madame Doucet volunteered the information that Mathias Poirier and Normand Bourque, two of the councillors of St. Marc, had been appointed to escort Dominic on his trip to Quebec City. She added that her husband was scheduled to drive them to Amos, and could perhaps give her a lift should there be room in his car. She cautioned Elizabeth that this was merely a possibility and that she should not depend on it.

Her hopes having risen at that offer, Elizabeth hastened to prepare Dominic's working clothes, as suggested by Monsieur le Curé. They consisted of a pair of overalls, a shirt, and a jacket. She made arrangements for a kind neighbour to mind the children during her absence, should she be fortunate enough to get to Amos.

Finally, after what seemed to be an eternity, and after she had made countless trips upstairs, where the window offered a better view of the main road and any approaching cars, the mayor arrived with the two escorts. Elizabeth was given transportation to Amos, but not a word was spoken to her throughout the seemingly endless trip.

On their arrival in town, Elizabeth expected to be taken to the hospital to see Dominic. Much to her horror and dismay, the car came to a halt in front of a building on which was inscribed the word "POLICE," where she was asked to get out.

With feelings of dread, fearful of what she might discover, Elizabeth walked into the building.

Dominic's first request of the town constable, after the latter had locked him up and switched out the light the previous night, was that a priest be brought to him. There were several priests in Amos, and all only a couple of blocks away. The constable promised to accede to that request. After a considerable interval of time had elapsed, and a priest had not put in an appearance, Dominic repeated his request more emphatically. When it became obvious to Dominic that he would not be visited by a priest, he asked that his family physician be brought to the jail.

All in vain!

He then begged for his family, for friends, or for a brother Knight of Columbus.

Everything was promised! Everything was denied!

Repeatedly, he pleaded to be taken to court in order that he might be told what wrong he had committed that would warrant his being detained behind bars. Eventually, he was forced to concede that he would not be granted a hearing, and that he would be denied even those most elementary notions of justice normally accorded to the worst criminals of the land. On meditating on the strange and puzzling happenings of the two previous months, Dominic was convinced that his was not an ordinary arrest but that worse was yet to come.

Although Dominic had never before been in a jail, he was aware of the fact that even the greatest criminals, when detained in prison, were given nourishment. That privilege was denied him.

In a final desperate attempt to obtain justice, Dominic again pleaded and begged of the constable to take him to court so that he might be granted the right to plead his case before a judge, if there was a case to plead.

His requests were ignored.

Eventually, Dominic's repeated insistences produced a visitor, who arrived accompanied by the constable. The man was a stranger. True, Dominic had asked to see a brother Knight of Columbus, and that man was a Knight of Columbus of Amos, but he did not come as a brother.

On entering the prisoner's cell, the visitor asked Dominic if he knew his identity. Never having seen the man before, Dominic assured him that he did not.

The stranger introduced himself as being Dr. Marcel Sarazin of Amos, and then asked Dominic his name.

Dominic replied, "I am Dominic Raina of St. Marc de Figuery."

The doctor ordered the prisoner to hand over the documents that he carried in his pockets. Not recognizing in the man a representative of the law, Dominic firmly refused to comply with that command. The doctor grabbed the prisoner and, with the assistance of the town constable, proceeded to give him an injection through his clothes.

It was shortly after the doctor's visit to Dominic that Elizabeth found herself on the street in front of the fire station trying to summon up the courage to face her husband. There was little time for hesitation. Mathias Poirier, one of the councillors of St. Marc who had been appointed to act as escort to Dominic on the trip to Quebec City, approached to conduct her to the cell. On entering the fire station he called, "Monsieur Raina."

Recognizing the voice, Dominic replied, "Oui, Monsieur Poirier." Then, raising himself from the cot at the back of his degrading enclosure, he came forward to greet his visitor and to ask him whether he knew when the doors of the cell would be opened.

Only then did Elizabeth, who had never before seen a cell, realize that Dominic was behind bars. She looked on speechlessly as Mathias Poirier told Dominic that the door would be unlocked at three-forty-five o'clock p.m. He then displayed the keys to the cell, which he had in his possession.

Those keys, in the hands of one of the six councillors of St. Marc, led Dominic to believe that the town of Amos had transferred his fate to the authorities of St. Marc. That action further suggested to him that the town of Amos had not found cause for punitive measures.

Dominic's first words to Elizabeth as she approached his cell were, "Now that I am behind bars, what is going to be done with my wife and poor little children?"

In a silent gesture of encouragement, Elizabeth handed him his prayer book, which she had brought from home.

Fearing that time might be limited, and that it might be unwise to waste it in unnecessary conversation, Dominic outlined a few important errands which he asked Elizabeth to attend to immediately. He instructed her to send a telegram to the Honourable E.G. Garland, Member of Parliament, House of Commons, for Bow River, Alberta. As a former fellow westerner, Dominic had great confidence in the Honourable Garland, and he wished authorities in the Province of Alberta to know of his dilemma. In the frightening situation in which he found himself, he felt motivated to grasp at any straw. He also asked her to pick up some stationery and stamps.

As she rushed down the street on her errands, Elizabeth encountered Napoléon Doucet and Normand Bourque. Both men signalled her to enter the car in which she had been driven to Amos. She explained to the best of her ability, since neither man could understand English, that she first wished to buy some stationery. After making her purchase she proceeded to the station, where she informed the clerk at the wicket that she wished to send a telegram. At that moment, her glance wandered to the window, through which she noticed that the four o'clock train from the west, en route to Quebec City, had pulled into Amos.

Forgotten, for the time being, was the telegram!

Present only was the awful realization that this was the train which was to take her husband four hundred miles away from home! To speak to him before he boarded the train was the only thing that mattered to her at the moment.

She rushed out onto the platform and raced frantically from train window to train window, in the hope of getting one last glimpse of her husband. She believed him to be in one of the coaches. As she was trying to locate him, she turned about and noticed him advancing along the platform under the escort of the two guards. She was appalled at his appearance of fatigue and illness.

While Dominic had been awaiting Elizabeth's return he was visited by Mathias Poirier and Normand Bourque, the two councillors of St. Marc who had been appointed by Monsieur le Curé Jules Michaud to escort him to Quebec City. One of the men unlocked the cell — a gesture that led Dominic to believe, for a few minutes, that he was to be conducted to the courthouse for the long-awaited hearing. He had not been informed that he was scheduled to be taken to Quebec City. Having assumed that he was aware of the trip, Elizabeth had not mentioned it during their brief time together. Dominic felt optimistic when he was escorted from the cell and out onto the street, but his hopes were quickly squashed when he was ordered to enter a car parked in front of the fire station.

Because the courthouse was only a few steps away, Dominic once again became wary and suspicious, and resisted entering the car. The guards did not force the issue, but conducted him along the street on foot. The trio proceeded, first in an easterly direction, then southward toward the station, where the train awaited.

Husband and wife were separated by a shoving, yelling, curious mass of humanity. The crowd appeared identical to the one that had gathered on that same platform, at that same station, at that same hour, approximately two years earlier, when Dominic and his family had descended the steps of the train from the west to set foot in Amos.

Finally, after breaking a passageway through the noisy crowd of spectators, the guards reached the door of the train with their prisoner. It was while they were attempting to shove him into the train that Elizabeth came face to face with her husband. As he was being forcibly pushed up the steps, Dominic pleaded, "Let me speak to my wife first." He snatched a moment to kiss her and to say, "Keep on praying and everything will turn out alright." It was under those degrading circumstances that Elizabeth had a last glimpse of her husband, as he was unceremoniously shoved into the coach. Moments later, the train pulled out en route to Quebec City.

Standing there on the platform, grieving, Elizabeth was approached by Napoléon Doucet. For the third time that day, he signalled her to enter his car. For the third time she refused, offering the excuse that she had to send a telegram.

On reaching the telegraph office, she transmitted the telegram, word for word, as Dominic had dictated. It informed the Honourable Garland that Dominic Raina, a former resident of Alberta, was being unjustly detained and tortured in the jail of Amos in the Province of Quebec.

On learning the nature of the telegram, the operator appeared angry. He remarked that it was a terrible telegram to send across Canada, and not very flattering to the Province of Quebec. He stated, further, that Dominic was not in jail, but was being transferred to a good hospital where he would be treated for his ulcers. Dominic had suffered for many years from ulcers of the stomach.

Weeping, Elizabeth retorted, "How do I know where they are sending my husband? I was told he was in a hospital and I found him in jail."

The man repeated that it was a terrible telegram.

To avoid argument, Elizabeth agreed to a slight rewording of the wire, but instructed that it vary as little as possible from the original dictation so that her husband's wishes might be fulfilled.

As the discussion reached its conclusion, Napoléon Doucet entered the office and approached the operator. He took him aside and the two men spoke briefly. When they had completed their discussion, Elizabeth approached the operator a second time in order to pay for the telegram. Napoléon Doucet then beckoned her to follow him. She was conducted to the car, where she did not protest when instructed to step in. She was then driven to the Continental Hotel, where Napoléon Doucet asked her to await his return while he attended to business matters.

Certain people at the hotel, noticing that Elizabeth was greatly disturbed and extremely weary, offered sympathetic consolation. The manager of the hotel, on learning the cause of her grief, became concerned. He commented that he had often bought produce from Dominic at the market and that he knew him to be a fine man. He went out to make enquiries concerning the arrest. On his return to the hotel, he appeared worried and agitated, and counselled Elizabeth not to remain alone with the children at St. Marc.

After a wait of about two hours at the hotel, Elizabeth was picked up and driven home by Napoléon Doucet. There, she was met by her children, who had waited impatiently her return, eager to learn what fate had befallen their father. With her children gathered around her, Elizabeth told them that their father was en route to Quebec City to an unknown destination. Feeling utterly helpless, mother and children wept together.

So began their fatherless life in hostile surroundings!

CHAPTER VI

ELIZABETH'S LONELY ORDEAL

"I bend but do not break." Jean de la Fontaine.

Elizabeth retired early to bed that night. She was totally exhausted, both physically and mentally. Too worried to fall asleep, she spent the night reviewing the events of the day. She tried, in vain, to make sense of all that had happened.

Repeatedly, she asked herself: "Why did everyone, in both Amos and St. Marc, know what was going on when I wasn't told a thing? Why was Dominic arrested? Where is he now? Will he ever come back? How will I cope alone with the children when I know so little French? Who can I trust?"

The language barrier took on momentous proportions. Because English was customarily spoken at home, Elizabeth had little opportunity to learn French. She was busy with the care of her family, and the only occasions on which she was exposed to French was when she and Dominic exchanged visits with the neighbours. She knew that she would have to depend on her bilingual children when conducting any matters of business. Her thoughts turned often to Mary. While she missed her greatly and wanted her back home, she was now gratified to know that she was in a safe place. She feared what the future might hold for the rest of the children and herself.

Early the following morning, Elizabeth roused her children and suggested that they all kneel down to unite in prayer that God help their father in his plight. She also asked for guidance from above on what course of action to take to bring him home again.

She eventually decided to phone the Taylors, one of the few English-speaking families in Amos with whom she had become acquainted and whom she felt she could trust.

In response to her telephone call, the Taylors drove immediately to St. Marc to discuss the matter at the family home. Elizabeth was convinced that Dominic had not been guilty of any offence. Since she wished desperately to know his whereabouts, she asked the Taylors to drive her to the Department of Colonization of Amos. She was convinced that the officials there could tell her where her husband was and that they would have the power to reunite him with his family.

The Taylors volunteered to go, themselves, to the Department of Colonization to see what could be done. They consoled Elizabeth with the promise that they would obtain Dominic's address, and assured her that they would send a telegram advising him that all was well at home and that he was not to worry over his family. With final words of sympathy and encouragement, and assurances that they would return the following day, the Taylors departed.

True to their promise, and generously bearing gifts in an attempt to cheer up the disconsolate family, they returned the following afternoon. They had succeeded in obtaining Dominic's address, which read: "Hospital of St. Michael the Archangel, Mastaï, near Quebec City, P.Q."

Since Elizabeth was unfamiliar with hospitals in and around Quebec City, she did not realize the significance of that address. She consoled herself with the thought that only a nice hospital could bear such a nice name. She was grateful to know that Dominic was not in jail.

Having been busily occupied before his abduction with the winding up of fall work, Dominic had not had time to cut fuel for the winter. Despite the fact that they were mere children, Johnny and Ralph assumed that responsibility. On November 26, while dragging logs, one swung over and badly injured Johnny's foot, causing it to swell and to become very painful.

On the following day, Elizabeth was visited by Royal Renaud, Inspector of the Department of Colonization of Amos, accompanied by a Knight of Columbus. Royal Renaud's companion volunteered the information that he was not connected with the Department of Colonization, although his office was located in the same building.

Noticing Johnny's bandaged swollen foot, which was causing him great discomfort, the gentlemen asked permission to examine it. After careful inspection, they advised Elizabeth to apply salt pork to the injured area. Home medications were used extensively throughout the community of St. Marc. It was only in serious cases that a doctor was consulted. It was unfortunate that Johnny did not have an opportunity to give the injured limb sufficient rest at a time when a man's job and a father's responsibility were resting heavily on his young shoulders. In spite of the treatment suggested by the gentlemen he limped for sometime afterward, and his foot never ceased to trouble him.

The original purpose of the visit of the two gentlemen was to enquire after Dominic's life insurance policies. Elizabeth informed them that they were with Monsieur le Curé Jules Michaud for safekeeping. On puzzling over the interest displayed by the visitors in that connection, Elizabeth reached the fearful conclusion that Dominic must be seriously ill. The gentlemen assured her that they had not had any news to that effect but felt it wise to have the policies in order, should something unforeseen occur. After having obtained all the desired information in connection with the policies, the visitors departed. The gentleman who had accompanied Royal Renaud had promised to make arrangements with a neighbour to deliver five dollars' worth of fuel to the house. Elizabeth greatly appreciated this act of generosity.

That same week, a kind woman of the neighbourhood drove to St. Marc to suggest to Monsieur le Curé that he organize a bee among the men of his parish for the purpose of cutting fuel for Elizabeth. The priest refused to consider the suggestion, explaining that he did not have enough fuel for his presbytery.

About a week after Dominic's abduction, and after the guards had returned from Quebec City, that same woman called on Elizabeth to give her a second-hand account of Dominic's trip. She recounted how much the guards had enjoyed the opportunity to travel to Quebec City. They had supposedly taken advantage of the trip to visit acquaintances there. They had also expressed amusement at how ravenously Dominic had eaten on the train. His hunger was understandable, since he had not been given nourishment of any kind for over twenty-four hours. The neighbour terminated her narrative by delivering the startling information that Elizabeth was expected to pay all the expenses incurred on that trip.

Elizabeth was incredulous to hear that she was expected to pay for her husband's abduction. Wishing to verify that rumour before allowing herself to worry unduly, she sent Johnny to phone Monsieur le Curé the following day to ask him for a verbal statement of the taxes owed on the property. The priest informed Johnny that the taxes had amounted to thirty-four dollars on the day of Dominic's arrest a week earlier, but that they had since increased by approximately one hundred dollars. From that statement, Elizabeth realized that the expenses of the abduction had indeed been charged to her.

On his return from the post office at St. Marc, on the evening of December 4, Johnny carried in his pocket a long-awaited letter from his father. Needless to say, there was much excitement at home when Elizabeth opened the envelope.

It was only when she read, "I find myself in an insane asylum where I have passed four days and four nights of terrible suffering," did she know the nature of the hospital in which Dominic was confined.

In that first letter, Dominic had copied, word for word, an article which he had read with interest in a French newspaper, and which he suggested Johnny translate to Elizabeth.

So great was her delight on hearing from Dominic that Elizabeth rushed to give the news to her nearest neighbour. On learning the contents of the letter, the neighbour asked Elizabeth if she thought that her husband would return. Feeling that there was no reason for her to think otherwise, she replied, "Why certainly." Her response produced incredulous looks among the people present.

The following day, after she had had time to think matters over more carefully, Elizabeth grew increasingly bewildered. Why was Dominic in an insane asylum? To whom could she go for an explanation? Monsieur le Curé seemed the logical person.

On reaching the presbytery, and on handing Dominic's letter to the priest, Elizabeth asked, "Father, did you think my husband was insane?"

Monsieur le Curé opened the letter and read in silence for a couple of moments. Then he started to laugh. He indicated a sentence in the letter, remarking, "See, your husband says he passed four days and four nights in terrible suffering." Elizabeth did not respond until the priest had finished reading. She then commented, "I cannot see, by that letter, that there is any insanity in my husband."

The priest conceded that Dominic could not be insane or the nuns who staffed the hospital would not have let the letter pass, as it was customary for them to read all the mail.

Monsieur le Curé later used that letter to convince the parishioners of St. Marc that Dominic was insane by pointing out to them that only an insane man would write both French and English in one and the same letter. Apparently bilingualism served as a criterion of insanity at that time.

Dominic's first letter home was followed shortly by a second one, in which he confided to Elizabeth that even during his greatest suffering he had continued to believe that two and two equalled four. He asked her to take good care of his day books, and to keep them from other people. He recalled to her mind that: "Father Michaud is the representative of God at St. Marc. Napoléon Doucet, as mayor, is the highest authority at St. Marc in all civil matters. Keep those things clear.

Father Michaud represents God; Napoléon Doucet represents Caesar. Act according to your conscience and be submissive to the law."

Since Dominic's departure, the atmosphere in the family home had become more sober. The responsibilities assumed by the older children increased dramatically. While the children continued to enjoy their friends at school, they occasionally became the victims of taunts, such as: "Your father is crazy. Your father is a fool." The children were assured by their mother that their friends were not intentionally malicious, but merely used the jibes as a means of settling youthful differences. The children accepted the truth of what their mother said. Nevertheless, the taunts were painful to them, and they banded together in their hurt and sorrow. The friendship and closeness that developed among the brothers and sisters would last throughout their lives and would be considered, by each one of them, to be the greatest of their riches.

Each day the children rushed home from school to be with their mother. They knew that they were her greatest comfort and that she needed them around her.

Thirteen-year-old Johnny had willingly taken over the chores and responsibilities normally assumed by his father. Nine-year-old Ralph was kept busy assisting Johnny in the barn, and in keeping the woodbox filled to feed the Quebec heater in the kitchen. Eight-year-old Clara had become her mother's "big girl" since Mary had entered the convent at Sturgeon Falls. When she was not helping her mother with the little ones, or was not occupied with her homework, she snuggled down beside the Quebec heater. Clara was always cold. She was also sad and frightened at the fate that had befallen her father. From the Quebec heater she derived warmth for both body and soul.

The family missed Dominic greatly and prayed together each evening for his safe return home.

Letters travelled back and forth between Sturgeon Falls and St. Marc, and between Sturgeon Falls and Mastaï. Mary had been told that her father was in a hospital in Quebec City. Although she exchanged numerous letters with him, she was unaware that the hospital in which he was detained was an insane asylum. The family had united in withholding that information from her in order to save her from needless worry.

Mary was lonesome for her family. Their frequent letters were the highlight of her life in the austere atmosphere of the postulate. During the first three weeks of December her loneliness was augmented by the fact that she could not open any of the letters received from her family. The Catholic church was celebrating the holy season of Advent. It was a time of penance and preparation for the feast of Christmas. As a sacrifice, all letters received by the postulants could not be opened before Christmas day.

After the completion of her third month with the Sisters of Wisdom, twelve-year-old Mary was garbed in the long black robe and white wimple of a postulant. Because of her new attire, she was accorded the respect shown the postulants by the day scholars, with whom they attended classes. As the postulants filed into the classrooms each day, the day-scholars always stepped aside so that they might enter first. That deference shown to her new status was a novel experience for Mary, and she tried hard to squelch her feelings of importance. Humility before God and one's fellow man was greatly stressed in the preparation for a religious life.

Elizabeth was dismayed when, on December 12, she received a statement of dues from the Provincial Secretariat at Quebec, Services of Asylums. It was signed by the Under-Secretary of the Province, and it informed her that she was indebted to the Services of Asylums of the province for the sum of ten dollars and forty-one cents, as half upkeep for Dominic Raina at the Hospital of St. Michael the Archangel for the period from November 24, 1934, to December 31, 1934. She was asked to transmit the payment immediately.

Elizabeth showed that statement to her friends in Amos. They advised her not to pay one cent. When she later showed it to Monsieur le Curé he reprimanded her for not having come immediately to him, and told her that she should not divulge to others matters of this nature.

The first piece of encouraging news to reach the family after Dominic's arrest came in the form of a letter written by a former inmate of the asylum. It was dated December 10, 1934, and, translated from French, it read:

> "Madame, I am going to give you news of your husband. He is in perfect health. We were both in the same hospital with the same illnes, and now I am back with my family since 8 December. I was one month and seven days. Your husband would be very happy to return among you. I talked to him all the time I was there and he asked me to write you as soon as I was out to give you news of him. I would be happy to see him among his family. I would not want him to pass Christmas day in the hospital. I will tell you what means to take so that he will be with you for Christmas. You have only to send him a money order for his passage and tell them to send him back as soon as he gets his money. I am sending you a copy of a letter which comes from his little daughter of Notre Dame de

Lourdes. When he is back with you I would like an answer and return me the copy that I am sending you of Mary Raina's letter because it is a souvenir for me. Do not worry as he is very well and I shall work for him until he is back among you. If you have not got the money to send him, answer me right away and I will attend to it myself. I am mailing him a letter at the same time as yours. I will give you my address . . . I am closing in wishing you much courage while awaiting the return of your husband among you.''

It was with great optimism that Elizabeth wrote to Dominic on December 15. She told him about the letter and how delighted she was to hear that he would be home for Christmas. She assured him that the neighbours had also expressed delight on hearing the good news. She told him that several of them had gathered at the house the previous day to thresh the wheat and bale the hay, and that Johnny was going to Amos the following day with a load of hay, which he would try to sell in order to raise the money required for the train fare home from Quebec City. Her letter was terminated with the words, ''We will all be looking for you not later than Saturday, 23 December.''

Unfortunately, the anticipation that pervaded the family that day proved to be short-lived. When Johnny went to Amos with the load of hay on the following day, he was advised by Mr. Taylor that it might be unwise to transmit money to Mastaï for his father's train fare at that time. Mr. Taylor felt that it might be more prudent to wait until an official notice authorizing Dominic's release had been received from the superintendent of the asylum.

Although she was disappointed, Elizabeth understood the wisdom of that advice. She explained the decision to Dominic in another letter the following day. ''But,'' she wrote, ''I am enclosing two dollars with which you can buy yourself a little gift if you do not make it home for Christmas after all.''

The official notice, signed by Dr. C.S. Roy, Medical Superintendent, and dated December 19, 1934, arrived shortly afterwards. Elizabeth was informed that Dominic was ready to return to his family, but that he should continue to rest for some time before returning to work. Dr. Roy instructed her to transmit money for Dominic's fare and that, upon its receipt, her husband would be conducted to the train. He promised to inform Elizabeth as to the date of his departure.

On receiving the happy news, Elizabeth immediately arranged to have the sum transmitted with the help of Mr. Taylor.

The next few days were passed in a flutter of excitement. Elizabeth and the children discussed and rediscussed the possible date on which Dominic would arrive. Since there was a train from Quebec City scheduled to come in on Thursday, it was concluded that he would be arriving then. With great excitement, Johnny left for Amos on Thursday, December 17, to meet his father at the station.

While doing the chores that evening, eagerly awaiting Johnny's return from Amos with his father, Elizabeth heard a rap on the barn door. Before her stood a neighbour, who had a phone in his home, and who bore the sad message that Monsieur le Curé had called with discouraging news for her. The priest had received a telegram from the asylum to the effect that Dominic had had a setback and that his homecoming would be delayed.

The bearer of that depressing news bore a second message. The Taylors had called, saying that they considered it prudent to keep Johnny at their place for the night. Consequently, Elizabeth did not have her little right-hand man to console her in her sorrow and disappointment. She had grown to rely on Johnny to help assuage the fears that accompanied the nights. Frequently, under the cover of darkness, the dog had been locked in the shed by unidentified prowlers while they explored the premises.

As Christmas day drew closer, Elizabeth and her children were forced to acknowledge that Dominic would not be home to celebrate with them. In addition to Dominic's absence, Elizabeth felt doubly pained to face Christmas without Mary. For the sake of the ones at home, she presented a cheerful front and made the occasion as festive as possible under the less than happy circumstances.

The ever-kindly and compassionate Taylor family provided gifts and treats for everyone at home. Elizabeth could find no words which could sufficiently express the gratitude she felt towards those true and loyal friends. She could not imagine surviving alone in Quebec, in what had become such fearful surroundings, without them.

In a letter to Mary, in late November, Dominic had asked his daughter what she wanted for Christmas. In her reply, Mary had asked for a pair of scissors. She was spending many hours learning to make buttonholes and patches, and the fine needlework for which the nuns were famous.

Dominic had written to Elizabeth asking her to get the finest scissors available for Mary, since it was the only thing she had requested. At Sturgeon Falls, the young postulants were given special treats on Christmas day, and all lessons were put aside. Games were played and picture puzzles put together. Mary's greatest joy, on that special day, was admiring the scissors she got from home.

On Friday, December 28, Johnny left for the Village of St. Marc carrying in his pocket a short letter written by his mother to Monsieur le Curé and Napoléon Doucet. In the letter, Elizabeth demanded that arrangements be made immediately for Dominic's return home for New Year's day. She pointed out that she considered the matter of the train fare to be the responsibility of the Municipality of St. Marc, since the municipality had obviously engineered her husband's abduction. The priest assured Johnny that he would immediately wire to the asylum sufficient money for his father's train fare home, and that he would insist on his prompt release.

Once again, hope and excitement pervaded the family home!

Johnny was among the crowd gathered at the station in Amos during the following days on which a train was expected from Quebec City. After repeated trips to town, and after repeated disappointments, he despaired of ever again seeing his father. He sat down one evening, after his numerous chores were done and his homework was completed, to write him a letter. It revealed how faithfully he carried the great burden and responsibility of being the man of the family during his father's absence. He wrote:

"Dear daddy:

I am writing to you now because I have a lot to tell you and you can never come home. We have two nice young cows, one we milk now and the other in the spring. One is 2 1/2 and the other 3 1/2 years old. Mr. Boutagne sent a sample of our wheat away, I think to Ottawa, to get the analysis but they said they did not have enough. We got $4.00 for first prize in green feed, and they kept $2.00 for your membership fee for 1935 . . . In 1934 there were 19 baptisms at St. Marc. One was Dominic Raina Jr. We sold three dozen eggs last week but now the chickens are laying less because it was cold. We had a real nice Christmas and New Year but it was the first that you were not there and we missed you, but I hope you will be back for the next. I am keeping track of all Receipts and Expenses and I want to be your bookkeeper when you come home so I can learn the trade. I have not been away to play with anybody since you left. I saw a lot of people with frozen faces. I went to Amos very often and I never froze mine. In fact I got to town with sweating face, hands and feet every time. Twice Mama put a big rock in the oven and made it real hot. I put my feet on it and it kept them warm till I got to town. I am giving the horse oats and she goes a lot faster than Mr. Lantagne's colt. Me, Ralph, Clara, and Louis went to mass today and Louis gave one cent to the Infant Jesus so you can come home by Tuesday. Dear daddy, do not worry about the Life Insurance Policies because Mamma gave them to Father Michaud for safekeeping and the Knights of Columbus put both your policies in order for some time so you would not lose either of them. Do not worry about that or anything. I know you worry because it is your duty to watch over us and you are not here, but do not worry just the same and take a real big rest as you have the chance and you do not have to stay up all Friday night to go to the market. I hope you can get a good job so you do not have to do that anymore because it is real hard for you to do. Does your stomach bother you anymore? I sure hope it does not. We are all feeling well. I hope you do not have to borrow glasses to read my letter, ha! ha! Your loving son, John Raina."

Elizabeth had become very uneasy over Dominic's continued and unexplained detention at the asylum. She publicly spoke, as best she could with her limited knowledge of French, to a group of parishioners at St. Marc the following Sunday after Mass. She emphasized that, since the Municipality of St. Marc was responsible for sending her husband to the insane asylum, it was up to that same municipality to arrange for his immediate return home. "I hope I shall not be forced to go to Quebec City myself to get my husband," she concluded.

On January 8, 1935, Johnny was told by some neighbours to warn his mother that Monsieur le Curé intended to either borrow on, or to cash in his father's life insurance policies, and that he intended to sell his parents' property for back taxes.

On hearing those rumours, Elizabeth and Johnny rushed to the presbytery at St. Marc. Elizabeth told the priest that as long as her husband was alive the insurance policies belonged to him and that no other person had a right to tamper with them. She stated, further: "You are wrong in assuming that there is any money to be borrowed on the policies."

Monsieur le Curé hotly contradicted that statement. He had misinterpreted an insertion in the policy stating that it was subject to a five-hundred dollar loan. He then produced the policy and pointed out that he could indeed borrow that sum of money. After considerable discussion, Johnny was able to make him understand that the insertion merely signified that his father had already borrowed five-hundred dollars.

Elizabeth learned, later, that Monsieur le Curé had taken the policies to a council meeting a few days earlier. There, he had convinced the members of the council that the Rainas were wealthy and could borrow five-hundred dollars any time they needed the money. During those years, before the erosion of the dollar, that seemed like an impressive sum to the poor settlers of the community.

When the discussion regarding the policies had terminated, Elizabeth asked, "What is all the fuss I hear about taxes?" She begged Monsieur le Curé not to add more worries to the great burden she already carried. She continued, "You have my husband in the asylum; now you are doing your best to render me insane. St. Marc is certainly the place from which to railroad people into the asylum." She assured the priest that if her husband returned — which she hoped he would — he would settle immediately for all the just taxes. If he should happen to die — which she hoped he would not — she would be enabled, as beneficiary of his policies, to pay them herself. "I do not, however, intend to pay the expenses of my husband's trip to the asylum," she added.

On hearing that, Monsieur le Curé sprang to his feet and dashed about in search of his Code Book.

"I do not want to see that book; put it back on the shelf," said Elizabeth, refusing to look at the volume. She assured Monsieur le Curé that if he had any doubts as to whether he would be able to collect the taxes she could put his mind at rest. She pointed out that she had nine tons of baled hay in the barn at home which could be sold. The money obtained would more than cover the just taxes. "Just taxes!" she emphasized for the second time.

Monsieur le Curé commented that perhaps the hay could be sold in the spring. He did not discuss the taxes further, nor did he tell Elizabeth how much money was required.

During the following days, several neighbours called at the family home in an attempt to buy hay. "I have promised my hay to Monsieur le Curé for taxes," Elizabeth informed them, on refusing to sell.

In a letter to Dominic, Elizabeth wrote:

"I did have a long visit with the priest at St. Marc last evening and I did show him a sample of your wheat, and I did also talk about our life insurance. They are perfectly safe there and are all in good order as the Knights of Columbus did arrange for that and I did think it would be lack of trust on my part to take them from him to give to someone else. Maybe I did say more than he wanted to hear but I said what I felt like saying."

On January 10, Elizabeth received a disconcerting letter from Dr. C.S. Roy, in which he informed her that Dominic had greatly improved since his arrival at the hospital, to the point where they had considered letting him go for the holidays. He added that, in the meantime, the patient had had a setback, making it necessary to delay his departure. He suggested that Elizabeth refrain from writing to her husband so frequently because her letters made him lonesome. Dr. Roy concluded by stating that Dominic was in perfect health, from a physical viewpoint, and that they would notify her when he had recovered sufficiently to leave.

Elizabeth replied to Dr. Roy by return mail asking him not to keep any of her letters from Dominic. She explained that she knew her husband better than anyone else knew him, and that he would be very worried if he did not hear from his family frequently. She asked whether she would be permitted to see her husband should she go to Quebec City.

After mailing that letter, Elizabeth felt a great urgency to go to Dominic, whether or not Dr. Roy approved. She made immediate arrangements to carry out that resolve. She sent Johnny to St. Marc the following day to notify Monsieur le Curé of her intention to try, herself, to obtain Dominic's discharge from the asylum.

Monsieur le Curé instructed Johnny to tell his mother to go to Quebec City if she wished, but that the council was not going to give her any money.

Elizabeth was annoyed at Monsieur le Curé's implication that she was seeking charity. Furthermore, she had been given to understand on a previous visit to the priest that he had already transmitted to Quebec City the money for Dominic's return ticket to St. Marc.

With the benefit of hindsight, it was imprudent and unnecessary for Elizabeth to notify Monsieur le Curé of her intention to go to Quebec City. But she still adhered to the commonly-held belief that a priest could do no wrong, and she fell in with the habit adopted by all the other parishioners of informing Monsieur le Curé of all important matters occurring within the family. The power and magnetism of the man was such that he invited confidences. Most of the settlers seemed to be unaware of their rights to privacy in their business dealings and personal problems. Their Catholic faith and unquestioned confidence in the clergy of their church had been deeply instilled in them from the cradle. It was understandable, under those circumstances, that the priest came to expect, and to wield, total power.

A few days prior to her scheduled departure, Elizabeth heard that an excursion was leaving Amos for Quebec City on January 18. It meant a reduction in the price of the return trip from twenty-five dollars to only seven dollars. Elizabeth considered that to be a good omen and planned her trip for that date.

On the evening of January 17, after her bags had been packed and all arrangements made preparatory to her departure the following day, Elizabeth received a letter from Dr. C.S. Roy in response to her letter of January 10. Dr. Roy advised her that Dominic was recovering slowly from his new phase of nervousness, and assured her that there were no objections to her coming to see her patient, but it was preferable that he rest another fifteen days before leaving the hospital.

Despite the doctor's suggestion that Dominic's stay in the asylum be extended, Elizabeth felt convinced of the importance of getting to Quebec City without further delay. Everything was in readiness at home for her imminent departure. She had arranged for some kind neighbours to take charge of her home and her children during her absence. Those particular neighbours were French Canadians who had immigrated from western Canada a short time earlier. They had lost everything in the brief time they had resided in the Abitibi. They arrived at the house early on the morning of January 18 to receive final instructions from Elizabeth before her departure.

At around noon of that day, Johnny drove his mother to Amos to catch the four o'clock train. Elizabeth carried in her purse the thirteen-dollar government financial aid cheque to cover all the expenses of her trip.

By now, when the planned trip to Mastaï was rapidly becoming a reality, Elizabeth was beginning to feel very apprehensive. The thought of undertaking such a venture alone took on enormous proportions in her mind. She had never before, in the whole of her life, ventured more than a few miles unaccompanied and, then, only in familiar territory. Elizabeth became physically ill thinking about what lay ahead. Nevertheless, she was determined to carry on with her plans.

On reaching town, Johnny drove his mother to the Taylor residence so that she might be more comfortable while awaiting the arrival of the train. He then went out to cash the cheque with which to buy her train ticket. At Elizabeth's suggestion, he went to the Bank of Commerce in an attempt to withdraw a few dollars from his father's account. The money was needed for the maintenance of the family at home during her absence. Because of his inability to produce the bankbook, which his father had carried on his person at the time of his abduction, that venture proved unsuccessful.

After giving final advice to Johnny, Elizabeth boarded the train at four o'clock. She was accompanied by Frank Taylor, who was a student at a school near Quebec City and who was returning to classes after the Christmas break. That fine young man had volunteered to sit with her on the train and to be of any help he could. His presence gave Elizabeth a great sense of security.

At about ten o'clock that evening, as the train was puffing monotonously on its way and as Elizabeth was dozing off to sleep, the porter entered the car and approached her seat. He presented Frank Taylor with a telegram. It had been wired by his parents and instructed him to give Elizabeth his return ticket to Amos. After their son's departure with Elizabeth, the Taylors had discussed the possibility that Monsieur le Curé had never wired the money for Dominic's train fare home, as he had indicated. In that event, they feared that Elizabeth would not have enough money to buy another ticket should Dominic be released. That thoughtfulness on the part of the Taylors proved to be fortunate.

The train reached Quebec City at approximately nine o'clock on the following morning. Elizabeth had not had much experience at travelling by herself and had no idea where the asylum was located. Young Frank Taylor took charge and, under his guidance, Elizabeth soon found herself on a streetcar en route to Mastaï, located about four miles out of the city.

On her arrival there, Elizabeth was overwhelmed by the size of the building and by the many doors. She was impressed by the large and beautiful statue of St. Michael the Archangel, after whom the institution was named, prominently displayed on front of the building. Elizabeth was at first uncertain how to gain admittance, but she eventually located the right entrance and was admitted by the doorman, who conducted her to a parlour to await Dominic.

After a short interval of time had elapsed, she was shocked to a state of speechlessness to see him approaching, his face bruised and battered almost beyond recognition!

CHAPTER VII

THE INCARCERATION

"No period of history has ever been great or ever can be that does not act on some sort of high idealistic motives, and idealism in our times has been shoved aside, and we are paying the penalty for it." Alfred North Whitehead.

Little did Dominic and Elizabeth suspect, when they were so cruelly separated under such humiliating circumstances, that when they should meet again it would be under equally humiliating circumstances. At Amos their separation was witnessed by the crowds gathered at the station. At Mastaï, their reunion was witnessed by the alert eyes of guards, behind the barred doors, and within the confining walls of an insane asylum.

In answer to his questions when the train pulled out of Amos on that fateful day of November 23, 1934, Dominic had been told by his guards, in a weak attempt at humour, that he was being conducted to the Provincial Parliament at Quebec City.

As darkness set in, Dominic was instructed to mount an upper berth in a coach that was occupied mainly by lumberjacks. There, he was given the first nourishment, consisting of several sandwiches and several cups of coffee, since his arrest on the previous night.

The injection administered by Dr. Marcel Sarazin in the jail at Amos had taken effect. Experiencing feelings similar to those of a person emerging from an anaesthetic, he talked freely with his fellow passengers. Gone, for the time being, were sorrow, pain, and bewilderment.

When sleep ultimately claimed their charge, the guards seized the opportunity to relieve him of his belongings. He had held in his possession his bankbooks, writing paper, envelopes, the Agreement of Sale of his land, and other important documents.

So passed the night of November 23-24.

Dominic became aware of the removal of the contents of his pockets when the train was nearing its destination the following morning. While he was putting on his overcoat, preparing to alight, he noticed an envelope protruding from Normand Bourque's pocket. On the left-hand corner of the envelope were written the words "Hanna, Alberta." Recognizing his property, Dominic indicated the envelope in question and asked to see it. The guard refused to turn it over, with the comment that it was of no importance.

When the train came to a stop on front of the station at Quebec City, Dominic was conducted down the steps and instructed to enter the back seat of a taxi. After positioning themselves, one on either side of him, the guards issued instructions to the driver. The taxi drove off. Headed for where?

On drawing up in front of a huge institution a short while later, and before entering the building, Dominic asked sarcastically, "Are these the Parliament Buildings?"

The guards replied in the affirmative.

The doors of the building were unlocked to admit the trio. The guards instructed Dominic to be seated. They submitted their report to authorities there, handed over Dominic's working clothes, and departed. Their mission had been completed.

Dominic was approached and encircled by several doctors. He sized up the situation immediately, and made them aware that he recognized them as being psychiatrists.

Questions! Questions! Questions!

Because Dominic possessed a knowledge of several languages, questions in French, English, Italian and Spanish were fired at him. Eventually, the psychiatrists united in giving their patient a physical examination. It disclosed the bruised area on his hip left by the injection administered in the jail at Amos by Dr. Marcel Sarazin. One of the doctors asked for an explanation of the bruise, appearing concerned when Dominic told him what had transpired.

On completion of the examination, Dominic was handed over to the two day guards of ward four. A much-needed bath, a few minutes later, served to invigorate him and eased his feelings of depression. But these more optimistic feelings were to be short-lived!

To his horror and bewilderment, Dominic was conducted to a cell — one of a group in ward four. That particular ward was located on the ground floor, and it was the one in which the very insane were confined. Dominic's cell was similar to the average prison cell. Its one little window faced the outside world, but it was at a height which did not permit the occupant to get a glimpse of that world. A little cot in one corner was the only article of furniture that the cell contained. Dominic was held in solitary confinement by a heavily wooded door reinforced with solid iron bars. Except on occasional instances, when the door was opened to admit guards or attendants, Dominic could not see into the corridor. A little sliding panel, cleverly constructed in the door, permitted guards to view the inmate without being observed by him.

Dominic found himself alone and within the constriction of a strait-jacket. Once again, as in the jail at Amos, he called for his family, for friends, and for a priest. His pleas merely served to try the anger of the guards, who now strapped him to his cot.

A special guard was assigned to serve meals to inmates confined to their cells. The man had an amazing ability to shove food down the throats of the most resisting patients, normally accompanying the chore with curses. Since Dominic's hands and feet were strapped to the cot, he was unable to feed himself. Although he had suffered for many years with a badly ulcerated stomach and his dentures had been removed, he did not resist the feedings. The meal usually ended with hot tea. On one particular day, Dominic noticed a cup containing a strange liquid standing on the tray. The unsavoury liquid was poured down his throat. Dominic did not know the nature of the liquid or why it was given to him, but it had the effect of turning his stomach into a torturous ball of fire. In pain and fright, he pleaded again for a priest.

All in vain!

Was there not a priest available within the whole of that huge Catholic institution run by nuns in the Catholic Province of Quebec? Not a person entered the cell to console the suffering inmate throughout those agonizing hours.

Eventually, when it appeared that they could not possibly get worse, things took a turn for the better. A guard entered the cell and relieved Dominic of his straitjacket. He returned his dentures and supplied him with the usual uniform worn by inmates. He was then led to a parlour about two cells away, where he found himself once again among people.

On glancing about his new surroundings, Dominic noticed a calendar hanging on a nearby wall. He studied it for a moment and noted that it was Wednesday, November 28, 1934. Four long days had passed since his arrest in Amos!

The parlour of ward four was large enough to accommodate about twenty people. In addition to providing living quarters during the day, it served as a dining-room for the inmates of the ward. It contained several chairs, a few tables large enough to seat six people each, and a cupboard which housed the necessary dishes and cutlery for the use of the inmates of the ward. The inmates were confined inside the room throughout the day by means of solidly-locked doors. The room did not offer any form of entertainment, nor was there literature of any kind.

Dominic managed to occasionally borrow a newspaper to help pass the endless monotonous hours. He also drew comfort from his prayer book and beads — the only items not taken when he was relieved of his possessions on the fateful trip from Amos to Quebec City. Immediately, upon being admitted among people, Dominic expressed a desire to write to his family. He was told that he must wait for a couple of days. The receipt of a telegram informing him that all was well at home offered some consolation.

Mealtimes always presented a certain amount of activity and diversion. Some of the patients were assigned the task of setting the tables. Others, who had been selected by the guard, were conducted down long corridors which led to the huge central kitchen. There, bread was piled into baskets and soup was poured into kettles, to be conveyed by the inmates to their respective parlours in the various wards. Although the meals were rather poor and rationed, *Le tabac canadien* was plentiful and was supplied liberally to the patients, who were also presented with clay pipes.

With the coming of night, Dominic learned that he was to share a plainly-furnished dormitory with several other inmates. Those patients who wanted to attend daily Mass were conducted to the chapel by the guards. Dominic was permitted that privilege for the first time on November 30.

During his first days in the parlour of ward four Dominic became acquainted with his fellow inmates, with nurses and orderlies, and with his attending psychiatrists Drs. Gustave DesRocher and George-Henri LaRue, and the young intern Dr. Barat.

As soon as he was permitted to write letters, Dominic began to correspond with his family. Although his mail was strictly censored and he could not freely discuss his experiences in the asylum, it was a comfort to be in touch with his loved ones again.

The experiences Dominic encountered while an inmate of ward four were varied and unusual. On one occasion, his assistance was requested in attending a violently insane man who was confined within a cell. The frightened guards warned him to be cautious, explaining that the man was dangerous.

Why was Dominic, branded as one hundred percent insane, requested to attend a brother inmate?

On another occasion, he was conducted by a guard down long corridors, which ended in an empty room on the ground floor of the building. There, he was handed a hammer and asked to do a minor repair job on a wide open window. The guard then departed, closing the door firmly behind him. Left completely unguarded, Dominic noticed that, by taking a short step out of the window and onto solid ground, perhaps an escape could be accomplished. He was overcome with fear and prudently resisted the temptation.

A stroll along the banks of the St. Lawrence River on December 3, in company with several fellow patients and under the surveillance of guards, was the first outing permitted Dominic during his confinement.

In a conversation with his attending psychiatrist Dr. LaRue, at the beginning of December, Dominic was told that he was being observed closely in an effort to determine whether he actually was insane, or merely pretending to be.

"What!" exclaimed Dominic. "I, pretending to be insane? No such thing! I freely admit to being sane."

Dr. LaRue commented that others were known to have done it.

Shortly afterwards, Dominic was led before a board of psychiatrists, one of whom carried in his coat pocket *L'Evenement* — the daily paper of Quebec City. On the portion of the paper protruding from the psychiatrist's pocket Dominic noticed a telegraphic despatch from Le Pas, Bolivia.

"That is either a mistake or a typographical error," he remarked, indicating the words "Le Pas." "It should read "La Pas," and not "Le Pas." After exchanging puzzled glances among themselves, and after a few moments of reflection, one of the doctors conceded that Dominic was correct and the newspaper was mistaken.

Ward fifteen, into which Dominic was transferred during the second week of December, was considered to be one of the better wards. It differed from ward four in that it boasted a separate dining-room which was attached to the parlour. Unlike ward four, the doors not only remained unlocked but were kept wide open throughout the whole of each day, although the patients were strictly supervised. Again, no literature or entertainment was offered. Dominic endeavoured to fill his time constructively by applying himself to the challenge of learning the Eskimo language from a fellow inmate who had been flown in from Thunder Bay.

In a letter home, Dominic wrote: "Everybody thinks my mind is okay. Probably you will have to take the first steps to get me out. I hope now to be home for Christmas. I am ready to go as soon as permission is given me to do so."

Although the letters he received from home were regular and contained cheerful news, Dominic could sense an undertone of sadness. He could not conquer the feeling that a powerful influence was at work to greatly harm his wife and children without their knowledge. He felt that he was urgently needed at home. Furthermore, he wished to spend the rapidly-approaching Christmas season with his family. He approached Dr. LaRue, and other officials of the institution, to insist on his release. The gentlemen suggested that, since his confinement was not costing him a cent, he should take advantage of the opportunity to get a few more days of rest.

A few days later, Dominic noticed Dr. LaRue engaged in conversation with a strange companion in the hall. Not having heard anything further concerning his release, he approached the doctor and asked him, in French, to give immediate consideration to his discharge and return to his family. Having evidently been recognized by Dr. LaRue's companion, who turned out to be Dr. C.S. Roy, the Superintendent of the asylum, Dominic was surprised to find himself being addressed by the man. Dr. Roy apologized for the delay, explaining to Dominic that as soon as the money for his train fare was received he would be released.

Dominic was under the impression that Mathias Poirier and Normand Bourque had transferred his bankbooks to the authorities at Mastaï before they returned to St. Marc. He proceeded to ask those authorities for their return, so that he could secure money for the train fare. Much to his dismay, he learned that the books had not been left with them.

The experiences Dominic encountered in ward fifteen were no less strange and varied than those encountered in ward four.

Very puzzling, was the fact that many of the supposedly insane inmates of this ward were permitted to violate freely one of the strictest rules of the asylum by carrying cigarette lighters on their persons.

Still more puzzling, was the fact that these same privileged few were the possessors of bunches of keys which enabled them to unlock numerous doors throughout the institution. Although it was strictly understood that the patients were not to leave the parlour under any circumstances, they did not hesitate to use the keys by coming and going constantly throughout the day, only to gather in the parlour in the evening.

A sharp slap in the face, delivered him one afternoon by one of a group of inmates marching in formation down the corridor past the parlour door of ward fifteen, caused Dominic to quickly turn about. As his eyes met those of his assailant, he was asked by the man, "Do you know who I am?"

"Certainly, I know you," asserted Dominic.

Dominic had recognized the man as the same who had poured the vile liquid down his throat on that unforgettable day in the cell of ward four when he was strapped to his cot. As the group disappeared around the corner he turned to his guard, who had witnessed the incident, and asked, "Was that man crazy, or a guardian of crazies?"

"You should not say crazy: you should say sick person," evasively replied the guard.

Christmas day of 1934 marked the first time the Raina family had been separated for the holiday season. Numerous letters were exchanged between Dominic and his family. Mary received many affectionate letters from her parents and brothers and sister. She particularly treasured Clara's letters because they gave so much of the news that Mary enjoyed hearing. She was also impressed at how well her little eight-year-old sister composed her letters, and her excellent spelling, when she had had so little formal instruction in English.

New Year's Day of 1935 ultimately arrived. The patients received treats and a nice meal from the kind nuns. They were extended the compliments of the season by the Superintendent, Dr. C.S. Roy, who made his rounds accompanied by Dr. LaRue.

Dominic had been instructed by Dr. LaRue, during a conversation in English shortly after his arrival at the asylum, to *Parlez français, je ne vous comprends pas* ("Speak French, I do not understand you"). Since Dominic's French pronunciation was better than his English pronunciation, he obligingly spoke French to the doctor thereafter. Consequently, he was surprised to be approached by the man one evening early in January and to be told in English to follow him. On being conducted into Dr. Roy's office, the Superintendent addressed him in French. Constantly and simultaneously, for several minutes, Dominic was questioned by the two psychiatrists, one speaking French and the other English.

Although Dominic expressed a natural desire to be released, he prudently refrained from protesting the inhuman treatment he had previously received at the asylum. He felt that the voicing of any complaints could merely aggravate matters.

From the interview, Dominic received the strange and certain impression that the psychiatrists had united in a decision to brand him with the official seal of insanity. The fact that a declaration authorizing his release had been written in December added to the irony of the situation. Dominic attempted to familiarize the doctors with the events leading to his arrest. He commented that, although they had probably dealt with hundreds of cases, they would discover that his was one of the most serious.

Dominic emerged from the interview feeling apprehensive. He had been previously assured by orderlies, guards, and doctors, that he was in a condition to be released, and that as soon as money for his train fare was received he would be allowed to leave the asylum. Especially frustrating was the fact that he had sufficient money in the bank to cover his train fare, but that he could not produce the money because his bankbooks had been lifted from his pocket.

Fearful about remaining any longer at the asylum, Dominic wrote to Elizabeth on January 8, urging her to come to Mastaï. On the morning of January 9, he attempted to smuggle out three letters written by him to different persons in Amos. They contained the simple urgent message, "Tell my wife to come at once." It was the first time since his confinement at Mastaï that Dominic attempted to break a rule of the institution, but he felt that the urgency of the situation justified the action. He was convinced that it was a matter of life or death!

In the meantime, additional horrors lay in store for him!

At seven-fifty o'clock, approximately ten minutes before bed time on the evening of that same day, Dominic was signalled by one of the guards to follow him. He was conducted down long corridors, which led to the parlour door of ward four. In answer to the guard's knock, the door — as if by prearrangement — was unlocked from within. Slowly it swung open to reveal a room, sinister in its total darkness.

As Dominic was ushered into that darkness an arm, belonging to a second guard, encircled his neck and dragged him backward across the floor farther into the room. The door then swung shut again, barring any possible escape.

Cruel and bloody was the scuffle which ensued between the three men in the blackness of that parlour! One guard grabbed Dominic's right arm and rendered it useless. The other guard possessed himself of a weapon from a nearby cupboard.

Tiens sa main! Tiens sa main! ("Hold his hand! Hold his hand!"), instructed the man to his companion as he made use of that weapon.

Just then the clock struck eight. Merciful deliverance! That was the time when the first guard was due in ward fifteen to conduct his men to the dormitory. That was the time when the second guard was due in ward four to replace the one whose duties were terminated for the day.

The room was flooded in light! It revealed the guards — one with a terrified expression on his face, and the frightened fleeing form of the second. It revealed Dominic, whose face was badly bruised and battered.

A nurse was summoned immediately. The night guard conducted the victim to the washroom. There was not a doctor available to Dominic when one was so desperately needed.

Too weak and discouraged to offer any resistance, Dominic was put into a straitjacket and again locked in a cell in ward four.

While he suffered intense pain throughout the night, he could hear guards constantly coming and going along the corridors. He could hear them stop in front of his cell to make use of the peep hole in the door. As day broke, the young psychiatrist Barat, whom Dominic believed to have been sent by the kind nuns on an unofficial visit, entered the cell. He took Dominic's pulse and commented, "Poor boy." The gentle nuns took charge. The meals served Dominic were the best he had had while in that institution.

On January 11, after his straitjacket had been removed, a sympathetic nun brought Dominic some mail which had arrived for him from home. She then handed him a pen and some stationery and asked him to write to his family. "What shall I write?" he questioned, knowing that he could not give cheerful news.

"Write from your heart," counselled the kind little nun.

The next day the door of his cell was unlocked and Dominic was once again permitted among people. His face was responding to the skilful ministrations of the nuns and was healing gradually.

Dominic received a most ironic letter from the Provincial Parliament at Quebec City shortly after his return to the parlour. The letter, dated January 11, 1935, was signed by George M. Bilideau, Priest, Services of Establishment, Parliament Buildings, Quebec. It invited him to call at the parliament buildings on Mr. Hormidas Magnan, who would give him a settler's certificate permitting him to travel at reduced rates when he was ready to return to St. Marc de Figuery.

Dominic could not imagine what had inspired that unusual communication.

Although the days that followed passed quite uneventfully, Dominic felt that he was running a race against time. He endeavoured to transmit to Elizabeth a silent plea for help. He hoped that she was taking the necessary steps to obtain his release as soon as possible.

On Saturday, January 19, 1935, after approximately two months of confinement, during which he had not received a single visitor, Dominic was informed that Elizabeth had arrived at the asylum.

"At last! At last! Do not return home without me!" pleaded Dominic on being reunited with Elizabeth. Appalled at the brutal treatment he had received, as evidenced by his still badly bruised face, Elizabeth had already resolved not to leave Mastaï alone under any circumstances. Prudently, she refrained from commenting on his injuries.

Because Dominic and Elizabeth had so long been separated there were numerous matters they wished to discuss. Their visit had barely begun when it was interrupted by a guard, who approached to conduct Dominic to the noon-day meal. Lunch was customarily served at the early hour of eleven o'clock.

Elizabeth was conscious of the fact that she carried in her purse a mere five dollars. All the expenses encountered throughout the remainder of her trip would necessarily be limited to that paltry sum of cash. How she wished that she could see Dominic again so that she could ask him what to do! Since the first Amos-bound train was not scheduled to leave Quebec City until Monday, she approached the doorman to ask his advice in securing cheap accommodation. The man suggested that she enquire at a sanatarium located near the asylum.

After entering the building, a short time later, Elizabeth was approached by a nun, who asked her whom she wished to see. Elizabeth replied that she was seeking a room for a couple of nights. The nun told her that the only room unoccupied was in the men's department, but she could have it if she wished. The men in question were mental patients receiving treatment there. Having no other alternative, Elizabeth followed the nun past a poolroom and up a long stairway. Because accommodation in this building appeared to be greatly superior to that of the building where Dominic was confined, Elizabeth assumed that the inmates were very important persons.

"You are not afraid?" queried the nun, on handing over the key to the bedroom in front of which they eventually stopped.

"I do not think I shall be afraid," hesitated Elizabeth.

Fearing that her five dollars might not be enough to cover necessary expenses, Elizabeth did not dine that noon. Weakness drove her to the dining room for dinner. Although the meal served her was appetizing she was too worried to eat more than a few morsels. She did not know whether she would be able to obtain Dominic's release. She feared that she might be admitted to the asylum too, since her husband had been locked up without apparent reason. She was concerned about the children at home.

The following morning Elizabeth attended Sunday Mass. When she returned to her room after the service, she discovered a nun closely examining some pictures of her children that had been left on the bedside table. The nun began immediately to question Elizabeth.

"Were you afraid of your husband?" she first asked.

"No, sister, I never had any reason to be afraid of my husband," replied Elizabeth.

"Did your husband drink? Did he beat you?"

Elizabeth again replied in the negative.

"Why was your husband sent to the asylum?" the nun asked, curiously.

Elizabeth answered, truthfully, that she did not know the reason.

No sooner had the nun departed when a cleaning woman entered the room. She, in turn, questioned Elizabeth and asked her whether she would be able to take her husband home.

"I don't know," was the truthful reply.

The second visitor departed, only to be replaced shortly by a third. She volunteered an account of Dominic's sojourn at the asylum. She explained that he had first been confined to ward four, but that he had later been transferred to ward fifteen, one of the better wards. She commented, reflectively, that she did not know what had happened to cause Dominic to be readmitted to ward four. She asked Elizabeth whether she would be able to take her husband home.

Once again, Elizabeth replied, "I don't know."

The visitor volunteered her opinion that if Elizabeth wished to take Dominic home no doctor could stop her. She advised Elizabeth to tell the doctor that she was taking him home, and then proceed to do so.

That unexpected information served to renew her courage, and to give her fresh hope and consolation.

That afternoon, Dominic and Elizabeth were permitted a short visit together. It was the last before the weighty questions foremost in both their minds would be answered. Would Dominic be released? Would he be permitted, the next day, to pass out of the doors of the asylum into the world, a free man once more? Would Elizabeth, in an unguarded moment, raise her voice too strongly in protest against the brutal treatment rendered Dominic, thereby lessening the chances of obtaining his release?

Promptly, the next morning, Elizabeth arose and prepared to meet with Dr. LaRue. She succeeded in obtaining an interview in his office shortly after nine o'clock.

"Do you think my husband was insane?" was the first of several questions she asked the psychiatrist. The man remarked that perhaps it was only what he had seen around him at Amos.

"Why was he sent to the asylum? If it was rest he needed I could have given him that at home."

The doctor gave no indication of having heard that second question.

"Why was my husband sent to the asylum?" persisted Elizabeth.

The doctor hesitatingly commented that Dominic was a foreigner and a communist, and with those gold mines nearby they had to be very careful about people.

Elizabeth was rendered speechless at that astounding explanation. She was fully aware that Dominic had never taken a special interest in gold. Furthermore, she knew that he had never at any time harboured an intention of belonging to a communist party, the tenets of which would be repulsive to him as a Catholic and as a Knight of Columbus.

Several equally weak excuses regarding Dominic's detention were offered by the psychiatrist, who then produced a form for Elizabeth to sign.

As she looked with suspicion at that document the doctor assured her that it did not contain anything of a serious nature, but that by affixing her signature matters would be greatly simplified should she wish to readmit Dominic to the asylum at a later date.

Elizabeth was horrified at that suggestion. To her knowledge, she had not sent him there in the first place. Nevertheless, she signed the document, remarking as she did so, "Oh well, I guess I can sign that if I have to, but you'll never see my husband back here again."

She told the doctor that she was worried because authorities at St. Marc had threatened to sell the family home to force her to pay the expenses of Dominic's abduction. Dr. LaRue advised her, emphatically, not to give those authorities a cent. She suggested that Dr. LaRue retain the money that Monsieur le Curé had wired for Dominic's train fare so that it could be applied to cover any expenses incurred at the asylum. Dr. LaRue replied that no money had been wired to Quebec City.

Much to her disappointment, Elizabeth was unable to obtain an interview with Dr. C.S. Roy, the Superintendent of the asylum. Nevertheless, she did obtain a card authorizing Dominic's release.

With that document of liberation in her possession, Elizabeth rushed immediately to Dominic. Together, after a final grateful glance at the statue of the mighty St. Michael the Archangel, they turned their backs on Mastaï and boarded the train for home.

When Dominic and Elizabeth reached Amos the following day they did not have sufficient money to pay for transportation to St. Marc. It was decided that Dominic would walk the ten miles home, while Elizabeth was able to get a ride in the mailman's already overcrowded sleigh.

CHAPTER VIII

THE LOSS OF A HOME

"Every man has by nature the right to possess property as his own." Pope Leo XIII.

The joy in the family home was boundless when Dominic and Elizabeth arrived home that evening.

The children had so much to tell their father and each one tried to out-talk the other. Among the more interesting news they conveyed was their account of how the neighbour who had looked after them during their parents' absence had spent the nights sitting in front of the window with a 22-rifle in his hands. Elizabeth was convinced that her fears of prowlers during Dominic's absence had been justified.

Although Dominic had arrived home on a Tuesday, very few people, including Monsieur le Curé Michaud, were aware of his presence at St. Marc. His first outing after his return was to attend Mass on Sunday, where he occupied the front pew of the church. When he entered from the vestry to say Mass, Monsieur le Curé blanched visibly on noticing Dominic in his customary spot. With a complete loss of composure, he turned and left the church without offering any explanation to his flock. After waiting in vain for the priest's return, the congregation concluded that he would not reappear and gradually vacated the church. For the first time, Mass was not heard that Sunday at St. Marc de Figuery!

Dominic's first days at home were spent intently studying all correspondence that had reached the house during his absence. He compared notes with Elizabeth and, bit by bit, fitted together the pieces of the puzzle which confronted him. Although Dominic and Elizabeth were convinced that they were the victims of considerable injustice, it was only then that the full realization of the seriousness and magnitude of the case became clear.

They were aware of the immediate need for action in order to obtain reparation and to prevent additional abuse by authorities.

So that they might gather the necessary evidence, Dominic began by sending Johnny to the presbytery at St. Marc to ask Monsieur le Curé to return the life insurance policies. The priest handed them over.

Dominic next called at Mathias Poirier's home in an endeavour to recover the articles that had been removed from his pockets on the fateful trip to Mastaï. Considerable discussion took place between the two men, resulting in Madame Poirier uneasily producing the wallet and returning it to its rightful owner. Because that was the only article returned to him that day, Dominic again called on Mathias Poirier on the following Sunday. That second visit resulted in the return of the stationery. Dominic was never able to recover the Deed of Sale of his land nor his bankbooks.

One evening, while reading the newspaper *La gazette du nord* of February 1, 1935, Dominic was surprised to notice a paragraph concerning himself. It appeared to be written by an individual who was unaware of the trouble he had experienced in the Abititi. The reporter commented that Dominic Raina, a former wheat farmer from Alberta, was making a fortune in the Abitibi, thanks to the cultivation of vegetables for the mining regions. He challenged others to do as well.

In his reply to that comment, Dominic stressed that: "Dominic Raina is not on the way to making a little fortune. He is rather on the point of being ruined!"

On their first visit to Amos after Dominic's return, he and Elizabeth called on Dr. Simard, their family physician. They wished him to examine Dominic's face, hip, and a toe that had been injured by a too-tightly restraining strap in the cell at Mastaï. The kind doctor remarked that the authorities at the asylum had overstepped their rights by so mistreating a patient.

As each succeeding day resulted in the exposure of additional injustices, Elizabeth's thoughts were drawn back to the papers she had been asked to sign by Monsieur le Curé on November 23, 1934. What did the papers signify? Suspicions persisted in racing through her mind. Elizabeth knew that she must find the answers. Johnny was sent to the presbytery to ask for a written explanation. He succeeded in obtaining a short undated note, in which Elizabeth was advised that the papers she had signed indicated the number of children, the properties and the insurance. She was informed that they had been sent to Mastaï, but she was assured that they did not bind her to anything.

Recognizing strength in unity, and believing that when he went anywhere alone he was in danger of a second abduction, Dominic felt that Mary was needed at home. By helping to care for her younger brothers and sister, Elizabeth would be free to accompany him on visits to authorities.

Coincidentally, at about that same time, Mary had become very lonely for her family and wished to return home. She had begun to question her suitability for the religious life and doubted that she had a vocation. Before Mary had left home, her mother had counselled her to indicate her feelings by means of a small ''x'' at the bottom left-hand corner of a letter, should she wish to return to her family. Elizabeth knew that the nuns would read her incoming and outgoing mail, and she felt that Mary might be reluctant to express such a wish in writing. When the ''x'' appeared, Mary's parents knew that they were wise in their decision to bring her home.

Years later, while Mary and Ralph were reminiscing about life in Quebec, Ralph remarked, ''If mother had not been smart enough to tell you to put that ''x'' at the end of your letter, you would have been too timid to tell the nuns that you did not have a vocation. Today, you would probably be an old fat Mother Superior with wooden prayer-beads dangling from your stomach.''

Since train connections between Amos and Sturgeon Falls were poor, Mary's parents did not want her to travel alone. It was necessary to sell the family horse in order to obtain enough money to go to Sturgeon Falls and return with Mary. Dominic felt uneasy when he left home alone to board the train at Amos. He remembered, only too vividly, the horrible fate that had befallen him on his last trip alone to Amos. His uneasiness increased when he noticed that his departure from the station was witnessed by officials of the Department of Colonization, whom he now thoroughly mistrusted. He was tense and wary until two-forty o'clock p.m. on the following day, when the train pulled into a little town on the Ontario border.

''Is this Ontario?'' he asked uncertainly, on turning to a passenger in a nearby seat.

''Yes, we are in Canada again,'' confirmed the man.

With a sense of relief, and experiencing the comfortable feeling of an exile who has just returned to his country, Dominic relaxed.

On the afternoon of Saturday, February 23, Mary was informed by a nun that her father had arrived to take her home.

Before being permitted to see her father, Mary was asked by the nun to remove her postulant's habit and change into the clothes she had been wearing when she arrived at the convent. Mary complied. She felt somewhat naked and immodest when her hair, which had been covered for three months, fell freely around her shoulders.

The nun next asked Mary if she would like to pay a farewell visit to the chapel. Mary was pleased to have a talk with God. She was deliriously happy to be going home, but she was somewhat reluctant to face all the other little girls at St. Marc. She knew that they would wonder why she had given up a privilege that had not even been offered them. Mary was confident that God would understand. Her relationship with Him was very much like her relationship with her parents. She felt secure in His love and in her ability to occasionally manipulate Him with promises if the occasion warranted it. She now promised Him that she would find a way to atone for her desertion, and left feeling confident that He would forgive her.

It was from her father that Mary learned, that afternoon, that the Hospital of St. Michael the Archangel was an insane asylum.

Dominic left Sturgeon Falls on that same day to return with his daughter to St. Marc de Figuery. Due to poor train connections, Dominic and Mary were obliged to spend a weekend in Taschereau, Quebec.

That Sunday proved to be bitter cold. Since Mary was recovering from the flu her father instructed her to stay indoors. He sauntered out alone to attend Mass in Taschereau's little church, the troubles at St. Marc temporarily forgotten.

As he approached the church he noticed, attached to the door, a Poster of Sale of properties to be sold for arrear taxes by the different municipalities of the Abitibi on March 7, 1935. On reading through the poster Dominic noticed his name standing out among the rest.

Although Elizabeth had acquainted him with the rumours that Monsieur le Curé had threatened to sell his land for taxes, Dominic had ignored it as being idle gossip. He had not received any official notice to that effect, and he knew that his taxes had been paid. The more he pondered over the matter the more incredible it seemed!

On returning to the hotel, he instructed Mary to bundle up warmly against the bitter cold because he had something important to show her. He took her to the church and asked her to read the poster on the door. "Mary," he said, "I want you to remember always what you have read here today, because you have just read about the coming theft of your home. Never forget that!"

It struck them as odd that the poster had not appeared in St. Marc, when it was customary for all such posters to be attached to the door of the church there, so that they might be read by all.

Mary was almost unbearably excited when she and her father took the train for the final lap of their trip home. When they arrived at the station at Amos on Monday they were too late to take the snowmobile to St. Marc. Since the horse had been sold to procure money for their trip, Johnny was unable to meet them at the station. They started the ten-mile journey home on foot.

After having progressed some miles, Dominic concluded that Mary could not possibly walk any farther that night. He told her that he would take her to a nearby farm home and make arrangements for her to stay until morning. Mary begged her father to let her continue along with him so that she could see her mother that night. Her father could not be swayed in his decision. He made arrangements with the mistress of the house to keep his daughter until morning and to put her on the snow-mobile for St. Marc the following day. He had forgotten to tell the woman that Mary had not eaten since that morning, so she was put to bed without supper.

The bed was located in a far corner of the attic, and Mary was so frightened in the eerie surroundings that she stayed awake all night. The following morning, bright and early, and long before it was scheduled to arrive, she waited at the roadside for the snowmobile.

Shortly after his return to St. Marc from Sturgeon Falls, Dominic proceeded to investigate the matter of the scheduled sale of his home for taxes. The investigation succeeded in disclosing some interesting facts.

Dominic learned that a specially-called municipal council meeting was held two days after his abduction. At that meeting, Monsieur le Curé had attempted to induce the councillors to include his land among the list of those to be sold for arrear taxes. The fact that Dominic had never neglected to pay his taxes was not taken into consideration. Dominic was told, unofficially, that at the same meeting the councillors were informed that he was scheduled to die two days after his arrival at Mastaï.

Dominic wondered what was meant by that astounding revelation and if it had any basis in fact. His thoughts returned to the unprovoked beating he had suffered at Mastaï. To what lengths would the guards have gone had they not been unexpectedly interrupted by the arrival of the night shift? After all, his incarceration at Mastaï was a drastic step to effect his removal from St. Marc. But surely this was just a rumour! Yet, strange things seemed to happen in the Province of Quebec!

The suggestion that his land be sold for taxes met with considerable opposition at that meeting. Some of the councillors protested the proposal on the grounds that Dominic might return. Consequently, the priest's wishes were not fulfilled on that occasion. But Monsieur le Curé did not waver in his resolve to sell the property. He merely bided his time.

At a meeting of the school board, held in his presbytery a short time later, he again presented the previously rejected proposal. In accordance with the Municipal Act of the Province of Quebec at that time, the right to authorize the sale of lands for arrear taxes belonged exclusively to the municipal council. The school board did not have any authority to deal with such matters. Nevertheless, it was at that meeting of the school board that Dominic's land was included on the list of sale. This was done despite the fact that the meeting had been declared illegal by one of the councillors, who had been unable to follow the discussion because of the deafening noise of the priest's radio located on the table beside his chair. The councillor felt that it had been turned on full blast for the explicit purpose of concealing the true nature of the business from many of those in attendance.

Joseph Lacoursière, one of the councillors, denied possessing any knowledge of the matter when Dominic approached him in early March. Napoléon Doucet, the mayor, also pleaded ignorance when publicly confronted. He denied possessing any knowledge that the Raina taxes had so surprisingly increased from thirty-four dollars to one hundred and thirty-four dollars in a few short days.

March 7, 1935 — the official day chosen for the sale, for arrear taxes, of lands covering the Abitibi East — ultimately arrived. A cloud of gloom hung over the Raina home! Despite all Dominic's and Elizabeth's protests the sale of their property was scheduled to take place that day. The actions of Monsieur le Curé Jules Michaud and his coterie of supporters were tantamount to theft, and the Rainas were only too well aware that they would soon be a homeless and destitute family.

At ten o'clock in the morning, while discussing that depressing state of affairs, they noticed a horse-drawn cutter carrying a strange man turn into their gate.

"Does Dominic Raina live here?" enquired the smartly-dressed stranger, on reaching the door of the house.

"Yes," confirmed Dominic. "What is your name?"

The visitor replied that he preferred not to reveal his identity.

To Dominic's bewilderment, and without having been invited to do so, the man then unhitched his horse and conducted it to the stable.

In the meantime, a second cutter carrying two gentlemen, whom Dominic recognized as being parishioners of St. Marc, turned into a neighbour's gate. As though by prearrangement, after unhitching and stabling their horse, they also came to the house. They explained their visit by expressing a wish to buy a hen. Coincidentally, their arrival gave them an opportunity to witness the conversation that ensued between Dominic and the first visitor. Dominic saw no reason why their curiosity should not be satisfied, and he courteously invited them to be seated. He then told his story to the stranger, who appeared eager to hear it.

The man was under the false impression that the Raina family had been settled in the Abitibi by the Department of Colonization at its entire expense. He appeared surprised to learn that Dominic had paid the five-hundred dollars of cash for his property, and that no money had been paid by any other source.

Although the man did not waver in his resolve to conceal his identity, some neighbours had seen and recognized him. They told Dominic that he was Mr. Mascotte, jailer at the Courthouse of Amos. Dominic never did learn under whose orders Mr. Mascotte was sent, nor why the other two gentlemen had chosen that particular time to visit.

In any event, it appeared that Mr. Mascotte did not intervene in the proceedings. This was evidenced by an undated and unsigned notification, written in Monsieur le Curé's familiar handwriting, which reached Dominic by mail on March 14, 1935. It informed him that Article 738 of the Code required that he be notified that his lot was sold for taxes on 7 March and bought by the municipality.

That note, though brief, was long in its significance. With it came a complete change in the atmosphere of the Raina quarters. Although the Raina family was permitted by the Municipality of St. Marc to remain in the house, they could not cultivate the land. While they had a place to live, they no longer had a home. Dominic had been robbed of his occupation as a farmer and of his means of obtaining a livelihood. Automatically, and of necessity, he turned his pen into an instrument for justice.

Letters! Letters! Letters!. Short letters, long letters, pleading letters, and accusing letters were mailed to authorities, both civil and religious. They were mailed to the humblest and the proudest, to the lowest and the highest.

As Dominic composed the letters, the children were kept busily occupied in writing copies for the family records. By so doing, they were made thoroughly familiar with the case in all its aspects, and it became indelibly impressed on their minds.

The family's thoughts were temporarily diverted from the loss of their home when news of the tragic death of Stanley Siscoe swept through the Abitibi. The former *coureur de bois* was well-known in mining circles as the discoverer of the Siscoe gold mines and President of the Cie Siscoe Extension.

Stanley Siscoe met his untimely death on March 25, 1935, when the pilot of his private plane was forced, because of a blinding snowstorm, into an unexpected landing on Lake Matchi Manitou near Senneterre, Quebec.

The two men attempted to signal for help, eventually parting ways in their own personal efforts to attract rescuers. The pilot was spotted and saved, but Stanley Siscoe's body was found on Lake Matchi Manitou, a victim of cold and hunger. He was lying on his back: his coat was thrown wide open and there were bank notes strewn all about him, in what was felt to be a gesture of despair when the victim perceived that all was lost and that wealth did not have the power to save him.

Dominic pointed out to his children that even riches, such as were amassed by Stanley Siscoe, did not have the power to guarantee life under adverse circumstances. He told his children that, even though the family was destitute, a good future might still be in store for them, while there was no future in store for Stanley Siscoe.

CHAPTER IX

IN SEARCH OF JUSTICE

"Injustice anywhere is a threat to justice everywhere." Martin Luther King Junior.

One day at the beginning of March, 1935, while standing with Dominic in the grocery store owned by Mr. Brunet, the Mayor of Amos, Elizabeth caught sight of the town constable. She was moved to compassion on noticing an expression of genuine sorrow clearly stamped on the man's face as he gazed fixedly at Dominic. Touching her husband's arm, Elizabeth whispered, "The town constable is in the store. Why don't you shake hands with him?"

Not only did Dominic agree to carry out that gesture of friendship, but he entered into a conversation with the man. Together, they reminisced over the events of November 23, 1934.

The constable told Dominic, in the presence of several people from St. Marc who were also gathered in the store, that he did not know why he had been given orders to arrest him. He said that, after the arrest, he had made numerous enquiries concerning his prisoner, and that not a word of complaint had been raised against him.

Dominic understood that the constable had acted on orders from superiors and that he regretted his involvement. In view of the tremendous power of the clergy of Quebec at the time, it was in the best interests of the "little man" to go along with the established custom of obedience, rather than fight a situation much bigger than himself. Although unjustified, the role played by the constable was understandable, and Dominic never bore any ill feelings towards the man.

Around the middle of March, Dominic felt that the time had arrived to pay Monsieur le Curé an unofficial visit. He was accompanied by Elizabeth and several sympathetic neighbours. In the presence of the witnesses, Monsieur le Curé admitted having mailed registered notices, as required by law, to the effect that their properties had been listed for

89

sale to at least twenty-five ratepayers of the municipality. He admitted that such a notice had not been mailed to either Dominic or Elizabeth.

During that same visit, the priest confirmed Dominic's suspicions that l'Abbé Charles Minette of the Department of Colonization of Amos was aware, on November 23, 1934, that he was on that day detained as a prisoner in the jail at Amos.

"Your wife should never have gone to Mastaï to get you," concluded the priest.

Mathias Poirier, one of the councillors of St. Marc who had accompanied Dominic to Quebec City, and who had since become sympathetic to his cause and had now accompanied him to the presbytery, held the floor next. He admitted taking Dominic's wallet and retaining it in his possession until January 27, 1935, when it was returned to its rightful owner. He stated that Dr. Marcel Sarazin had declared Dominic one hundred percent insane in the jail at Amos on November 23, 1934, despite the fact that the doctor was not a psychiatrist. He admitted, further, having carried in his pocket a certificate of insanity on the trip to Mastaï and transferring it to the authorities there.

Around that time, Dominic became aware that false rumours, to the effect that the Knights of Columbus had paid the premiums due on his life insurance policies, had been well publicized throughout the Abitibi. He learned, further, that Monsieur le Curé had corresponded with the Great West Life Assurance Company and had obtained confidential information from them with regard to his policies. On hearing that disturbing news, Dominic was motivated to write a letter of reprimand to the company for having transmitted personal information to third parties with respect to his policies during his absence. He asked them for copies of the pertinent correspondence.

In their reply to Dominic, the Great West Life Assurance Company informed him that they could not reveal such information without first obtaining authorization to do so from Monsieur le Curé Michaud, who was the acknowledged third party with whom the company had corresponded.

Permission from Monsieur le Curé was obtained. A portion of the correspondence, which sufficed to prove that no premiums had been paid on the policies by the Knights of Columbus, was then mailed to Dominic.

It was during this period that the identity of the Secretary of the Municipal Council was kept carefully concealed from the public. In an attempt to find that person, if such a person existed, Dominic called on Claude Thérien. The man was a good friend of Monsieur le Curé, and

Dominic hoped he could shed some light on the mystery. To no avail! Monsieur le Curé appeared to be the only one who knew the identity of the secretary, but he refused to divulge that information.

While it was customary at St. Marc to hold council meetings in the basement of the church immediately after Mass on Sundays or on Holy Days of Obligation, in certain cases - when they were classified as secret meetings - they were held in the presbytery.

On April 19, 1935 (Good Friday), the basement of the church was the scene of an interesting and well-attended municipal council meeting, conducted in such a manner as to conceal the identity of the secretary. Dominic again endeavoured to locate the man who held that office, but Monsieur le Curé declared that he did not have to reveal that information if he did not wish to do so.

At that meeting, Dominic offered his gold wedding ring in payment of taxes, but Monsieur le Curé refused to accept it. He further made the astounding request that Dominic pay the premiums due on the eight hundred dollar fire insurance policy that had previously been taken out on the buildings located on the land which was no longer in Dominic's possession!

Elizabeth, who was present at the meeting because she no longer permitted Dominic to go anywhere unescorted, was unable to restrain herself another moment. She arose and demanded, "Monsieur le Curé, why did you sell our land?"

The priest replied that it had been sold for five dollars of arrear taxes. The fact that it was not customary in rural municipalities to sell lands for taxes until a ratepayer had fallen at least three years in arrears had been ignored. Monsieur le Curé was aware that Dominic had bought his property through the Department of Colonization less than three years earlier, with the assurance that it was clear of back taxes.

"Why did you not ask me for five dollars?" Elizabeth demanded next. The priest replied that he could not ask her for five dollars because her husband was ill.

"If you felt that I could not pay even five dollars, how did you expect me to pay the expenses of my husband's trip to Mastaï?"

A shrug of his shoulders constituted Monsieur le Curé's reply to that second question.

"What were you intending to do with my seven little children and myself if my husband had not come back? You were going to put us on the road, weren't you!" she accused.

Again, the priest did not reply.

Becoming increasingly annoyed at the questions to which he appeared unable to supply satisfactory answers, Monsieur le Curé abruptly terminated the meeting.

During the following days, Dominic's search for the secretary continued. A good friend and neighbour eventually wrote to the Department of Municipal Affairs, Parliament Buildings, Quebec City, in order to learn the identity of that person. The official reply, dated April 25, contained the information that Mr. Claude Thérien was the Secretary-Treasurer of the Municipality of St. Marc de Figuery.

Why had Claude Thérien pleaded ignorance when previously approached by Dominic?

The most obvious reason was that the Quebec Municipal Act clearly stated that a person could not occupy the roles of secretary-treasurer and municipal councillor of the same municipality at one and the same time, and Claude Thérien was already a councillor.

Because Monsieur le Curé was disturbed at his failure to induce Dominic to pay the premiums due on the fire insurance policy, he repeated the request in writing on April 25. In his reply to that letter Dominic combined a refusal to be responsible for the premiums with a suggestion that Monsieur le Curé take out an insurance policy against the fires of hell.

During May of 1935, Dominic received an interesting letter from a businessman of Amos. The letter informed him that the Honourable Hector Authier, Member of the Legislative Assembly for the Abitibi, was aware of the sale of his land. He was assured that the politician was convinced of the unlawfulness of the sale, and wished him to know that the family was not required to vacate the premises. He also transmitted a promise that an investigation on the whole case would take place immediately.

In fulfilment of that promise, Royal Renaud, Inspector of the Department of Colonization of Amos, was assigned to the role of investigator. In that capacity, he called promptly on Dominic and Elizabeth.

Unfortunately, Royal Renaud endeavoured to persuade Dominic to make certain ridiculous false statements. For instance, he wished Dominic to declare that he had, himself, expressed a desire to go to the asylum. Royal Renaud stated, further, that the investigation revealed that Dominic was scheduled to die two days after being admitted to Mastaï. This was the second time that Dominic was told that his death had been predicted on his transfer to Mastaï. But then, at St. Marc de Figuery at that time, truth was often stranger than fiction!

Dominic became suspicious of the Honourable Hector Authier's motives. Why was he so willing and anxious that an investigation be conducted on the case? Dominic and Elizabeth hoped that it was because he wished justice to be done. Because the clergy was so well protected in the Province of Quebec, they feared that the Honourable Hector Authier might be more anxious to find a loophole in the case whereby Monsieur le Curé Michaud could be exonerated of guilt, than he was in obtaining justice for their family.

Dominic wrote for help to the notorious Duplessis, who was then commencing his political career; to Mr. Bellac, the Member of Parliament for Pontiac at the House of Commons; as well as to the Department of Justice, Ottawa.

At a council meeting held in the basement of the church at St. Marc on May 8, Monsieur le Curé again brought up the matter of the premiums due on Dominic's fire insurance policy. Believing that his angry written refusal to pay the premiums would have served to prevent any further discussions on that particular matter, Dominic was amazed at the priest's persistence. At that meeting, Monsieur le Curé produced a letter which he had received from the Secretary of the Mutual Fire Insurance Company stating that in order to prevent the policy from lapsing it was required that a two-dollar premium be paid immediately.

Dominic knew that he was not responsible for the payment of the premium, since the Municipality of St. Marc had confiscated his property. He did not evince the worried reaction expected by Monsieur le Curé. He arose, picked up the letter from the Mutual Fire Insurance Company, and examined it closely.

"Do you find anything wrong with the letter?" challenged the priest.

Before replying, Dominic picked up a piece of paper, which he noticed had been turned face-downward on the table in an obvious attempt at concealment. "No, not at all, but here is the receipt proving that you have already paid the two-dollar premium," he replied, on indicating the piece of paper.

After the laughter had subsided, Dominic asked, "Who was responsible for sending me to the asylum?"

"The Municipality of St. Marc," promptly answered Napoléon Doucet, the mayor.

"Dr. Marcel Sarazin of Amos," contradicted Monsieur le Curé. He promised to defend the Municipality of St. Marc, and to assume personal responsibility for any expenses it might become involved in with regard to the case.

At that point, Dominic and Elizabeth left the meeting. They knew that nothing constructive could be accomplished when Monsieur le Curé was in complete control. They learned, later, that the priest had seized the opportunity afforded by their departure to pronounce Dominic "either crazy or crooked."

On May 13, Dominic received a letter from W. Stuart Edwards, Deputy Minister, Department of Justice, Ottawa, to whom he had previously written informing him of the family's dilemma and asking for assistance in obtaining justice. In his letter, the deputy minister informed him, with regret, that the Federal Crown had no jurisdiction in the matter of his case and could not act. In the Province of Quebec, such matters were under provincial control.

Dominic questioned the wisdom of a law which permitted Canadian provinces full internal control over matters of justice within their boundaries. He felt that there should be a change in the Constitution permitting federal authorities to intervene when a province failed to protect its citizens.

One evening the children overheard their father saying to their mother: "Unless drastic changes are made in the Province of Quebec, and unless it is given a thorough cleaning, I can see the day when we will have a revolution in Canada. I can see the day when the waters of the Ottawa River will be flowing with the blood of the innocent mingled with the blood of the guilty." The children never forgot those words.

As the weather turned warmer, neighbouring farmers attended to the task of planting their crops. Dominic and Elizabeth looked with sorrow across the fields which they had once called their own. Their land had been industriously cultivated the previous autumn in preparation for planting in the spring of 1935, but the fertile fields now lay in abandonment. A generous neighbour invited Dominic and Elizabeth to plant a small garden for their use on his land.

Knowing that in the publicity of his case lay his only safety, Dominic posted on the most conspicuous corner of the public road, adjacent to the property, a sign which read: *"Against human and divine law this place was sold. We are ready to move out at orders of authorities."*

The notice was read by many, and remained posted for months, but no protest was raised and no orders to vacate were given the family.

Up until the time of Dominic's abduction, Elizabeth's main occupation and interest in life had centred around the care of her husband and children. She had never, at any time, entertained a desire to correspond with politicians or men of importance. Nevertheless, she felt that the time had come for her to join her husband in expressing written protests. In spite of a grade four elementary school education, she began by writing of her own volition, completely unassisted, a letter to the Honourable Hector Authier. In her lengthy letter, dated May 20, 1935, she recalled to his mind, step by step, the tragic experiences she and her family had suffered in the Abitibi. She went on to ask:

"Does the Province of Quebec want us to walk out? What were the plans if my husband had not come back? Was I going to be put on the road with my seven little children? Or did they want me to apply to the Province of Alberta to look into the matter? If my husband makes his Will or transacts any business will it be legal or will it be of no value? I am ready to walk out of the Province of Quebec if what was done to us was right or lawful, but at the same time if I am forced to walk out I will have to tell the story of what was done to us. I may say, that when we told the people in the west that we were going to Quebec some of them told us that they were indeed very sorry for us because the French Canadians were going to take off our shirts. Shall we go back to Alberta and tell them that they were right? That the French Canadians not only took our shirts but our very country? But we still have a very high opinion of most of the people of Quebec. I would like to say much more but my grammar is very poor and I want to make a copy of this to send to the Cardinal Villeneuve.

I am asking for reparation of honour . . . How is the brand going to be taken off our seven children as coming from a father declared one hundred percent crazy? I may admit I do not know the code, but I use the code of common sense. My conscience tells me that where things like that are permitted, not only I do not call those people Canadians but I cannot call them Catholics. As true Canadians we are supposed to fight to keep our country clean and honest, and as Catholics we are to give a good example in our actions and do not do to others what we do not want others to do to us. I also believe that when we are sick and call for a priest and people supposed to be Catholics, and priests are denied us by authorities, it is time to wake up. I may say that in the west, surrounded by Protestant friends, if my husband had called for a priest they would have brought one from 150 miles if necessary."

As Dominic read the letter he realized that, in its daring accusations, it far surpassed any he himself had so far written. While he agreed that it should be mailed, he greatly feared the possible consequences of such a boldly-written truth. He was especially apprehensive in view of the fast-multiplying rumours that attempts were under way to again have him committed on charges of insanity.

He did not doubt that Elizabeth's letter would result in a response of some kind. He and Elizabeth lived in a state of uneasy suspense, which each passing day of silence only served to increase.

On June 2, a member of the Junior Chamber of Commerce of Amos called at the family quarters, bearing two hand-written copies of the letter. Assuming friendship, the man advised Elizabeth not to say a word to anyone in connection with the case. He pointed out the wisdom of maintaining silence, and assured her that if she cooperated she would be treated as a queen.

Elizabeth replied, "I do not wish to be treated as a queen. All I want is some justice for my family."

On their way to Mass, on that same day, Dominic and Elizabeth encountered Royal Renaud. They urged him to tell his friend, the Honourable Hector Authier, that they were awaiting an immediate official reply to the letter Elizabeth had written to him. They added that they did not appreciate being approached by emissaries urging them to silence.

From the pulpit of the church, that Sunday, Monsieur le Curé announced, to the delight of the expectant parishioners, that a ten-minute meeting of the municipal council would take place in the basement of the church immediately after Mass.

A great deal of sparring normally took place between Dominic and Monsieur le Curé at those meetings. While it was not intended by either man, their encounters offered a great deal of amusement. Attendance at the council meetings by the male population of St. Marc had increased dramatically. Elizabeth's habitual presence had caused the female attendance to rise from zero to one.

At his desk, glowing with self-importance and surrounded by the municipal council, sat the assistant-secretary, Monsieur le Curé. Silently, he scrutinized the faces of his audience.

Apparently satisfied at the expressions of anticipation and curiosity manifested there, he declared the ten-minute meeting open. He then held the floor with the delivery of a nine-and-a-half minute speech. It terminated with a significant glance at Dominic, and the words "All done," clearly spoken in English for Elizabeth's benefit.

"All done," quickly became the local joke in St. Marc. "All done" replaced the customary *"Bonjour"* when friend met friend during the following days.

Because Elizabeth was convinced that Dominic lived in great peril at St. Marc, she urged him to ask the family physician to certify his sanity. The doctor declined, remarking that it was police he needed for protection and not a psychiatric evaluation.

Elizabeth continued to fear for the safety of her family. With a feeling of urgency, she sent a telegram to the Federal Department of Justice, Ottawa. In it, she pleaded: "Send at once two federal policemen to escort self, husband and seven children out of the Province of Quebec."

Around that time, Dominic was astounded and angered to receive a presumptuous notice from Monsieur le Curé informing him that, at a special meeting of the municipal council, it was agreed that Johnny would be granted permission to quit school to work at the gravel pits because his was "a special case." The priest was undeterred by the fact that Johnny was an exceptionally bright thirteen-year-old student, compelled by law to attend school. Dominic and Elizabeth had not been consulted in the matter, and they felt that to be a further infringement of their rights.

Johnny had attained a higher level of education than was customary among the local children. The teacher had never been called upon to teach the level of mathematics at which Johnny had arrived. She was at a loss how to handle the problem, since she could not understand the subject. Johnny took his new book home and spent several hours poring over it. His perseverance paid off, and by the end of the evening he knew exactly what to do. The next day at school he taught the problems to the teacher, who then fulfilled her obligation by teaching them back to Johnny.

Dominic had high expectations for Johnny, as he did for all of his children, and it was of great importance to him that they received a good education. One of his greatest fears and frustrations, in view of the events encountered in the Province of Quebec, was that he would be financially unable to realize the dreams he had for them.

Dominic was constantly appalled at the low priority given to the education of the school children of rural Quebec. How could they hope to compete, scholastically, with the children in the rest of Canada when their own superiors kept them down?

Dominic and Elizabeth often spoke, and puzzled over, the nature of the papers Elizabeth had been asked to sign by Monsieur le Curé on the day of Dominic's abduction. They decided to again visit the priest, and to insist that he acquaint them with their contents.

When they reached the presbytery, a couple of hours later, they were surprised to find Monsieur le Curé carefully studying a typewritten copy of the letter written by Elizabeth to the Honourable Hector Authier.

Indicating the letter in question, Elizabeth asked the priest if he disagreed with any of the charges it contained. After careful consideration, Monsieur le Curé acknowledged its entire truthfulness.

Wishing to get to the purpose of the visit, Elizabeth insisted that she be shown a copy of what she had been asked to sign on November 23, 1934. After considerable evasiveness, the priest arose and crossed the room to his desk. From the drawer, he withdrew a *blank* Form of Authorization, such as was used to send insane people to the asylum. He told Elizabeth that she had signed one of those, although he did not tell her how he had filled in the blank spaces.

Elizabeth was appalled at this deception on the part of a priest whom she had trusted implicitly in his role as a representative of God. Although she had been asked to sign that paper, Dominic and Elizabeth were aware that at the time of her signature the arrest had already been made. Furthermore, arrangements had already been completed for Dominic's transfer to Mastaï.

''What! You asked my wife to sign a thing like that! You should serve a term in Bordeau for asking a woman to sign a paper authorizing you to send her husband to an asylum!'' burst out Dominic, as he glared at the grinning priest.

''Oh, before I go to Bordeau, you will go to Mastaï again,'' laughed Monsieur le Curé, in the full confidence of his power and influence. He again accused Dominic of being either crazy or crooked.

The case grew in strangeness and magnitude as time went on. Another anonymous visitor put in an appearance on June 18, under the disguise of a medicine salesman. Jauntily, he stepped out of his car! With a flourish, he attempted to sell his products. He selected a bottle of perfume and presented it to Elizabeth.

''I never use perfume,'' said Elizabeth, who did not buy cosmetics of any kind.

The salesman then turned to Mary and gave her the perfume. It was under those unusual circumstances that twelve-year-old Mary came to be in possession of her first unforgettable bottle of perfume.

Olive oil! Dominic must buy some olive oil! All Italians like olive oil! The salesman selected a tempting-looking bottle of the greasy liquid and endeavoured, again unsuccessfully, to push his products.

On so doing, he mentioned that he had 'happened' to see a copy of the letter written by Elizabeth to the Honourable Hector Authier.

"The Province of Quebec does not like that letter at all, he informed Dominic and Elizabeth.

Elizabeth retorted, "Whether they like it or not, they have to accept it because it is true."

At his departure, the salesman assured Dominic that he was convinced that he was not insane.

With each passing day the Raina family became poorer, and justice seemed more unattainable. Monsieur le Curé, enveloped in the protecting folds of his soutane, appeared more and more confident in his position of unquestioned authority.

On June 19, in an effort to curtail what he considered to be the priest's unethical business practices, Dominic mailed a petition signed by himself and several neighbours to His Excellency Bishop Rhéaume of Haileybury. Permission was asked to bring Monsieur le Curé before the civil courts, but satisfaction was not obtained. From the pulpit of the church, Monsieur le Curé advised his flock that it was useless for them to mail protests to the bishop, as His Excellency did not believe in their veracity. He felt secure in the bishop's protection since he, too, mailed petitions bearing many signatures to His Excellency. The school children reported to their parents that Monsieur le Curé had asked them to copy their fathers' names on a petition he was sending to the bishop.

On one occasion, it was rumoured that Monsieur le Curé had given a poor widow of the parish a one-hundred pound bag of flour in order to secure her signature for his purposes.

Dominic was told by some neighbours, at the beginning of July, that Bishop Rhéaume had visited Amos and that a secret meeting in connection with his case had taken place with His Excellency in attendance. Dominic and Elizabeth wondered why they had not been invited to attend so that they might present their grievances.

An important meeting of the municipal council was held in the basement of the church at St. Marc in early July. There were at least forty ratepayers of the municipality and several guests from Amos in attendance.

Dominic seized the opportunity presented by the meeting to further publicize his case. He distributed at least twenty-five hand-written copies of the declaration that he had previously received from Monsieur le Curé stating that the papers signed by Elizabeth on November 23, 1934, did not bind her to anything.

As the recipients of those copies studied the written declaration, the assistant-secretary, Monsieur le Curé, arose to deny having ever written such a statement.

"Is that your handwriting or not?" demanded Dominic, who had anticipated the priest's denial and had already approached his desk for the purpose of displaying the written declaration.

"Yes," muttered Monsieur le Curé, as he fixedly studied the missive.

"You can read it, but don't you dare steal it!" warned Dominic, clasping the evidence.

"That is nothing! When a priest asks a woman to sign a paper authorizing him to send her husband to the asylum, well . . . that is nothing!" said Dominic, turning to the interested audience.

"Mr. Raina is either crazy or crooked," was the priest's customary claim used in defence against Dominic's accusations. He followed the insult with a promise that he would obtain a certificate to that effect from Dominic's family physician on the following day. A certificate of insanity or a certificate of crookedness? wondered Dominic. He retorted that the proper place and time to analyze heads was right then and there at the council meeting. He suggested that several doctors and policemen be summoned for that purpose.

The assembled council members appeared unnerved by that suggestion. One brave councillor arose and tendered his resignation. Joseph Lacoursière, a second councillor, explained that he had no part in the Raina case and also offered his resignation. Adélard Corriveau of the school board next arose, to officially confess that it was the school board, and not the municipal council, that was responsible for the sale of the Raina property.

Although no enmity had that evening been displayed toward them by the councillors, Dominic and Elizabeth reached the house in a state of worry and uneasiness. They were only too well aware of the power and influence of Monsieur le Curé, and of the danger they were in as a consequence.

On July 9, Elizabeth sent out an appeal for protection to the Honourable R.B. Bennett, the Prime Minister of Canada.

In reply to that appeal, a letter dated July 17, 1935, was received from the Department of Justice, Ottawa. Elizabeth was advised that the matter was one for the attention of the provincial authorities, because the administration of justice, both civil and criminal, came within the purview of the provincial government.

During a visit with Monsieur le Curé that summer, Dominic asked the priest why he had not visited him in jail. Monsieur le Curé replied that since Dominic had received the Sacraments of Penance and Holy Eucharist two days prior to his arrest he did not need a priest.

Around that time, Dominic made enquiries concerning the telegram he had asked Elizabeth to send to the Honourable E.G. Garland on the day of his arrest. He was horrified to learn, though unofficially, that the telegram had been reworded and seriously falsified, stating that Elizabeth had sent her husband to the asylum. Perhaps attempts were underway to undermine her credibility.

On July 14, 1935, Dominic wrote to the Department of Municipal Affairs, Quebec City, with regard to the theft of his property. In his letter he stated, "My trial is the trial of the whole Taschereau administration . . . I have no political colours, but I am against bandits, kidnappers, thieves, and 'Secret Rule'."

CHAPTER X

THE SITUATION WORSENS

"Every man is equally entitled to protection by the law."
Andrew Jackson.

A great political meeting was scheduled to take place at Amos on July 23, 1935. Maurice Duplessis, Leader of the Opposition of the Quebec Legislative Assembly, was scheduled to be the main speaker. All previous efforts to obtain redress for the wrongs inflicted on them having failed, Dominic and Elizabeth pinned fresh hope on the new party, *l'Union nationale,* which Duplessis represented.

It was with great confidence in the ultimate triumph of justice that they left for Amos to attend the meeting on the scheduled day.

Very encouraging was Duplessis' speech, promising honesty and justice should he come into power. Long and loud was the clapping which resounded through the hall! That evening, Dominic and Elizabeth were given the opportunity to speak privately to the future leader of Quebec, who promised to look into their case. He told them that after his election he would have enough jails built to house all the criminals of Quebec.

Dominic and Elizabeth took advantage of the trip to Amos to call on Dr. Simard. They wished to verify whether or not the doctor was in town on November 23, 1934. While confined to his cell, Dominic had been denied the right to see his family physician. Earlier that month, Royal Renaud had declared the doctor had been absent from town on that day, but the physician confirmed that he was indeed in Amos on November 23. He had, in fact, performed two operations at the local hospital. He also informed Dominic and Elizabeth that Monsieur le Curé Michaud had called at the office two weeks earlier. True to the threat he had made at the council meeting, the priest had insisted that the doctor give him a certificate of insanity on Dominic. Dr. Simard had refused, telling the priest that he not only considered Mr. Raina to be completely sane but smarter than anyone else at St. Marc.

During a previous visit to Dr. Simard, the physician had told Dominic and Elizabeth that a single doctor (Dr. Marcel Sarazin) did not have the authority to declare a man insane in the first place.

With the end of July came the haying season once again, and how abundantly it grew that year! Along with the haying season came a frustrating note from Monsieur le Curé Jules Michaud. It informed Dominic that the Municipality of St. Marc de Figuery had sold the hay from Lot 39, Range 3, Figuery, to Mathias Fortier on July 26, and had given him permission to put it in the barn.

Determined to protest this latest assault on the property, Elizabeth resolved to go again to Amos.

As she walked down the main street of the town, worried indecision clearly evident throughout her bearing, she was met by Mr. Mascotte, jailer from the courthouse of Amos. He stopped her to enquire what was the matter.

"Oh, they are hauling away the hay, and I can't bear it! I just can't bear it!" Elizabeth tearfully informed him.

After some consideration, Mr. Mascotte suggested that she call on Mr. Ladouceur, the lawyer.

Mr. Ladouceur pointed out the difficulty in doing anything with the case, explaining that the reason Monsieur le Curé did all those things to the Raina family was because he knew he was so well protected.

To whom could she turn next, wondered Elizabeth. The Mounted Police! They always get their man! Standing before the local representative, Elizabeth confidently recounted her troubles.

"It is unbearable for me to remain at St. Marc under these circumstances. Will you please put me in jail, so that I may be accorded a trial," she begged.

The policeman, who had not been authorized to step into the provincial department, counselled her to go back to St. Marc and to have patience.

"But I may get very angry and shoot someone. What will you do with me then?" asked Elizabeth, who could barely refrain, under those frustrating circumstances, from taking the law into her own hands.

Later on in the season, the family was again visited by the man who had previously called under the disguise of a medicine salesman. On this occasion, the man stated honestly that the purpose of his visit was to discuss the case. He suggested certain courses of action whereby he felt the family might obtain redress for their just grievances.

Although his suggestions were appreciated, they did not keep the family from becoming daily more destitute, and the children were often hungry. They attempted to survive on any nourishment that could be culled from the land.

The children had picked great quantities of berries throughout the summer. Earlier in the season, they had discovered a patch with seemingly endless acres of strawberries on the far side of Lac d'école. With meager lunches and numerous containers, they had invaded the berry patch each day as soon as the dew was off the grass. On one occasion, when their containers would not hold all the berries they hoped to pick, they filled their new straw hats with the overflow. As Elizabeth watched them coming down the road happily licking their fingers, which were covered with the berry juice that was seeping through their hats, she smiled at their obvious enjoyment. Although the hats had been bought at great financial sacrifice, she did not reprimand them. She suggested that they put them outdoors to dry, assuring them that the colour would be greatly improved once they were dyed permanently by the rich red berry juice.

The children were learning from their father the great importance of sticking together through the tragedy that had befallen the family. Dominic was a philosophical man who tried to instill his principles into his children at every opportunity. He pointed out to them that a family, or a municipality, or a nation, was similar to a chain — only as strong as its weakest link. He stressed that if the family was to survive its reverses even its weakest link must be very strong. The children took their father's teachings seriously because they considered him to be very wise and they trusted him implicitly. They did not worry about the future. They felt secure in their parents' love and wisdom, and depended on them to solve the existing problems.

At the house, food was becoming more scarce each day and the children were often hungry. The roof of the house was badly in need of repair to prevent the rain from leaking through. Clothes were wearing out. Some of the children were in need of medical attention. Further delay in the return of their home, and the consequent means of earning a livelihood, could only result in tragedy.

In desperation, Dominic and Elizabeth appealed for legal assistance to Felix Allard, the Crown Attorney at Amos. He assured them that when authorities did not deny the accusations, the silence on their part was an admission of guilt. He displayed genuine interest in the case and promised to write immediately to the Attorney General at Quebec City with regard to the matter.

Dominic and Elizabeth took advantage of their trip to Amos to call on Mr. Ladouceur, the lawyer whose help Elizabeth had previously sought in connection with the procurement of a copy of the papers that she had been asked to sign on November 23, 1934 — the day of Dominic's abduction. The lawyer had promised that he would act and that all expenses for his services would be charged to the Municipality of St. Marc de Figuery. He had not yet accomplished anything, but he again renewed his promise. He instructed Elizabeth to call back at a later date.

Elizabeth returned to his office in early August.

As she was walking down the hall that led to the lawyer's office she heard the voice of Monsieur le Curé Jules Michaud inside the room. When the priest emerged, he wore a satisfied expression on his face and directed a triumphant look at Elizabeth. Elizabeth feared that, as a representative of God, he had again found protection for his actions. Her suspicions were confirmed when she met with a distinctly changed attitude on the part of Mr. Ladouceur. He told Elizabeth that he could believe Monsieur le Curé just as well as her, and that he had decided not to handle the case.

Elizabeth feared that she was now up against a stone wall everywhere she turned. Disappointed as she was at the outcome of her visit, she could understand why the lawyer had been swayed. Not only was Monsieur le Curé a representative of God, but he was a man who exuded great power and charm. She was merely a humble settler's wife. What chance did she stand with the lawyer against such odds? In fact, what chance did she stand anywhere in the Province of Quebec, where the clergy ruled supreme and where the federal authorities were impotent to enforce justice?

Felix Allard, the Crown Attorney who had previously expressed an interest in the case, had not accomplished anything.

With the mental image of her undernourished children constantly before her, Elizabeth again called on the Mounted Police. In spite of the fact that they were powerless to defend the case, Elizabeth knew that she could always rely on them for sympathy and understanding. During the course of her conversation with them that day, the policemen advised Elizabeth to write to the provincial police at Noranda.

Elizabeth was reluctant to tell her family, on arriving home from her ten-mile trip on foot from Amos, that she had again failed to obtain either food or legal assistance.

The letter to the provincial police was written, as well as another one to His Excellency Bishop Rhéaume of Haileybury.

The hopelessness of the situation was undermining Elizabeth's strength.

Two days later, she lay very ill in bed surrounded by her worried family. On August 13, she wrote to the Mayor of St. Marc, advising him that she was holding the Municipality of St. Marc responsible for her family's dire circumstances. She begged that food and clothing be sent to the house, not as charity but as the beginning of reparation. The mayor returned the letter with the explanation that he could not act because he did not understand English.

On the following day, Dominic wrote an angry letter to the mayor. He reprimanded him for his failure to act on his wife's letter. He pointed out that:

> "For your information, I must tell you that English is an official language in Canada, and that if you do not understand it, it is up to you to get an interpreter. I am returning my wife's letter translated into French as literally as possible. I do not know if you know the code, but remember that by declaring Dominic Raina insane that does not give you the right to starve the Raina family."

Dominic asked the mayor under what laws he assumed the right to condone such atrocities. He added, "Are we living in Canada or amongst the wild tribes of Africa? If you are unable to reply in writing I shall take it as another evidence that you are in the wrong."

Because that letter was completely ignored by the Mayor of St. Marc, Elizabeth wrote to the Mayor of Amos on August 17, acquainting him with recent events. She stated: "If we are guilty, why not bring us to court and give us a chance to testify in public and let the people of Canada be the judges in our case?"

Because Elizabeth's recovery was progressing much too slowly, she wrote to the provincial police begging them to send a doctor to her bedside. The police did not respond. When Elizabeth eventually recovered she visited them in Amos. Constable Turnbull, the provincial representative for the region, attempted to justify his failure to send a doctor to visit her by telling her that he had gone to the presbytery at St. Marc, accompanied by the Health Officer of Amos. After a lengthy visit with Monsieur le Curé it was too late to call on Elizabeth.

"It was I who was ill, not Monsieur le Curé Michaud!" Elizabeth exclaimed angrily, on being given that incredulous excuse.

After considerable discussion, the constable asked that Dominic be summoned to verify dates of events so that they might take down notes. A minor investigation was that day conducted on the case by the provincial police.

Elizabeth took advantage of her trip to Amos to again call on Felix Allard, but the Crown Attorney declined to act on the case, explaining that he could not work free of charge. Elizabeth promised him that she would pay him for services rendered as soon as her confiscated home was returned, but he was unwilling to accept such uncertain terms of payment.

On September 4, a letter reached Dominic from the religious authorities, under the signature of His Excellency Bishop Rhéaume of Haileybury. In his letter, the bishop instructed Dominic not to write to him about his troubles. He pointed out that the government authorities should deal with his case because the clergy did not manage the civil law. He ended his letter by extending his blessing.

One evening, while Dominic was reading some papers which had accumulated around the house, he came across an article dealing with his unjust abduction. It appeared in the *Voice of the Prairies* column of the *The Saskatchewan Farmer* of September 5, 1935. While Dominic did not know who was responsible for the article, he was gratified to see that his case was being given some publicity. He felt that in publicity lay his greatest safety, and that of his family.

The effects of malnutrition were making themselves felt in the family quarters. At the beginning of September, Elizabeth deemed it advisable to take Mary to the family physician for a checkup because of her rundown condition.

Mary's father wrote a note to the school teacher explaining his daughter's absence. It read: "My daughter Mary cannot go to school because she has to go to the doctor. My children have not the means to buy the necessary books for school because the school board stole our land."

After giving Mary a thorough examination, the doctor diagnosed the problem as a pair of badly infected tonsils and stressed the need for an immediate operation. He wrote a note to that effect, which he instructed Elizabeth to deliver to Felix Allard, the Crown Attorney. The doctor prescribed that Mary adhere to a strict liquid diet for a couple of weeks. It was an easy prescription to follow because the wells on the Raina quarters were filled with water, but the cupboards were bare of food.

The Crown Attorney refused to accept the note transmitted by the doctor. The provincial police also declined to act.

Elizabeth next visited the Royal Canadian Mounted Police, who phoned the Department of Colonization in Amos and urged the officials there to give immediate attention to Mary's medical problems.

The phone call served no purpose other than to rouse the anger of the department. On the evening of that same day, Royal Renaud was sent to the family quarters to protest the publicity given to Mary's case of tonsillitis.

The discussion on the subject of Mary's tonsils having eventually terminated, Royal Renaud retreated into deep thought. Finally, turning to Dominic, he asked where he stood with respect to his church dues, pointing out that if his dues were not paid up the authorities had the right to sell his land.

"Did you call on us as Inspector of the Department of Colonization, or as a representative of Monsieur le Curé Michaud?" asked Dominic. He was well aware of the fact that in the Municipality of St. Marc church dues and taxes were supposed to be entirely unrelated and that, according to the Municipal Act, lands could not be sold on account of arrears in church dues.

Royal Renaud ignored that question. He next asked Dominic whether he had a certificate from his doctor proving that he was not insane. At that point in the conversation, Dominic wondered whether the man was, himself, qualified to carry such a document. He replied, "Show me your certificate of sanity, and I'll produce one too."

He next asked Royal Renaud why the Honourable Hector Authier did not reply to their letters.

"Hector Authier is wealthy and he does not need the Raina family," was the somewhat irrelevant reply.

Dominic pointed out that he did not wish charity from Hector Authier, explaining that, as a member of the Legislative Assembly at Quebec for the Abitibi, the man was a servant of the people and it was his duty to try to obtain justice for the people.

On meeting Elizabeth at church one Sunday shortly after the visit, Royal Renaud asked her why she always accompanied her husband wherever he went.

"Oh, I have to guard him so that he will not be stolen from me a second time," replied Elizabeth with her never-failing sense of humour. "If I had been more careful, perhaps they could not have stolen him the first time."

In mid-September, accompanied by Johnny, Dominic called on the provincial police at Amos, only to be told that they had not yet received from Premier Taschereau, the Attorney General, the authority to enforce justice. They suggested that Dominic write to Premier Taschereau himself.

"I have already done so," replied Dominic.

Constable Turnbull advised, "Well, write again, and tell him that I said so."

Dominic could not understand how the provincial police could expect an unprotected settler to accomplish what they, as enforcers of the law, could not themselves accomplish. He agreed, with reluctance, to their suggestion.

Dominic again protested the failure of the provincial police to call on his family, when they had so often been invited. Constable Turnbull commented that they had secret police. Venturing a guess, Dominic asked if it was the medicine salesman. The constable did not offer a denial.

On September 18, Dominic and Elizabeth received a letter from the Office of the Deputy Attorney General at Quebec, to whom they had written with regard to the case, at the advice of the Department of Justice, Ottawa. In that letter, they were informed that the Office of the Deputy General was not authorized to intervene in the matter.

After months of futile effort, Elizabeth had now reached the conclusion that there was no justice to be found in Amos.

Feeling that the Raina case was both a religious and a civil matter, she called on l'Abbé Charles Minette. As a priest, and as an official of the Department of Colonization, the man was a representative of both the religious and civil authorities. She informed the priest that she was considering renting a truck to drive herself and her family to the feet of His Excellency Bishop Rhéaume of Haileybury. She asked for any information he could give her as to the rental cost of such a truck.

Her request roused the anger of l'Abbé Minette.

He replied that Cardinal Villeneuve had already written to ask why her family was being persecuted. He denied that this was the case, and told her that on payment of the tax arrears the property would be returned to the family. Then, pointing to his head, he commented that Dominic was "sick, sick, sick."

Determined to not return home without groceries, Elizabeth approached a pawnbroker in order to pawn all her jewellery, the total value of which had amounted to one hundred and twenty dollars at the time of purchase. It consisted of her diamond engagement ring, her watch (an engagement gift from Dominic), a gold cross and chain, and her gold wedding band.

"Keep your wedding ring," counselled the dealer. He offered Elizabeth ten dollars for the remaining pieces.

Elizabeth's sorrow at parting with those precious keepsakes was compensated for by the pleasure she derived from watching the children enjoy the first full-course meal served them in many days. She hoped that the money for the redemption of her jewellery might somehow be found before the time ran out.

Dominic and Elizabeth were much encouraged on receiving an invitation to be present at a meeting scheduled to be held at the courthouse in Amos on September 21, with regard to their grievances. They were met by several policemen, who informed them that an investigation on their case was in progress at Quebec City.

Great was the anticipation that pervaded the Raina quarters throughout the following days, as the family awaited the outcome of the investigation!

Because the Honourable Hector Authier had refrained from replying to her letter of May 20, Elizabeth again wrote to him on September 25. She suggested that he abstain temporarily from his efforts at winning the elections, so that he might turn his thoughts and time to so trivial a matter as the procuring of justice for poor persecuted settlers.

As the days passed, it became increasingly evident that the Honourable Hector Authier intended to ignore Elizabeth's letters. She did not waver in her resolve to force the man to action, or to a statement of some kind. She decided to visit him in his office.

A few days later, she sat on a bench in the upstairs hall of the Department of Colonization awaiting the return of the temporarily absent Hector Authier. Eventually, he came up the stairs in the company of another lawyer, who appeared to be a friend. As he entered his office, Elizabeth arose and followed him inside.

"Oh . . . oh yes!" stammered Hector Authier, on learning the identity of his visitor. He asked Elizabeth whether she had received his letter, while shifting papers back and forth across his desk as though in search of some lost object.

Elizabeth replied with an emphatic "No."

He then offered the contradictory explanation that the reason he had not written was because he did not wish to become involved in the Raina case.

Elizabeth placed special emphasis on the injustice of Dominic's abduction. Hector Authier replied that if it was an error, an error was only an error.

"Yes! An error is only an error, but not to be paid by me!" burst out Elizabeth.

Hector Authier admitted that, although he was not a practicing lawyer, he was convinced of the illegality of the sale of the Raina property. He suggested, as though in sudden inspiration, that she consult a lawyer.

"I have no money with which to pay for lawyers," retorted Elizabeth.

The Honourable Hector Authier then asked who was advising her.

"My advisor is up above and He does not charge me a cent," replied Elizabeth.

The politician then commented that if her home was stolen she could always get another one.

Elizabeth was relieved that he did not say that if her husband was stolen she could always get another one.

Hector Authier's flippancy with regard to her situation convinced Elizabeth that, once again, nothing would be accomplished.

The weather was now growing cold and frosty — a forewarning of another rapidly-approaching northern winter. The problem of fuel would again present itself. With that worry in mind, Dominic wrote a note for the signature of Napoléon Doucet, under date of October 16, 1935. It read:

"To Whom it May Concern:

The Municipality of St. Marc de Figuery, undersigned, declares by the present that Dominic Raina of St. Marc de Figuery has the "right" to cut wood for his use on lot 39, Range III, Figuery."

To the great annoyance of Monsieur le Curé, the mayor unconcernedly signed that significant slip without first consulting him.

Elizabeth had visited the provincial police frequently over a period of several months, and each time she was refused any assistance and directed to seek recourse from the clergy. On October 23, after having been turned away once more, she presented herself, with angry determination, at the presbytery of St. Marc.

"See that I get these supplies immediately!" she directed, on handing the startled Monsieur le Curé a list of the family's needs. "If you don't, I shall publicize our case throughout the streets of Amos."

The flustered priest, in an attempt to prevent that threatened exposure of his activities, assured Elizabeth that he would give the matter his imm-diate attention. Bearing groceries and clothing, valued at fourteen dollars and fifty-nine cents, he called on the Raina family in the early afternoon of that same day.

Because the family had been forced to spend several evenings in total darkness, Monsieur le Curé further gave Dominic a cash donation of twenty-five cents with which to buy oil for the lamps. In a manner that implied favouritism toward the family, the priest cautioned Dominic not to tell anyone that he had donated a quarter.

While their parents worried over their welfare, and while the Raina children understood only too well the troubles that had beset their family, they were able to find the silver lining in the cloud. To their great delight, they were now compelled to wear the same heavy rubber boots that they had so coveted on their arrival in the Abitibi because their parents could no longer afford to buy them leather shoes. As their boots stood steaming behind the stove each evening, they sat around the kitchen table contentedly scratching at their chilblains while attending to homework. With the wonderful resilience of childhood, and the admirable philosophy of their parents to guide them, they were happy laughing little children.

At the end of October, Royal Renaud again called on the Raina family. During that visit, Dominic expressed a wish that arrangements be made by the Department of Colonization for the immediate deportation of his family to his former home in Alberta or to the Department of Justice in Ottawa.

Royal Renaud ignored the request. The purpose of his visit was to ask Dominic to sign a relief cheque, and to swear that he had consented to turn it over to Monsieur le Curé in payment of the groceries the priest had previously delivered to the family. Royal Renaud appeared to be unaware that an insane, or supposedly insane, person should not be requested to make sworn statements. Dominic refused to comply with that request on these grounds. He further mailed a letter protesting the inefficiency of their inspector, Royal Renaud, to the Department of Colonization's head office at Quebec City.

Nonplused, Royal Renaud again called on the Raina family at the end of November. He brought with him three cheques — the ones for the months of September, October, and November, respectively. Each cheque was valued at thirteen dollars and seventy-five cents. Royal Renaud retained the cheque for the month of September, again explaining that it was to be given to Monsieur le Curé in payment of supplies that the family had received from the priest in October. Since Dominic was out in the woods cutting fuel, he transmitted the cheques for October and November to Elizabeth. Before his departure, Royal Renaud told Elizabeth that he would return to have Dominic endorse the September cheque before giving it to Monsieur le Curé.

When the day appointed for the redemption of Elizabeth's jewellery from the pawnbroker's ultimately arrived, Dominic was forced to sell the cream separator in order to obtain the necessary cash.

As winter approached and the weather grew harsher, the lack of food again became the family's greatest problem. Their supply was supplemented by Johnny's efforts at hunting, but a few bush rabbits did not suffice to feed a large and growing family.

On one unforgettable day in November, Elizabeth tearfully watched Johnny leave for a hard day of manual labour, carrying in his lunch-kit a few slices of dry bread as sole nourishment. Once again, she was motivated to confront Monsieur le Curé and to demand groceries. Again, she threatened to expose the case on the streets of Amos as a means of securing the necessities of life for her children. Monsieur le Curé contacted the Department of Colonization of Amos, and urged the officials there to assume the responsibility on this occasion.

As a result of the priest's telephone call, one of the agents of the Department of Colonization brought out a few groceries and some clothing in the afternoon of that day.

Realizing how desperate were their circumstances, and wishing to prove his friendship and goodwill by himself protesting the privations the Raina family suffered, a kind neighbour wrote a letter of admonition to the Department of Colonization of Amos. He pointed out that Mr. Raina could relieve the hunger of his chickens by killing them, but he could not use that method to relieve the hunger of his children.

At the beginning of December, Dominic heard that Royal Renaud was retaining in his possession a certain cheque that rightfully belonged to him. He immediately notified the Quebec Provincial Police, and asked that action be taken at once to recover the cheque and to have it transmitted to him. As had come to be expected, satisfaction was not obtained. Dominic's efforts merely served to draw to the Raina quarters an angry Royal Renaud. He shouted that if Dominic did not stop acting crazy the Department of Colonization would no longer concern themselves with the welfare of the family, but would permit them to die at St. Marc. He then produced the September relief cheque, which he had in his possession, and presented it to Dominic with the request that he sign it and hand it back.

On the reverse side of the cheque was clearly stamped, in both French and English, the following warning: "This cheque must be endorsed by the payee or his attorney duly appointed in writing. Any other original endorser renders himself liable to prosecution according to the law."

Royal Renaud was still determined to transmit the cheque to Monsieur le Curé in payment of the much-disputed groceries which the priest had donated to the family.

Dominic refused to acknowledge Royal Renaud as a go-between for himself and Monsieur le Curé. He was determined to retain his right to conduct his own business, and to reimburse the priest himself if he wished to do so.

Having met with that resistance, Royal Renaud pocketed the unendorsed cheque, again threatening to transmit it to Monsieur le Curé and ensuring that the family would receive no more cheques.

On the following day, Elizabeth was invited to visit Monsieur le Curé at his presbytery. On her arrival there, the priest opened a drawer of his desk, from which he removed the much-disputed cheque. Completely disregarding the warning on the back, he presented it to Elizabeth with the request that she endorse it.

"No! It is made out to my husband. If he wishes to endorse it he can do so, but don't expect me to ever again sign anything for you!" Elizabeth told the priest in a manner that defied contradiction.

"No?" asked Monsieur le Curé, eyeing the coveted cheque which he held in his hand.

"No!" emphasized Elizabeth.

On December 11, the Department of Colonization of Amos was ordered by the town police to hand over to Dominic Raina the cheque that was intended for him. The department ignored the order, and Dominic never did gain possession of that badly-needed relief cheque.

CHAPTER XI

CONTINUING INVESTIGATIONS

"Unlimited power is apt to corrupt the minds of those who possess it; . . . where law ends, tyranny begins." William Pitt, Earl of Chatham.

Dominic and Elizabeth felt humiliated at being forced to rely on help to feed their family. They were angry when Monsieur le Curé told them that they were living on charity. The priest also publicized, at a council meeting, the fact that he had donated twenty-five cents to pay for oil for the Raina lamps.

Claude Thérien of the municipal council, a good friend of Monsieur le Curé, had previously sent his son to haul some wood for the Raina family because they no longer had a horse. He also related this particular act of charity.

Feeling that they could no longer endure those bitter insults, Dominic and Elizabeth resolved to reimburse Monsieur le Curé and Claude Thérien to the best of their ability. Since they did not have any money, they decided to reimburse the men with chickens.

At their father's instructions, and with three of the family's remaining hens in a box on their sled, Mary, Ralph and Clara set out for the Village of St. Marc on a cold evening in mid-December.

"Now don't bring them back," Dominic told his children as they left on their errand. He had instructed them to leave two of the chickens with Claude Thérien, and one at the presbytery with Monsieur le Curé.

Claude Thérien was angry and articulate when the children set the poultry down upon his kitchen floor. He shouted that he did not want the chickens, and that he would kill them and throw them behind the barn if they were not removed at once.

"Daddy said we were to leave them here," quaked the children before the thunder of his wrath.

In a kind endeavour to lift the responsibility from their shoulders, Madame Thérien suggested that perhaps they had better keep them.

"No!" stormed her angry husband, in a tone of voice that forbade further contradiction.

So, with the three hens still in their possession, the children proceeded to the presbytery. "We'll leave them all with Monsieur le Curé," they agreed.

From his combination office and library upstairs, where he was busily engrossed in adding up figures, Monsieur le Curé called, "Come right up," in response to the raps at the door.

Up went the children, bearing chickens in their arms.

"These are in payment for the coal-oil," they volunteered, on meeting the priest's astounded gaze.

Once deposited on the office floor, the hens peered nervously at their new surroundings. Apparently they recognized on the top shelf of Monsieur le Curé's library a suitable roosting place and, with a flutter of wings, sought their perch!

As he tried to catch the frightened chickens, the priest yelled that he had no use for them and did not intend to keep them. He then climbed on a foot-stool and, after several attempts, managed to capture the now loudly-cackling poultry, while the children looked on with ill-concealed interest and amusement.

"Perhaps you could cook them," they suggested innocently, in an attempt to be helpful. Their words merely served to further aggravate Monsieur le Curé, as he handed over the poultry and told them to "Get them out of here!" After the door had closed behind them, the children burst into gales of laughter as they relived the scene of Monsieur le Curé becoming entangled in the folds of his soutane in his attempts to catch the hens. They were delighted that he had opted not to keep them.

The Christmas season of 1935 arrived. Since Dominic had not received a relief cheque for December, the family knew that holiday festivities would be non-existent. While material comforts were lacking, the family was partially compensated by the abundance of warmth and humour within their tightly-knit circle.

In mid-December, Dominic composed, for publication in a widely-read newspaper in the Abitibi, a quiz for the holidays. It listed the following questions:

1. How many bandits took part in the kidnapping of Dominic Raina?
2. How many among them will be converted by 1 April 1936?
3. How many lies were sent to Mastaï with Dominic Raina?

4. How many miles did Mrs. Raina travel on foot this past summer to chase off injustice?
5. How many relief cheques addressed to Dominic Raina did he not receive?
6. Where are the above-mentioned cheques at present?
7. When will the Municipality of St. Marc return lot 39, R. III, Figuery, stolen from Dominic Raina?
8. How many dollars will be deposited in the two bank books stolen from Dominic Raina before returning them?
9. When will Duplessis replace Taschereau?
10. How crazy (in percentages) is Dominic Raina?

RULES:
1. Entries are free to all contestants.
2. The contest finishes on 1 April 1936 (April Fool's Day).
3. Final decision on 30 April 1936.

PRIZES:
1. For correctly replying to all the questions — 100 lbs. of mixed first-class grain.
2. For the first reply received — five cords of wood from Lot 58, R.I, Figuery.
3. For the second reply received — three cords of wood as above.

Address your replies to "Dominic Raina, The Fool, Figuery, P.Q."

A couple of days later, Elizabeth wrote a letter to Monsieur le Curé, warning him that:

"...I hope that you will be able to locate our lost cheque before Christmas, otherwise you may expect us to spend the holiday season with you. It would give you and Royal Renaud a wonderful chance to study my husband's head. If you have the time perhaps you could also give us a statement in writing as to the amount of charity given by the municipality to the Raina family between December 1932 and December 1935. I would like to publish the total given us as well as the total stolen from us. I believe that the theft of the hay alone would more than suffice to pay for any charity received and which is so often discussed at St. Marc."

Christmas day marked the fulfilment of a ten-month request made by Dominic to the Great West Life Assurance Company that they send one of their representatives to call on him. The Mayor of Amos, visited the Rainas in that capacity, although he was not an official agent of the Great

West Life Assurance Company. The purpose of his visit was vague and nothing was accomplished by his presence.

New Year's Day of 1936! The beginning of another unforgettable year in the Province of Quebec! On that day, in accordance with a tradition widely spread throughout French Canada, the Raina children gathered around their father to receive the paternal blessing and good wishes for the New Year.

On January 6, the first council meeting of the Municipality of St. Marc of the year took place. At that particular meeting, Napoléon Doucet offered Dominic employment at his lumber camp. Dominic knew that the mayor would not consider employing a person whom he believed to be insane. He recognized in the offer an opportunity of obtaining a public admission of his sanity, so he asked, "Do you feel that I am sane?" But Napoléon Doucet refused to commit himself to a reply. Elizabeth considered it imprudent for Dominic to go alone to the lumber camp when threats were still under way to have him again declared insane and returned to Mastaï. Because it was impossible for her to accompany him to the lumber camp, located approximately thirty miles south of St. Marc and near the Siscoe mines, she begged him to turn down the offer of the job.

Dominic and Elizabeth were only too well aware that their monthly relief cheques were insufficient to permit a family of nine members to survive. They knew that they must find a means of supplementing those paltry cheques in order to secure the necessities of life for their children. Unfortunately, there was no employment to be found at St. Marc, and to work at a distance from home posed a real threat to Dominic. And so it shortly became necessary to again approach Monsieur le Curé for groceries.

The priest responded by issuing Dominic with a written begging order. It stated that he should pass from house to house in order to obtain the necessities of life for his family. So that they might have food to put upon the table, the Raina family became beggars in the Province of Quebec.

Dominic begged from grocers, clergymen, officials, farmers, and people of nearly all walks of life, for food for his family. As he did so, he bore a placard on his chest which read: *"After having robbed us of everything, the authorities sent us to beg. We are obeying orders. Give us a little charity."* A nickel here, a promise there, dry peas, salt pork, and loaves of bread — some dry and almost indigestible — constituted the family's assurance of survival throughout the winter of 1936. They were the beggar family; their names now bearing the double stigma of beggary and insanity!

During that winter, perhaps the most poverty-stricken one of their childhood, the Raina children depended greatly upon each other for companionship and fun. Johnny, who was of a versatile and inventive nature, fashioned a parchesi board and dice from a discarded plank. Each day, after they had completed their homework and daily chores, the children gathered around the kitchen table and played tirelessly at that game. Mary enjoyed writing and composing lyrics for the entertainment of her brothers and sister. With Johnny's hearty laughter as encouragement, she worked endlessly at her literary projects. Never were the words of a composer more greatly appreciated than were her amateur efforts!

As the family's plight continued to be desperate, the written protests to authorities, both civil and religious, became more numerous.

The Honourable Maurice Duplessis, in whom Dominic and Elizabeth still had confidence, was again reminded of the urgent need for restitution. The Prime Minister of Canada, the Right Honourable Mackenzie King, was also informed of their plight, when they wrote to him on February 25, 1936. His Excellency Bishop Rhéaume of Haileybury was also kept current on the course of events.

In a communication to the bishop, Dominic asked permission to bring Monsieur le Curé Jules Michaud, Parish Priest of St. Marc de Figuery, and l'Abbé Charles Minette, Missionary of the Department of Colonization of Amos, before the Ecclesiastical Tribunal.

One day, Dominic and Elizabeth decided to write joint letters, to be posted by registered mail, to the Honourable J. Blackmore, Member of Parliament, House of Commons, and a citizen of Alberta. They acquainted him of their desperate situation, and begged his assistance.

While so many other letters had been ignored, the letter to the Honourable J. Blackmore produced immediate results. At a time when their situation appeared most discouraging, the family's hopes skyrocketed on receiving a very encouraging reply from that member of parliament. In it, he stated that he was much distressed on receiving their rather pathetic letters, and was wondering what would be the wisest course to take. He promised that he would make every effort to learn the whole truth of their unfortunate case and to see that they got justice. He assured them that he would take the steps which seemed to be wisest under the circumstances. He promised that an investigation would be conducted on the case soon, and that he would write again to keep them informed. He reminded them that Quebec was mistress of her own house, and that it was almost impossible for other parts of the Dominion to make Quebec authorities give justice to people within the borders of Quebec. He promised, however, that what could be done would be done.

Dominic and Elizabeth were convinced that, regardless of the outcome of his efforts, the Honourable J. Blackmore had a real understanding of the case and what they were up against in the Province of Quebec. His letter not only offered a ray of hope, but they felt less isolated in their tragedy as a result of his promise to take positive action.

In early March, Dominic received a letter from M.J.E. Gregoire, the Mayor of Quebec City, with whom he had exchanged correspondence. In his letter, Mr. Gregoire commented that extraordinary things were happening in the Province of Quebec, and that the law was not always at the service of righteousness. He pointed out that the people of the province were becoming more and more aware of the fact that there were two measurements, for the poor and the rich, for the reds and the blues. He expressed hope that radical changes would take place in the near future.

While begging on the streets of Amos in mid-March, Dominic and Johnny were met by a member of the Royal Canadian Mounted Police. He informed them that instructions had been received from Ottawa authorizing an investigation into their case. This was the result of the promises made by the Honourable J. Blackmore in his recent letter, that he would take whatever action he deemed feasible in regard to the matter. The investigation was scheduled to begin the following week.

At around the same time, equally encouraging news reached Dominic from the religious authorities. In a letter from His Excellency Bishop Rhéaume of Haileybury, Dominic was granted permission to bring Monsieur le Curé Jules Michaud and l'Abbé Charles Minette before the Ecclesiastical Tribunal.

Dominic was informed of the large expenses that would be involved in such a procedure. He was made responsible for the selection of a priest to act as a lawyer at the tribunal. Still believing the Catholic Church to be the protector of the persecuted, Dominic was undeterred in his resolve. He remembered the contents of a pastoral letter, issued by His Eminence Cardinal Villeneuve and read recently from the pulpits of all the Catholic churches throughout the Province of Quebec, in which the cardinal stated that the Ecclesiastical Tribunal was intended for the protection of both the rich and the poor.

Insofar as the matter of choosing a priest to act as his lawyer was concerned, Dominic assured His Excellency that there were several possibilities. He indicated that he would be willing to accept Reverend Father Chagnon from the nearby Parish of Lamotte, or Reverend Father Lapointe of Amos, or Reverend Father Cyr of Les Pères Monfortains, or any other priest that His Excellency might suggest.

It was only a week later that Dominic received a disappointing reply to his letter. The bishop surprisingly revealed a change of mind. He now indicated a desire to avoid the Ecclesiastical Tribunal. He suggested that Dominic endeavour to effect a reconciliation with the priests involved in his case, rather than to consider taking them before a tribunal. The bishop's letter ended with the words: "I bless you so that you will understand your duty of Christian in the sense of pardon and of charity."

Although beggary had permitted the Raina family to escape starvation, Dominic had not developed a taste for that particular occupation and he hoped that the situation would prove to be temporary. He was greatly encouraged to learn from a neighbour, in early April, of a rumour suggesting that the long-awaited investigation by the Royal Canadian Mounted Police was in progress; a member of the force was scheduled to call at the house in the very near future to take down statements on the pertinent facts of the case.

In confirmation of those rumours, Constable Desrosiers, a young and enthusiastic Mounted Policeman, presented himself at the family quarters at four-thirty o'clock p.m. on April 7, 1936. He was attired in full dress uniform and was completely armed. From the time of his arrival, all throughout the night, and until six o'clock on the following morning, Dominic and Elizabeth were interrogated by the constable. He relaxed only briefly, every couple of hours, to accept a cup of coffee and to completely circle the house outside with gun in hand.

The children were awed and deeply interested in the drama unfolding in the house. They sensed the tenseness of the atmosphere and the importance of the investigation. Mary and Clara, from the vantage point of their beds in the kitchen, merely pretended to be asleep throughout that unforgettable night. They listened to every word of that lengthy interrogation so that they could reveal everything they had heard to their brothers the next morning.

During the days following the investigation, Dominic and Elizabeth called repeatedly at the office of the Royal Canadian Mounted Police of Amos. They were assured that all their statements had been verified as true, and were promised that the case would be settled in a short time.

On June 4, Dominic addressed a letter to the "Department of Injustice" of St. Marc de Figuery. He asked that the letter be presented for consideration at the next municipal council meeting. It revealed his ever-present sense of humour:

> "I propose, in the event that insanity should become a contagious disease at St. Marc, that an insane asylum be constructed on Lot 39, R. III, Figuery, stolen from the Raina family. I also propose that Royal Renaud, Inspector of the Department of

Colonization of Amos, and Jules Michaud, Priest at St. Marc, be appointed to the positions of alienist doctors of said asylum at an annual salary of two thousand dollars each. I further propose that Taschereau and Authier be named Honorary Presidents of the asylum. Finally, I propose that the word ''fool'' be replaced by ''mentally unbalanced,'' on the grounds that the former term is too vulgar for usage in what is hoped will be a high-class institution.''

During the summer of 1936, His Excellency Bishop Rhéaume of Haileybury visited Amos to bestow the Sacrament of Confirmation on the children of the town. In vain, Dominic and Elizabeth attempted to discuss their grievances verbally with the bishop. A second unsuccessful attempt to meet with His Excellency was made two weeks later, when he paid the customary triennial visit to the little parish of St. Marc de Figuery.

Shortly afterwards, Dominic and Elizabeth learned that the bishop was scheduled to visit St. Mathieu de Figuery (a little parish situated across the Harricana River and approximately four miles from the house). They were determined to meet with His Excellency before he left the Abitibi, so they attended the confirmation services at St. Mathieu. When the bishop eventually left the church for a nearby school they followed closely at his heels. At long last, Dominic and Elizabeth were able to speak personally to His Excellency Bishop Rhéaume of Haileybury!

Elizabeth acquainted the bishop with the injustices of which he had already received numerous accounts in writing. She begged him to accord her a second audience in the presence of Monsieur le Curé Jules Michaud. The bishop replied that he did not believe that Monsieur le Curé had asked her to sign papers, and that he did not wish to stand between her and the priest.

His Excellency departed from the Abitibi a few days later, having made no effort regarding the Raina case. Dominic and Elizabeth were forced to admit that it was useless to hope that the clergy of their church who were in positions of power would exercise that power on their behalf.

Once again, as neighbouring farmers turned to the task of sowing their crops, Dominic and Elizabeth were drawn to look with sorrow across the fields of the land which they had once called their own. They were saddened at the sight of the weeds that now grew in such rich and disgraceful abundance on the fertile acres of soil. Dominic and Elizabeth had always taken great pride in their land and its appearance. They did not wish to be the subjects of unjust criticism by strangers passing by, and perhaps looking with disgust at those neglected fields. Dominic felt that, in all fairness, the blame for the neglect should be directed at the authorities who were responsible. He posted on a corner of the field near the public road, where the weeds grew green and luscious, a large and prominent sign, reading: *"Experimental Farm of the Municipality of St. Marc de Figuery."*

On Sunday, June 14, the Raina family was visited by Constable Desrosiers, the Mounted Policeman who had previously conducted the investigation on their case. He instructed Dominic to contact Napoléon Doucet with regard to Mary's need for an immediate tonsillectomy. Dominic followed the constable's instructions, but they were ignored by the mayor.

Shortly afterwards, Dominic attended a meeting of the school board, held in the customary meeting place of the basement of the church at St. Marc. He was accompanied by Elizabeth and several neighbours. Since Dominic's return from the asylum at Mastaï, the settlers of St. Marc had gradually divided into two factions. There were those who sided with Dominic, and those who sided with Monsieur le Curé. Men who had never before contradicted the priest in anything now openly expressed their views, often in favour of Dominic. St. Marc had become an interesting and stimulating place to live. Young people gravitated to the meetings in numbers that had never been seen before the advent of the Raina case!

At this particular meeting of the school board, Dominic insisted that he be shown the exact place in the books dealing with the sale of his property. He wished to learn who had put forth the proposal, by whom it was seconded, and by whom it was passed. Although, in accordance with the Municipal Act, he had a right to that information, it was refused him.

Dominic wrote again to the Knights of Columbus of Amos. His letter was dated June 30, and in it he begged the order to act seriously on his case, "In the interest of the Catholic Church and for the honour of the Province of Quebec." He added, "If you sincerely believe, as Catholics, that you have acted properly, you should gladly help me to spread the news from Halifax to Vancouver what the Taschereau administration has done to the Raina family."

Ironically, rumours reached the family at the beginning of July that Monsieur le Curé had publicly insinuated that Dominic was afraid to meet with His Excellency Bishop Rhéaume. That news motivated Dominic to write again to the bishop, reassuring His Excellency that he would be pleased to meet him any time. He concluded his letter with the words: "I hereby reiterate my complete obedience to the authority of the church."

Throughout all those months of tragedy, Dominic's love of his religion and his church had remained undiminished. He was saddened beyond words at the unrestrained power of the clergy in Quebec. He was aware that power of that nature could only prove detrimental to the church. He felt the importance of greater control over local priests by their superiors if the church was to retain its mission of justice and compassion. But, like so many other Catholics, he was powerless against an institution that had stood unchallenged for centuries.

In the role of evaluator, and accompanied by the councillors Fortier and Dupuis, Monsieur le Curé visited the property that had been confiscated from the Raina family and placed on it a value of eleven hundred dollars! While the health of their children gradually deteriorated, Dominic and Elizabeth fought for restitution, but were unable to recover a cent of the money that might have served to prevent that deterioration.

Ironically, the family was compelled to carry out various tasks assigned them by Monsieur le Curé in order to obtain their monthly relief cheques. One such task was assigned them on July 20, by means of a note transmitted to them by the priest. In it, they were instructed to pull all the daisies on the public road, from Monsieur Alphonse Cloutier's place up to the river at Monsieur Forêt's, if they wished to receive their relief cheque by Wednesday evening.

Dominic and Johnny were absent from home the day the note arrived. Since the family depended on the relief cheque to replenish the non-existent grocery supply, Mary was put in charge of the younger children while Elizabeth pulled those countless daisies single-handed.

The Raina's were not alone in their persecution.

Among the other persons exploited by Monsieur le Curé was a poor widow who had a large family. She was once instructed to cut a number of fence posts. Although the assignment was given her during the winter when the snow stood deep upon the ground, her cheque was not transmitted to her until the completion of that task. Another poor widow, who had been unjustly relieved of her property, was instructed to scrub the large floor of the school in order to obtain her cheque.

Again that summer, as in the previous year, Dominic and Elizabeth witnessed the hay from their property being cut and hauled away. There were twenty-two large loads harvested that year! They witnessed, further, the cutting and destruction of three treasured young apple trees. The trees had been obtained by Dominic from the Dominion Experimental Farm at Ottawa two years earlier, and that year had finally rewarded them with blooms.

As in the previous year, when she felt that she could no longer endure those continued ironies, Elizabeth visited the Mounted Police at Amos, insisting that action be taken on her family's behalf.

The Mounted Police advised her to return to St. Marc and to be patient a little longer. Although she followed their instructions, it shortly became necessary for her to inform them that Dominic's relief cheque was held up and the family was in dire straits. She wrote:

> "When I called at your office the last time I was in Amos you did suggest to me to return to St. Marc, which I did, but I really do not see any reason why I should be asked to remain any longer on Lot 39, R. III, since the Municipality of St. Marc claims it is theirs. At present I am killing all my chickens because we have no feed for them. Next we will be obliged to kill our cows because we have no hay for them for winter . . . School will commence next week. My children have not clothes to go to school and not books required . . . Must I remain here to dig my own grave to bury myself and my family?"

It was during that desperate period that a dry goods salesman chose to peddle his wares throughout the Village of St. Marc. Among the materials he displayed, when he called on the Raina family, was a pretty piece of cotton. It had a white background splashed with tiny blue flowers. School was due to start within the next few days, and Mary wanted a dress for the new school term. She knew that she must have that piece of cotton. With the thoughtlessness of youth, she begged and pleaded for the material until she succeeded in breaking down her mother's resistance. The material was priced at fifty cents for the entire piece. The money represented more than a day's supply of groceries for the entire family. But Elizabeth reasoned, at that point, that the material for a dress for thirteen-year-old Mary was more important than groceries for the family. She combed the house in search of money, and came up with forty-three cents. The salesman closed the deal for that amount.

At Mary's insistence, she was allowed to make the dress completely unassisted and without the benefit of a pattern. Mary wore her dress with great pride and satisfaction. Never, ever, was she so proud and delighted with a single piece of clothing! When her friends at school pointed out that one side of the collar was rounded, while the other side was pointed, Elizabeth advised her daughter to tell them that it was the latest fashion for collars that year.

What Elizabeth lacked in formal education she more than made up for in wisdom and common sense. Never did she show anything but complete confidence in her children's abilities to accomplish anything they undertook. She might easily have held her own among the best trained child psychologists in the country! On one occasion, when Johnny and Mary vied for the privilege of baking a cake for dinner, their mother settled the dispute with her customary wisdom. She selected a recipe for a marble cake, assigning the baking of the dark batter to Johnny and the white batter to Mary. What had started out as an argument ended in the children happily baking the cake together.

If Dominic and Elizabeth were becoming weary of writing letters to authorities, the Raina children were becoming even more weary of writing copies for the family records. Nevertheless, the letters continued to be written because there appeared to be no other avenue of obtaining justice, if justice was ever to be obtained.

On August 29, Dominic wrote a letter to the Honourable Emile Lesage. His communication read:

> "Now that you are our representative, I am applying to you, not for a favour but simply for something to which I am entitled: justice. You must know something about my case. At Amos and St. Marc de Figuery they try to hush up the matter and the provincial authorities are unable to reply to our letters. The present Attorney General, the Honourable Maurice Duplessis, when he was at Amos around July 23, 1935, had promised to give attention to our case, but I am still awaiting a reply. It is in your Province that the biggest crime in Canada has been committed and I trust you will find time, first: to see that the necessities of life are immediately supplied to the Raina family, second: that the investigation regarding the Raina case be made public."

Two days later, Dominic took the remnants of Elizabeth's only pair of shoes to Amos to show them to authorities there. A kind merchant eventually gave him a donation of three dollars with which to buy her a new pair.

Dominic and Elizabeth realized with awful certainty that before many weeks should pass a northern winter would again envelope the family in cold and hunger. They shuddered at the prospect of spending another such winter in the Province of Quebec.

In desperation, Dominic wrote to the Department of Labour at Quebec City asking for employment. His letter, dated September 1, 1936, read:

> "I, the undersigned, father of seven young children, humbly ask for work to enable me to provide the necessities of life to my family. The Attorney General and some Quebec members

are somewhat aware of the education I have, and of my qualifications. I speak and write the two official languages. We are completely destitute, and without means of subsistence for next winter. At Quebec, they know the reasons why. As far as references are concerned, I could give you many . . . I am acquainted with farming, municipal administration, old-age pension, principles of co-operative societies, etc. . . . I humbly ask for some kind of work or employment immediately so that I may provide for my family who are homeless and in the greatest need. I make this request as a Catholic and as a Canadian, for the honour of the Province of Quebec and to cover up in the most honourable possible way the terrible crime which the Taschereau administration has committed against me and my family.''

CHAPTER XII

LAST MONTHS IN QUEBEC

"We may be personally defeated, but our principles never."
William Lloyd Garrison.

With all their available resources going towards food, there was no money to spare for badly-needed repairs on the house. The dampness which pervaded the rooms every time it rained, due to the badly-leaking roof, added an even greater threat to the family's health. While it had previously been possible to place the beds between the leaky spots by the skilful shifting of furniture, such a feat was now impossible as all the spots were leaky and the rain seeped through everywhere.

On the morning after one particularly rainy night, during which the family shivered under wet blankets and water stood in puddles on the floor, Dominic summoned several neighbours in as witnesses of the fact. A report of the situation was then made to the Royal Canadian Mounted Police of Amos, who instructed Dominic to bring the matter to the attention of Napoléon Doucet. The mayor arranged to have the roof repaired with pitch, but the man assigned to do the job was inexperienced and matters were not improved, as was uncomfortaly discovered the next time it rained.

During another wet and discouraging night, Elizabeth did the only thing she could to try to solve the problem. She wrote, once again, to the Royal Canadian Mounted Police. Her letter, dated September 15, 1936, informed them that:

"It is a quarter to eleven at night that I am writing to you. I would rather be in my bed taking my much-needed rest but it is raining outside and also inside, and our prison is flooded. My bed is soaked and the beds of my children. I am moving the beds here and there so that they can get a little sleep. So long I have been trying to be as patient as I possibly could, now I can do so no longer. If you would be here to see for yourself what we must put up with you would never blame me for asking you to put me in prison. I can no longer, under present conditions, remain on Lot 39, R. III, stolen from us. I am ready for authorities to either deport us out of the Province of Quebec or to be put in prison if what was done and is done us is right. It is not my pleasure to write to authorities in the manner I am doing but because I am forced by injustice to do so. Tomorrow I will beg from neighbours for the stamps to mail you the present. I am begging of you to give the above full consideration.''

At that point, when the family had indeed hit rock bottom, an encouraging letter arrived from the Honourable Emile Lesage in reply to Dominic's previous letter to the man. In his communication, he commented on Dominic's letter, and assured him that he sympathized greatly with the dilemma in which the family found itself. He instructed Dominic to call on Mr. Georges Duchemin of the Land Office at Amos, promising that Mr. Duchemin would provide the necessities of life. He suggested that Dominic show the man the present letter as a means of introduction. He concluded by repeating that he felt convinced justice could be obtained through Mr. Duchemin.

Although Dominic and Elizabeth approached Mr. Duchemin on several occasions, their visits proved futile and they became further frustrated.

The children had settled back into their routine of doing homework around the kitchen table each evening. Whereas it had always been customary for the children to finish up their evenings by playing parchesi or cards, the boys had adopted the habit of retiring earlier than usual. Johnny, Ralph, and Louis shared a room, and seemed to gravitate toward it with unusual enthusiasm each evening.

Puzzled at this unexpected development in the habits of her sons, Elizabeth wondered if they were ill. The mystery was solved in mid-October. While making the beds in the boys' room one morning, their mother was assailed by the unmistakable odour of dill-pickles permeating the atmosphere. She examined the huge crock of pickles that she had prepared throughout the summer, and which occupied a corner of the bedroom, only to discover that most of them had disappeared. Therein lay the answer to the boys' eagerness to retire early each evening.

During those days, the lives of the Raina family fluctuated like emotional seesaws: periods of discouragement were followed by renewed hope and confidence.

Dominic and Elizabeth once again became confident in the ultimate settling of their case, on receiving a letter from the Honourable

J. Blackmore, House of Commons, Ottawa. In the communication, dated October 6, Mr. Blackmore informed them that he had received a letter which led him to believe that soon their case would be placed before the Honourable Maurice Duplessis, the new Premier of Quebec. He again explained that their provincial government must give them justice if they were to receive justice, and that he could do nothing but take the matter up with the proper officials of Quebec.

Dominic and Elizabeth felt that, whatever the outcome of his efforts, the Honourable J. Blackmore had done all in his power to help them and they were deeply grateful.

In mid-October, a nurse and doctor presented themselves at L'école du lac to vaccinate the local children against diphtheria. It was customary to give each child a reward of fifteen cents on the administration of the inoculation.

After submitting bravely to the vaccination, six-year-old Louis Raina, without discussing his intention with anyone, ran to a neighbour's house to buy a loaf of bread with his fifteen cents. With great pride, he presented it to the family at the dinner table. For the first time, in several days, each member of the family enjoyed a slice of delicious freshly-baked bread with the customary bowl of porridge.

Among the neighbours at St. Marc were many dear and loyal friends who proved their goodwill in diverse and touching ways.

One such demonstration of their regard and support took place in the form of a letter to the Honourable Maurice Duplessis. The communication bore twenty-one signatures, and it was dated October 30, 1936. Translated from French, it contained the following plea:

> "We, the undersigned citizens of the Abitibi and ratepayers of the Municipality of St. Marc de Figuery, County of Abitibi, P.Q. request of you justice for one of our citizens, Mr. Dominic Raina, who, during the past two years, has been unjustly deprived of his property by the Municipality of St. Marc de Figuery, thereby causing great suffering to himself and his family. We are therefore asking that you resolve to have returned to Mr. Dominic Raina that which is rightfully his and place him again in a situation deserving of honest people. Trusting that our request be given consideration and that justice be given to these people deserving of it . . ."

Dominic and Elizabeth were touched, almost beyond words, to learn that their warm and humble neighbours had written to the highest authority in the Province of Quebec on their behalf.

During that fall of 1936, Dominic and Elizabeth called at the presbytery of Amos to beg of Reverend Father Lapointe, a superior of Monsieur le Curé Michaud, to intervene with the priest on their behalf, but their effort proved futile. It seemed that no member of the Catholic hierarchy was prepared to admonish members of their own ranks, nor to instruct them to assume responsibility in the case.

Elizabeth was expecting another child. Because she had always experienced complications at the birth of her babies, she called on her family physician, asking him to come to the house at the time of her confinement.

Dr. Simard protested that she would die if she remained at St. Marc for her baby's birth. He instructed her to go immediately to the Hospital of Ste. Thérèse (Amos' only hospital) and to secure a Public Assistance Form from the superior there. He told her to present it to the Mayor of St. Marc for his signature, and to then bring it back to him immediately, whether or not the mayor had agreed to sign it. It was important that it be sent to Quebec City as soon as possible. Dr. Simard assured Elizabeth that he would attend to her during her confinement, but stressed again that the event must take place in the hospital.

In accordance with the doctor's instructions, a form was immediately obtained and transmitted to Napoléon Doucet.

On numerous occasions throughout the following days various members of the Raina family returned to St. Marc to get the form. Each time, they were told that the mayor had not yet signed it. Eventually, Dominic approached Napoléon Doucet to insist that he return the document at once. Dominic was told that it had been transmitted to Monsieur le Curé, who had signed it and forwarded it to Quebec City.

A short time later, Dominic received a letter from the priest. It was written under date of October 25, and it contained the worrisome information that at a special meeting of the Municipality of St. Marc de Figuery it was decided not to sign the Form of Public Assistance requested for Elizabeth. The priest pointed out that Elizabeth's case was an ordinary one which could be passed at the house, as was done by other women of the parish. He added that only a few of the richest ladies of Amos passed their confinement at the hospital, and if they began it for one at St. Marc they might be obligated to continue for the others.

Dominic was outraged!

How could Monsieur le Curé possibly consider himself qualified to decide in such a life or death situation when he was not a doctor? How could he determine whether or not a woman was in a condition to pass her confinement at home without first having given that woman a medical examination? How could he presume to judge Elizabeth's particular case when he was ignorant of the circumstances surrounding the births of her babies?

Eventually, the Taylor family of Amos took it upon themselves to bring the matter to the attention of Dr. Martel, the local Health Officer. The doctor immediately sent his assistant and nurse to visit Elizabeth. They assured her that provisions had been made for a private room for her at the hospital, and instructed her to report there immediately when she had her first contractions.

That occasion marked the first time throughout their married lives that Dominic and Elizabeth were forced to depend on charity at the birth of one of their children. Never before, had they been obliged to endure such bitter humiliation.

Remembering the assurances given her that provisions had been made for her hospitalization, Elizabeth did not worry unduly when she went into labour on the morning of December 4, 1936. Little did she guess the mortifications which were in store for her at the Hospital of Ste. Thérèse!

On her arrival there, she was told by the superior of the hospital, who was aware that she had just undertaken a ten-mile journey by sleigh from St. Marc, that she could not be admitted because arrangements had not been made for her hospitalization.

Too ill to comment, and not wishing to pass her confinement in a hospital where she felt so unwelcome, Elizabeth turned to Dominic and begged him to take her back to St. Marc.

On noting the increasing discomfort of the patient the nun relented somewhat, and asked Dominic and Elizabeth to be seated while she made further enquiries into the admission policies of the hospital.

The enquiries eventually disclosed, after what seemed to Elizabeth to be an eternity, that arrangements had indeed been made for her admission to the hospital. Furthermore, it was revealed that all the expenses covering one week of hospitalization had already been paid, and that all the arrangements had been taken care of by two English-speaking families of Amos.

The physical examination that was conducted on Elizabeth served to confirm her fears that her child no longer lived, and that her own life was in grave danger. The fact that her family physician was unavoidably absent from Amos at that time did not offer reassurance.

Five days later, Elizabeth gave birth to her lifeless baby under the care of Dr. Marcel Sarazin — the man who had declared Dominic one hundred percent insane in the jail of Amos on November 23, 1934. In spite of severe misgivings at the time, Elizabeth felt that Dr. Marcel Sarazin gave her the best possible medical attention, and she credited him with saving her life.

Dominic took the body of his stillborn baby daughter to the presbytery at Amos, so that arrangements could be made for her seclusion in the vault of the town pending burial in the spring.

In spite of that loss, the family was profoundly grateful when Elizabeth's strength was restored and she was able to return to St. Marc on December 19.

During one of Dominic's visits to the post office at St. Marc, which was run by the mayor, Napoléon Doucet remarked that Quebec and Ottawa appeared to be ignoring his letters. He told Dominic that he did not notice any replies coming through. Napoléon Doucet's manifestations of unfriendliness towards the family were not confined solely to Dominic. At about that same time, Clara was given three pennies by a friend. With great enthusiasm, she raced to the store, which was also run by the mayor, and selected the candy she wished to buy. Napoléon Doucet refused to make the sale, explaining that the three cents could be put to more practical use in the Raina family.

On the Sunday before Christmas, Monsieur le Curé looked down upon the members of his flock from the pulpit of the church and warned them that if they had not paid their church dues their relief cheques would be withheld. Although Dominic had always contributed generously to the church, he was now numbered among those who did not pay their dues. He deeply resented the priest's financial manipulation from the pulpit, and his threat to retain the cheques intended for those who could ill afford to do without them.

The unfolding of the New Year of 1937 marked the first visit to the Raina quarters by an officer of the provincial police.

Dominic pointed out to the man that his family could no longer survive on promises. He asked that the necessities of life be accorded them pending the conclusion of the investigation begun on his case ten months earlier by the Royal Canadian Mounted Police. To no avail!

During January of 1937, Dominic and Elizabeth received a letter from Mr. Georges Duchemin of the Department of Colonization of Amos, in which he informed them with regret that their relief cheque for the month of January had not yet arrived. He assured them that it would be transmitted to them without delay as soon as it was received at the office.

George Duchemin emphasized that he understood the pressing needs of the family, but pointed out that more had been done for them than for others even worse off. He suggested that they contact Monsieur le Curé Michaud who, he felt, would procure any necessary provisions for them.

That letter was one of the most significant to ever reach Dominic and Elizabeth in that it denoted the completion of a circle. The case had been referred back to Monsieur le Curé Jules Michaud, from whence it had originated!

Dominic and Elizabeth were appalled to realize that, after two years of incesssant attempts at obtaining redress for the injustices done to their family, they were right back where they had started. Furthermore, they took exception to Mr. Duchemin's remark that more had been done for them than for others worse off. Mr. Duchemin neglected to point out that, among the families assisted, the Raina family was the only one that had been rendered dependent on charity because of the confiscation of their property and, consequently, their means of earning a living!

Municipal elections were held in the little Municipality of St. Marc de Figuery in mid-January. The elections resulted in Napoléon Doucet's defeat. The new mayor, Joseph Corriveau, was possessed of admirable insight and common sense, and Dominic hoped he would ensure a more just administration of municipal affairs.

The new mayor's first move was to assert independence from Monsieur le Curé. In early March, the priest took it upon himself to dispatch notices calling a special meeting of the municipal council. As was customary, those notices were boldly signed in his capacity of, "Jules Michaud, Priest." Joseph Corriveau took exception to the presumptuousness of Monsieur le Curé invading what he considered to be his territory.

In a manner that defied contradiction, and to the great astonishment of the priest, the newly-elected mayor declared the meeting illegal! He pointed out that Monsieur le Curé did not have the authority to call a meeting without having first consulted the council. But Monsieur le Curé had been permitted to overstep his rights for too many years. He was unwilling to relinquish the reins which he had so long been permitted to hold under the protection of his clerical robes, and noisy and ridiculous was the bickering that followed the new mayor's reprimand.

Elizabeth listened to the dialogue between the priest and Joseph Corriveau in silent amusement. Turning to Dominic, she whispered, "Why don't you suggest that psychiatrists be brought in to analyze heads; I think this would be an ideal time in which to do it."

When Dominic transmitted that suggestion to the council, Monsieur le Curé hastily arose and grabbed his lamp. With the parting words, ''The meeting is finished,'' he dashed from the room, leaving the council in total darkness.

Dominic and Elizabeth were much encouraged to notice that winds of change were slowly, but surely, sweeping over the council. The submissiveness of the councillors to all Monsieur le Curé's suggestions, so noticeable during Dominic's early days at St. Marc, was now far less flagrant. Dominic was impressed at the courage and self-assurance with which the new mayor conducted himself at the meetings, and by the support and respect he was receiving from his councillors. Dominic was becoming more and more confident that a better future was just around the corner at St. Marc de Figuery, insofar as local politics were concerned.

Monsieur le Curé did not appear to share that confidence.

''Why do things so persistently go wrong at St. Marc?'' he pleaded, as he looked down upon his flock from the pulpit of the church one Sunday in March.

''Things so persistently go wrong at St. Marc because the leader at St. Marc is crooked,'' wrote Dominic to Monsieur le Curé, in response to the priest's plea for enlightenment.

In an attempt to contradict his previous words, Monsieur le Curé denied that he had stated that things go wrong, but rather that he had said, ''If they go wrong, why do they go wrong?''

Being uncomfortably aware that Dominic stood in constant danger of a second abduction, and knowing that the welfare of her children was at stake, Elizabeth felt that definite steps must be taken to leave the Province of Quebec as soon as possible, Her resolve was fortified when she was told, on one of her trips to the Justice Department in Amos, not to expect justice in Quebec if she could not speak French.

There was a second pressing reason that motivated Elizabeth to convince Dominic that it was time to leave the province. Girls married young at St. Marc de Figuery and their daughters were growing up quickly and were noticing, and being noticed by, the local boys. Elizabeth felt that life was difficult for the women of rural Quebec, and she did not wish her daughters to be part of that life.

Dominic and Elizabeth mailed notifications of their intended departure from the Province of Quebec to the authorities who had failed them.

One such notification was mailed by Elizabeth to the Honourable Minister of Justice and Attorney General of Canada, under date of March 12. It read in part:

"I regret to inform the Minister that I am fully decided to move my family out of the Province of Quebec. . . I protest more than ever the treatment that my husband did receive by authorities in the Catholic Province of Quebec.

On going out I will give my word of honour that I will tell the truth to people of all nationalities and creeds what was done to us in Catholic Quebec by authorities who claim to be Catholics . . . Upon my husband and his family they did pile sufferings, upon themselves they did pile dishonour and shame. I will start my journey for the freedom of my family penniless even if we did bring into this province $1,700 in cash and $7,000 of life insurance. I am still ready to have the head of my husband analyzed well in public, together with the heads of the ex-mayor, Napoléon Doucet, Jules Michaud, the assistant-secretary, the councillors and ex-councillors. This also is refused me. I will keep informing the Royal Canadian Mounted Police of my whereabouts."

Dominic and Elizabeth also mailed a letter to the Honourable Maurice Duplessis, the Attorney General of Quebec, informing him of their intention to leave the province.

A letter, appalling in its significance, was received by Dominic and Elizabeth from the Honourable Emile Lesage, Member of the Legislative Assembly, Quebec, dated March 22, 1937. It was in reply to a request by Dominic that he be given a copy of the investigation previously carried out on the Raina case. The Honourable Emile Lesage's letter contained the discouraging information that it was not possible to procure a copy of the investigation, which was conducted by the old administration. He added that the present government was not responsible for what was done by the old one.

At the last council meeting attended by Dominic and Elizabeth at St. Marc de Figuery, they made a final plea for the return of the property which had been taken from them. Although they offered to pay all the just taxes against the property in question, and although the councillors were themselves in favour of the proposal, Monsieur le Curé Michaud again succeeded in preventing such a positive act of restitution.

At the end of March, Dominic and Elizabeth sold their few remaining effects for one hundred and seventy-five dollars. They hoped the money obtained would take them out of Quebec, so that they could fight their case from the safety of Ontario.

So that the God of Justice might stand guard over their confiscated home, they left an emblem of their faith, in the form of a favourite crucifix, hanging upon the kitchen wall.

On March 31, the family's few remaining personal possessions were packed into boxes, the windows barred, and the doors locked. Parents and children looked, for the last time before their departure from St. Marc, at the place that had spelled such disaster to the family.

At the home of Elzéar Laroche, one of the many friends who had stood by the family throughout their months of tragedy, they spent their last night at St. Marc de Figuery.

Very early on the morning of April 1, 1937, after having posed for farewell pictures at the request of their dear friends, the Raina family was driven to Amos to take the train in search of freedom.

While Dominic bought the train tickets at the station in Amos, Elizabeth visited officials of the town to notify them of the family's departure from the Abitibi.

"I have come to tell you that we are today going out of the Province of Quebec," she told Constable Desrosiers, on presenting herself at the office of the Royal Canadian Mounted Police.

"Where are you going?" enquired the constable.

Elizabeth replied that they were first going as far as North Bay, Ontario, but that she did not know whether they would stay there or go on. She explained that they would have to reassess their financial situation after their arrival there. She invited Constable Desrosiers to look the family up should he ever happen to come their way.

After warmly assuring her that he would do so, Constable Desrosiers expressed sincere regret that nothing had been done for the family in the Province of Quebec. Dominic and Elizabeth never harboured any feelings of animosity towards the Royal Canadian Mounted Police. Although they were unable to obtain redress for the wrongs inflicted on the family, Dominic and Elizabeth were convinced that the failure of authorities to effect a second abduction was due to the watchful eyes of those policemen.

After notifying the officials of the Department of Colonization of Amos of the family's imminent departure, Elizabeth proceeded to the presbytery to pay her last official visit in the town.

Father Dudomaine asked the purpose of her visit and enquired whether it was the same old thing. Elizabeth informed him that the family was, that day, leaving the Province of Quebec. She asked if he would kindly, in the spring, attend to the burial of her baby. The astounded priest assured here that he would do that, and enquired where they were going.

Elizabeth informed him that they were going to North Bay, Ontario. For the second time that day, she volunteered the information that she did not know where they would go from there.

Several neighbours from St. Marc de Figuery were among the crowd of spectators gathered at the station at Amos. They had come to see the family off. They advised Dominic and Elizabeth to keep up their wonderful courage, and expressed sincere regret at seeing them leave under such sad circumstances.

Dominic and Elizabeth, in turn, genuinely regretted the necessity of leaving their friends and neighbours. They never blamed any of them for the tragedies that had befallen them. They were aware that the people were under the domination of the priest and, through years of conditioning, knew of no other course of action than to follow his instructions without question. They had been victimized, as the Raina family had been victimized.

The Raina children had spent many happy hours of their childhood playing with their little friends at St. Marc de Figuery. Their French Canadian peers had treated "the little English children" with much affection on their arrival in the Abitibi and throughout the years that followed. It was with mutual regret, and a promise to exchange letters, that they tearfully said good-bye.

At approximately one-thirty o'clock on April 1, 1937, the Raina family boarded the train that would take them out of the Province of Quebec.

From the window of their car, they looked back upon the Town of Amos, and upon the Church of Ste. Thérèse, as that bulwark of the Catholic faith of northern Quebec slowly faded from sight!

This picture was taken on front of the house at St. Marc de Figuery on March 31, 1937, after the doors were locked prior to leaving to spend the last night in Quebec at a neigbours' home. The Rainas left Quebec on the following day, April 1, 1937.
The Raina family - Back Row - Johnny, Mary, Clara, Elizabeth, Dominic, Nicky, Ralph. Front Row - Louis, George.

CHAPTER XIII

FIGHTING THE CASE FROM ONTARIO

*"Truth has no special time of its own. Its hour is now —
always." Albert Schweitzer.*

At one-forty o'clock p.m. on the memorable day of April 2, 1937,
the train carrying the Raina family crossed into the Province of Ontario.

Despite a new sense of security, Dominic fully realized that he would
never be as free as his fellow Canadians until the unjust stigma of insanity
was effaced from his name. Nevertheless, he exhilarated in the knowledge
that he could now go about unescorted. Gone was the constant haunting
fear of a second abduction! Though destitute, he could again look with
confidence to the future.

There remained but one hundred and twenty-five dollars in Dominic's
possession when the family reached the town of North Bay, Ontario, at
four o'clock on that day.

No sooner were they settled in a small hotel when Dominic and
Elizabeth set forth to call on His Excellency, Bishop Digman. He accorded
them the kindest reception they had so far met with since the beginning
of their numerous pleas to the clergy for help in obtaining redress.
Although the bishop was unable to offer practical assistance, he listened
sympathetically to their story and his words of encouragement were sincere and kind.

True to their resolve to keep authorities informed of their whereabouts,
Dominic and Elizabeth then reported to the provincial police. Once again,
they were deeply touched at the kindness they encountered there.

Realizing the extremity of their poverty, and fearing that their hopes
of obtaining justice at the Department of Justice in Ottawa might prove
futile, authorities at North Bay invited the family to settle in the town.
They urged Dominic to contact the town clerk for assistance.

At North Bay, as all throughout the country at that time, the depression had struck at countless families and rendered them dependent upon

relief. Dominic and Elizabeth decided against taking advantage of the kindness and generosity of the officials at the town hall, as they did not wish to be an added burden on the already overcrowded town. They resolved to go on to Ottawa to present their case before the Federal Parliament.

It was with hope and confidence, in spite of the few remaining dollars in their possession, that the Raina family reached the capital of Canada, just before dawn on the morning of April 4.

After securing accommodation for the family at a modest hotel on Rideau Street, Dominic and Elizabeth got in touch with the highest authorities of the land.

That first day, they contacted the Honourable Victor Quelch, with whom they were well acquainted, and who had succeeded the Honourable Gardiner as Member of Parliament for Acadia, Alberta.

On April 5, they gained admission to the Parliament Buildings, where they were kindly received by the Honourable J. Blackmore — the man who had initiated the investigation conducted on their case by the Royal Canadian Mounted Police, and who was well acquainted with its contents. They also met the Honourable J. Bradette, Member of Parliament for Cochrane, Ontario. Although the Honourable Bradette was familiar with conditions in and around Amos, he was unable to offer any constructive advice.

On that same day, Elizabeth notified the Honourable Minister of Justice, by means of a letter, of her family's arrival in Ottawa. She wrote:

"This is to inform you that my husband, seven children, and self, are in the city since Sunday morning. We have been advised by some clergy to approach the Minister. It is indeed hard for me to make public our case to all Protestant members for the reason that the injustice to us was done by a member of our Catholic religion. Please give the above due consideration. We are penniless."

On April 7, in accordance with instructions received from authorities, Dominic and Elizabeth called on a high official of the Department of Labour, who listened with interest to the account of their troubles.

During the evening of that same day, a news reporter from *La presse* called on Dominic and Elizabeth at the hotel in which they were staying. He suggested that they delay giving their story to the press. He flattered them and treated them royally. Drinks were ordered, in spite of their reluctance to share in a celebration at that worrisome time. Assurances that positive action would be taken to settle the case were emphasized repeatedly. Dominic and Elizabeth suspected that this was merely another attempt to hush up the case.

When Elizabeth's reaction to the promises appeared to be lacking in enthusiasm, and when her reluctance to believe too strongly in mere words became evident, the reporter asked her what she was worried about.

She replied that she was worried because the family had no money and nowhere to go.

In a manner that implied that her troubles were indeed over, he counselled her to just put her head on her pillow, to go to sleep, and not to worry.

At that time, it became necessary for Dominic to notify the proprietor of the hotel that he had exhausted his funds, and that he could no longer pay for accommodation. Not only did that kind gentleman permit the family to remain at the hotel, but on several occasions donated free meals. His wife generously permitted Elizabeth the use of her sewing machine and provided her with some clothing to make over for the children.

Although only fifteen and undernourished, Johnny was given employment involving heavy manual labour on a dairy farm, at ten dollars per month. The farm was located several miles from Ottawa, so Johnny had to be separated from the family.

On April 11, Dominic wrote to the Apostolic Delegate, the highest dignitary of the Holy Catholic Church in Canada. He attempted to give the clergy, once again, the opportunity to settle his case. He felt that only, in this way, could unfavourable publicity to his religion be avoided. As a good Catholic, the thought of publicizing his case to people of other creeds pained him greatly.

On April 13, Dominic and Elizabeth contacted the Ottawa Welfare Bureau. That charitable organization secured living accommodations for the family on Wellington Street in Ottawa, where they shared a crowded tenement with two other families.

Numerous authorities were contacted and acquainted with the Raina family's experiences in the Province of Quebec. Although they were invariably sympathetic, and all agreed that restitution should be made, the family was always referred elsewhere.

Following a visit to the Department of Labour, an official there exchanged telegrams with Monsieur le Curé Jules Michaud with regard to the Raina case. The Ottawa Welfare Bureau, in turn, exchanged correspondence with Dr. Simard in Amos. As a result of the communications, Dominic and Elizabeth were assured that all their statements had been corroborated. Various other authorities had also confirmed that the family was the recipient of a great injustice. The family was advised that it would be unwise to return to St. Marc de Figuery in the event that the property should be returned.

Shortly after their departure from St. Marc, Dominic and Elizabeth received a letter from Elzéar Laroche, one of their former neighbours and their dearest friend. In it, they were informed about a telegram that Monsieur le Curé had received from the Department of Labour, asking for a statement of the Raina taxes at the time of the sale of their land. Elzéar Laroche mentioned that the telegram had been received by the priest at six o'clock p.m. on April 5, while a council meeting was in progress, and that an immediate reply had been requested. He added that Monsieur le Curé still did not want to turn the books over to the mayor, and that when he received a letter from the bishop that did not please him he stated that the bishop did not know the Code.

During their early days in Ottawa, Dominic and Elizabeth were assured by members of the Royal Canadian Mounted Police that not a single point had been raised against them in the investigation that had been conducted on the case. To their great disappointment, they were not permitted to read the investigation because of its confidentiality. They were told, unofficially, that if they were to know the entire contents of the investigation they really would go crazy.

Although those reports were encouraging, and very much in their favour, they did not serve to lighten the worries that weighed down so heavily upon Dominic and Elizabeth. They had long ago discovered that promises, though numerous and encouraging they might be, do not serve to nourish hungry children.

As time went on, it became more and more evident how impossible it was for other provinces in Canada to interfere with the non-administration of justice in the Province of Quebec. For that reason, Dominic again attempted to obtain redress through the Duplessis administration, by writing to the Honourable Emile Lesage, Member of the Legislative Assembly at Quebec.

Due to the depression and the resultant high unemployment, Dominic was unable to find work of any kind. The family had not resided in the city long enough to entitle them to relief, nor to make them eligible for free clinical care. Consequently, they were dependent on various Ottawa charitable organizations for the necessities of life.

That spring, Mary's tonsils were removed without cost by a kind Ottawa doctor to whom she had been referred. The operation took place at the

Grace Hospital, where she was given free hospitalization by the Salvation Army.

But while Mary's health improved, Johnny's declined. Dominic and Elizabeth were becoming more and more concerned over Johnny's wellbeing. He was an undernourished teenager who was doing a man's work on a dairy farm. In a letter, dated May 24, he wrote:

"Dear Parents: I received your letters and thank you. I am coming home on the weekend if I can get some money and fine weather. The apples are in bloom and it sure looks nice. I usually write every Sunday but I didn't yesterday because whenever I sat down to write last evening I had to pull their car out of the mud . . . I can sure milk cows. I milked only 19 (by hand) last evening. If you get a farm I hope you will need me because I would earn a lot more at home. I will be home the first nice Sunday."

That letter was followed shortly by another one, in which Johnny commented: "We hardly ever finish work before ten o'clock p.m. and start at five o'clock a.m. I am well, but real tired and my legs are sore".

Because of their large family, Dominic and Elizabeth wished to move to more favourable surroundings than those in which they lived on Wellington Street. They eventually succeeded in locating a little house situated three miles from Ottawa on the Metcalfe Highway, near Billings Bridge, Ontario.

The generosity of the Salvation Army during those destitute days was unlimited. Not only did they supply a truck for the family's transportation when they took possession of the house which had been rented for them, but they also supplied some much-needed furniture.

In return for the use of the house, Dominic and Elizabeth made arrangements with the landlord, who had a large dairy farm nearby, to milk his many cows each morning and evening. Johnny was brought home, and was also given employment on the farm. Although the work was just as strenuous and the hours were just as long as at his previous place of employment, Johnny was delighted to be with his family again. The rest of the children were equally excited when Johnny returned. He had brought a pair of rabbits with him as a gift for his brothers and sisters, and many happy hours were spent with the new family pets.

The soil on the property on which their temporary home was located was rich and fertile. Dominic and Elizabeth planted a large garden, which provided the family with fresh vegetables in abundance.

Mary, Ralph and Clara spent the summer months picking strawberries and raspberries for local farmers. They were paid three cents for each one-quart box they picked. The wages were considered to be reasonable at that point in time. The children enjoyed picking berries and they never tired from their days spent in the berry patches of the community. Each child strived to be the one to pick the most boxes on a particular day. With a reputation for being industrious berry pickers, they never lacked for work.

A second job at which Mary, Ralph and Clara worked throughout the summer, when they were not needed in the berry patches, consisted in pulling weeds from local gardens. That was a job they did not like at all! They spent as much time mumbling and grumbling while they pulled the weeds as they had spent in laughing and chattering while they picked the berries.

A third job, and it was the worst of all, was picking potatoes at the end of the summer. In rain or shine, carrying heavy pails of potatoes, they worked from morning until sundown. With great difficulty, Mary and Ralph managed to struggle through the day, but Clara nearly dropped from exhaustion as she carried the heavy pails. Elizabeth had tempting meals of freshly-picked vegetables awaiting their return each evening. The children delved into them, like the field hands that they were, and then elected to go straight to bed. Nevertheless, all members of the family remained united in the struggle for survival, and they appeared to be succeeding.

During their early days in Ontario, the Raina children exchanged numerous letters with their friends at St. Marc de Figuery. Dominic and Elizabeth received periodic reports on interesting activities taking place at the council meetings, as they exchanged letters with their former neighbours.

In letters to Dominic and Elizabeth, in July of 1937, the Laroche's informed them that much dissension was taking place among members of the Municipal Council of St. Marc de Figuery since their departure. They were interested to learn that nearly all the parish was attending the meetings. Unlike his predecessors, Mayor Corriveau was not prepared to accept Monsieur le Curé's interference in the council. He opposed the priest's unethical acts in almost as strong a manner as Dominic had opposed them during his days at St. Marc de Figuery.

In a second letter to Dominic and Elizabeth, shortly afterwards, the same neighbours told them that, at a recent council meeting, the mayor did not wish Monsieur le Curé to take a seat, so the priest angrily removed the lamp and left with his three loyal councillors. Since the people were left in darkness, they had to go and find themselves another lamp.

That letter was followed almost immediately by one from a second former neighbour. It contained the interesting news that the council had been dissolved. Monsieur le Curé Michaud had refused to hand over the books to the mayor, telling him that if he wanted them he would first have to find them.

The mayor complained to the Department of Municipal Affairs at Quebec City, resulting in the Deputy Minister coming to St. Marc bearing a letter from the bishop instructing Monsieur le Curé to relinquish the books.

Another letter from Madame Elzéar Laroche, received during August, imparted the interesting information that the council was all dissolved and another election was being scheduled. She added that the municipal books were still at Quebec City, and after they were examined those of the school board would come next. She commented that all the cleaning up was happening just as Dominic had predicted it would, and everyone was saying that they were beginning to see that he was right. She said that her husband Elzéar thought it might be a good idea for Dominic to write to the Minister of Municipal Affairs for his land while the books were in Quebec City. She asked him to tell Elizabeth that she had taken her place to go to argue with Monsieur le Curé and to go to the meetings.

The Rainas were touched and heartened to learn that Madame Laroche was now attending the council meetings to argue with the priest. She was a woman of great courage, and a true pioneer in the cause of women's liberation in rural Quebec in an era when a woman's role was still one of subservience.

Feeling lost and strange, after having so long attended schools where French alone was taught, Mary, Ralph, Clara and Louis resumed their studies of the English language at the public school of Ellwood, near Billings Bridge, Ontario.

Although Mary had already passed the equivalent of her high school entrance examinations in Quebec, it was necessary for her to produce an Ontario certificate before being accepted for admission to an Ontario high school. Her parents felt that it would be to her advantage to repeat grade eight in English; the only English instruction she had had in over four years was during the four months she had spent in the convent at Sturgeon Falls.

Financially, Dominic and Elizabeth were unable to send Johnny back to school that fall. The younger children, required by law to attend school, could no longer contribute to the family coffers as they had done throughout the summer. As a consequence, even greater financial responsibility was placed on Johnny's shoulders.

Dominic and Elizabeth continued to direct their efforts towards regaining possession of their lawful property at St. Marc de Figuery. Their efforts were reinforced more firmly than ever when, on December 30, 1937, they received the ironic news that the property had been resold at a handsome profit, by the Municipality of St. Marc de Figuery, to Antoine Lantagne — a former neighbour.

The transaction took place with the understanding that the Municipality of St. Marc would reimburse the buyer at current wages for any improvements made on the property, should he be required to return it to the Raina family at some future date.

"Try to forget!" counselled the civil authorities. "Forgive those who did you wrong!" counselled the clergy. As they looked with sorrow at their underprivileged children, Dominic and Elizabeth tried, but in vain, to forget. As they cringed from the thought of the possible consequences that constant deprivation might eventually bring to those children, they tried, but in vain, to forgive.

So that she might secure some assistance for her children, Elizabeth began the new year of 1938 by again writing to the Minister of Justice and Attorney General of Canada. Her letter, dated January 8, read in part:

> "Your Honour: As suggested by you some time ago, I did appeal to the Attorney General of Quebec but to date no answer, so I have come to the conclusion that, after all, what was done to us was done in Canada under the British flag. It is from Canada that I ask justice. As Canadians we have a right to expect that.
>
> . . . While in Alberta, we had six children. My husband, in each case, was able to provide for the medical attention for my confinement, and the medical attention of any member of his family that required any, and continued to do so until the day of his kidnapping in Amos, P.Q. on November 23, 1934 . . . I am expecting a baby sometime in March. Will I have medical attention during my confinement?" . . .
>
> Will I be forced to go to the Parliament as soon as the House opens to put my case before the members? I hope I will be spared that terrible strain until after my confinement at least . . . For the love of my children, so long as I have a bit of

life, I shall battle that the brand each one of them carries as coming from a father declared one hundred percent insane will be taken off properly. What answer will my five sons give to Canada, if one day they may be called to give their lives for Canada and the British flag after what has been handed them?''

Because her family lacked so many of the necessities of life, Elizabeth also wrote to the Provincial Police of the Abitibi Patrol, asking them once again to attempt to recover Dominic's stolen relief cheque for the month of December 1935. In their reply, the police informed her that because the offence had taken place over two years ago, and being of such a small amount, they were not justified in incurring any expenses in the matter. Dominic and Elizabeth felt this to be an unusual reaction to a theft.

A discouraging letter was also received from the House of Commons, Ottawa. It was written on March 1, under the signature of the Honourable Angus MacInnis. He again informed Dominic and Elizabeth that there was no hope of the federal members being able to do anything for them. He admitted that they all agreed there was a justified grievance but the difficulty was to get the authorities in the Province of Quebec to deal adequately with the case. He assured Dominic and Elizabeth that he had talked their case over with quite a number of people, and they were all convinced that justice had not been accorded them. He expressed regret that they were unable to help them.

On 19 March, 1938, James Joseph Raina was born.

The older children were excited to learn of little Jimmy's safe arrival, and to know that their mother had successfully survived his birth. Each new baby was welcomed into the family with great enthusiasm.

Elizabeth bitterly resented having her children regarded as objects of charity. She was also weary of answering incessant prying questions of the charitable organizations upon whom the family was dependent for help. For those reasons, she determined to take her children to the Parliament Buildings to again beg for justice within those walls.

''I shall absolutely refuse to leave until they do something for us,'' she promised Dominic on the morning of April 25, 1938, as she left with all her children on that errand.

The family was scrutinized with ill-concealed interest by the policeman on guard when, shortly after ten o'clock, they entered the doors of those impressive buildings and looked with awe about them.

Elizabeth approached the information desk with the intention of asking permission to see the Honourable Victor Quelch. On so doing, she noticed the Honourable Réné Pelletier walking down the hall. She approached the man, recalled to his mind the injustices inflicted on her family in the Province of Quebec, of which he already possessed a thorough knowledge, and demanded immediate action on the part of the honourable members.

When he discovered that she did not intend to listen to mere promises, the Honourable Pelletier invited Elizabeth to be seated with the children in the waiting-room pending his enquiries into the matter.

The silence that enveloped the family, and served only to add to the tenseness of the atmosphere, was broken shortly by the sound of determined footsteps coming down the hall. As all glances turned curiously towards the door, the Honourable Réné Pelletier again came into view. He was accompanied by a second man, who enquired as to the purpose of the visit. Elizabeth replied that she wanted at least fifty dollars a month with which to feed her family while the various authorities continued their investigations. She pointed out that Johnny was ill and should not be forced to do a man's work on a dairy farm to help to feed the family.

Communications were immediately exchanged with the Department of Colonization of Amos, resulting in the department forwarding the startling information that the Raina family had been well treated by them while residing in their province, and that if they returned that same treatment would be resumed.

As she shuddered at that possibility, Elizabeth replied that she would much prefer to rot on the streets of Ottawa than to return to such treatment.

After considerable further discussion, she was asked if she would agree to accept a property in Quebec. Elizabeth interpreted the offer of a substitute property as an admission of guilt in the confiscation of the first one by Quebec authorities. She agreed to accept a substitute only if it was situated near Hull, Quebec, and in sight of the Federal Parliament Buildings across the river. She told the honourable members that if the property was nearby, the family could rush across the border into Ontario should the need for protection from further possible abuse by Quebec authorities arise.

Having delivered her ultimatum, Elizabeth glanced at her children — a message urging patience in her eyes. Then, leaning comfortably back in her chair, she stubbornly told the honourable gentlemen that she did not intend to leave the Parliament Buildings until satisfactory action had been taken to ensure the necessities of life for her children. When the members threatened to call in the police, she urged: "Go ahead! They are our best friends. At least if we are locked in a cell we will be accorded a trial, and that is what we have been waiting for."

Swiftly and ominously the honourable gentlemen left the room, leaving the Raina children to await developments.

With the announcement, "The chief is here," the gentlemen returned shortly to conduct the family to an office to meet the man in question. He was surrounded by several aides, who regarded the family with ill-concealed curiosity.

While their mother was being interrogated, the children looked with interest and grudging admiration at those impressive uniformed men. Darkly, in their minds, loomed the image of huge confining bars.

By the exercise of all his powers of persuasion, the man eventually succeeded in inducing Elizabeth to take her family to Red Cross headquarters. Unwisely, she left the Parliament Buildings without having accomplished a thing. Elizabeth regretted not having remained true to her resolve not to leave without first obtaining action on the part of authorities there.

The Red Cross people, who had previously investigated the Raina case and who were convinced of the unfair treatment the family had received, gave them charity. While so doing, they stressed that the family's welfare was the responsibility of either the Minister of Justice or the members of parliament.

Carrying her baby in her arms, Elizabeth next proceeded with the children to the Department of Justice.

Although she was unable to meet the Minister of Justice himself, she did succeed in seeing his secretary. When she insisted that the investigation made on the Raina case by the Royal Canadian Mounted Police be published throughout all the newspapers of Canada, the man explained that they could do nothing because they were only poor Liberal members.

The clock in the Justice Building now clearly indicated that evening was drawing near. The children were becoming uncomfortably aware of the fact that they had not had anything to eat since early that morning. Johnny was due back at the dairy farm to assist at evening chores. Once again, the family was forced to admit defeat, and to return home.

On April 26, in compliance with instructions from the federal authorities on her excursion to the Department of Justice the previous day, Elizabeth wrote to the Honourable Emile Lesage, Member of the Legislative Assembly for the Abitibi. Her letter informed him that:

> "Yesterday, with my eight children, I was in the office of the Federal Minister of Justice seeking redress for the injustices done to my husband, myself, and all my family. The Minister was absent and his private secretary suggested I take the matter

up with you. You stated to us that the present administration at Quebec is not responsible for the wrongs that we received under Taschereau's administration. Most emphatically I disagree with that point of view of yours.

. . . Our family is destitute. If we are right, as we firmly believe, in our claims against authorities, it is your bound duty as our representative to see so justice will be accorded us. If you believe us in the wrong, the charges being of a very serious nature, I do hope that you do not throw into discard the elementary notions of justice, of British fair play, and you will see that all possible facilities of a fair public trial be accorded us.''

Elizabeth objected to Mr. Lesage's statement that the Duplessis administration was not responsible for the wrongs rendered the family under the Taschereau administration. She felt that, by condoning those wrongs, the Duplessis administration had also put itself in a position of guilt.

The children had now been back in English school for several months and had made many friends. They were leading two separate lives — the days at school when they considered themselves to be normal, and the days at home when they could not be separated from the case. Their friends were completely unaware of the drama that had been their lives for several years. The children never talked about it. Elizabeth welcomed their friends with her usual warm enthusiasm, and they often shared the family's meagre rations. Insofar as the local children were concerned, this was just another family hard hit by the depression.

The Raina family survived mainly on baked beans all throughout that winter. The children's sandwiches, during the whole school term, consisted of two slices of home-baked bread filled with baked beans.

Ellwood school was a one-room schoolhouse. Although the teacher was a busy lady, she was also fair in her dealings with the pupils. As a punishment for arriving late for class, the offending pupil was made to stay indoors during recess. A strong believer in promptness, Dominic customarily urged the children out of the door at such an early hour that they were always the first ones to arrive at school. One day they decided to be late. As well as wanting to impress their friends with their naughtiness, they were curious to know what went on inside the school classroom during recess. On the day chosen to carry out their plan, they hid in a ditch to chat and to ensure that they would not arrive at school until long after classes had begun.

When they boldly, and importantly, put in a late appearance, the teacher looked pensive for a few moments. She then announced to the class that since it was the first time the Rainas were late they must have a very good reason, and it would be unfair to punish them for a first offence. The children were disappointed that their plan had backfired and had not incurred punishment. They never bothered to be late again.

On May 3, Dominic once again wrote to the Honourable Maurice Duplessis. His letter read:

"On July 23, 1935, at 8.30 p.m., in the parish hall, Amos, P.Q., while you were the leader of the opposition, my wife gave you a letter begging for justice. You promised us then to look into our case. Since that day you did become Premier; you received a lot of letters from us and several from other parties begging you to give us justice. You ignored it all. Probably you will also put this in the same place that the people of Quebec will put you later on. If I am yet writing to you it is not so much with the hope of getting justice from you but for the main purpose of obeying orders, as authorities in Ottawa told us dozens of times to take the matter up with you.

Magistrate Strike in Ottawa today sentenced a 19-year old youth to the Reformatory for at least six months for snatching a purse. You, Mr. Duplessis, Minister of Justice (?) of Quebec, so far you did not permit the arrest of a single party guilty of my kidnapping, or the stealing of valuable papers from my pockets and of all my earthly goods. You have been warning the West to keep their hands off the pockets of Quebec. I simply say: Quebec, you have put your fingers unlawfully into my pockets. I do demand from Quebec the immediate return of all the property stolen from me and proper reparation to myself and family. If you want to apply your padlock to some useful purpose I hope you will begin with the arrest of my kidnappers.

I can supply you with a list of the biggest criminals of Quebec if you really are interested in doing some cleaning. You are not going to clean Quebec of the Communist element by simply giving protection to parasites and bloodsuckers. If you want to give me a trial in Quebec City I am game to get there. But, remember, I want a fair, wide open public trial, with full freedom to choose my own defence; a trial from the Department of Justice, not the Department of Secret Rule. I am a rebel of the Department of Secret Rule, but I do obey orders of all duly constituted authorities, and I am glad to accept hanging if pronounced criminal . . ."

On May 3, 1938, Dominic called on the parish priest at Billings Bridge, Reverend Father Louis Lee, to notify him that the family was again without food or fuel. Father Lee arranged for him to call on the Apostolic Delegate.

Feeling grateful that he was at last to be granted an audience with that great dignitary of the Holy Catholic Church, Dominic was admitted into the luxury of the palace. Instead of the justice he had come to seek, he was given a charitable donation of seventy-five cents. So, for two whole days, the Raina family survived on the largesse of the Apostolic Delegate!

A week later, Elizabeth wrote to the Federal Department of Justice at Ottawa. Her letter read in part:

"While at Parliament with my eight children on 25 April seeking for justice I was told by the Honourable Réné Pelletier that if I went back to Quebec I would receive help. On May 3rd I wrote to the Honourable Réné Pelletier asking him what place I should go and what provision and protection my family would have.

. . . We are continually asked by authorities to forget and start over again. Would authorities tell us exactly how this can be done? Now I will be obliged to keep my children out of school because I can't give them any lunch. We do not come in on relief or justice. We honestly believe that the decision taken by authorities to starve a peaceful family composed of ten members in order to cover up a terrible crime committed against that family is not only a criminal act but stupid to the extreme. I repeat, in closing, that my family is out of food."

CHAPTER XIV

THE STRIVE FOR INDEPENDENCE

"To dry one's eyes and to laugh at a fall, and baffled, get up and begin again." Robert Browning.

During the spring of 1938, Dominic and Elizabeth spent considerable time in planning a course of action for the coming summer. In a country where justice was apparently unknown, and where charity was often bitter, they knew that only by complete unity and cooperation could the family once again become entirely independent. Because they had been so successful at market gardening during their first years in Quebec, they reasoned that the best means of becoming re-established might again lie in the cultivation of the soil.

In order that they might be enabled to sow a larger garden than had been possible the previous year, Dominic moved his family to a place located approximately one mile from Ottawa on the Metcalfe Highway. The property was situated on four acres of fertile land, and into that land went hope and countless hours of labour.

Each working member of the family was made responsible for contributing a share to the common good of the entire family.

Dominic and Elizabeth tilled and weeded the soil from dawn to dusk. Johnny continued his work on the dairy farm. Mary found a job cleaning the house and preparing lunch for a business couple who lived nearby. Thirteen-year-old Ralph and eleven-year-old Clara were assigned the task of pulling a little wagon loaded with produce to the doors of residents of Ottawa South. On their own initiative, they soon secured regular customers and learned to become first-class salesmen. Pulling a heavily-laden wagon several miles each day was far too strenuous a job for the two young children, but they carried on uncomplainingly.

As the days passed, it became increasingly evident to Dominic and Elizabeth that Johnny was unwell, although the local Health Officer had failed to diagnose an illness. Their constant worry over Johnny's health motivated Dominic and Elizabeth to again resume the battle of the pen.

Elizabeth wrote to the Right Honourable W.L. Mackenzie King, Prime Minister of Canada, under date of June 13, 1938. Although a reply was received from the Prime Minister's office, it did not offer the hoped-for encouragement.

A letter reached Dominic at the beginning of July from a friend at St. Marc de Figuery. In it, the man reassured Dominic that he had never been forgotten, and that he was always on his side as in times gone by. He reminded him that his offer to defend him against Monsieur le Curé still stood firm, and that the priest had not changed for the better. He also mentioned that at a recent council meeting those present talked about him and expressed a wish that he could find someone to defend his case.

Dominic and Elizabeth were deeply touched at those continued assurances of loyalty from their dear friends at St. Marc.

With the coming of fall, the younger children of school age were enrolled in the separate school of St. Thomas Aquinas at Billings Bridge, Ontario. Mary was compelled to continue domestic employment because her parents could not afford to send her to high school, and because her wages were needed to help to support the family. It was a great disappointment for Mary, whose ambitions were thus frustrated by the family's needs, but she understood why they must take precedence over her own.

Mary was aware that her parents shared her disappointment. Elizabeth had noticed, on her many trips to offices of high authorities in search of justice, the enviable jobs occupied by the smart young secretaries in those offices. She was often heard to comment to Dominic, after such a visit, ''Do you think that our daughters will ever be able to get a decent education, so that they can become secretaries?'' Mary feared, from the vantage point of her young years, that even such a humble dream could never materialize for her.

Meanwhile, numerous and varied were the lawyers approached by Dominic and Elizabeth, both in Hull and in Ottawa. While many of the legal practitioners showed an interest in the case and might have tackled certain of the minor grievances, the seriousness and enormity of the more major charges undoubtedly deterred them. Was it possible that if one link was touched the mighty chain might crumble down and prove too great a case to fight? The fact that Dominic and Elizabeth were financially unable to promise payment no doubt also served to discourage them.

Nevertheless, various authorities continued to conduct investigations into the Raina case. Their progress was usually pathetic, but their discoveries were occasionally humorous.

Months of research by their parish priest at Billings Bridge, Reverend Father Louis Lee, served only to produce from His Excellency Bishop Rhéaume of Haileybury the astounding report that Monsieur le Curé Jules Michaud of St. Marc de Figuery was the most saintly priest in that entire diocese. It further revealed that many priests from surrounding districts approached him for advice!

Dominic wondered whether the nature of the advice consisted in revealing to them the most effective methods whereby to bow into submissiveness any unruly settlers in their parishes? Or was the nature of the advice in any way connected with the purchase of gold mine shares?

In early November, Dominic received a letter from Elzéar Laroche of St. Marc de Figuery. Its contents contradicted the report regarding the saintliness of Monsieur le Curé, described by Bishop Rhéaume in his recent letter to Reverend Father Louis Lee.

In his letter, Elzéar Laroche reported that the books of the municipal council and the school board had been taken away from Michaud and that he could no longer do wrong via the books. He credited Mathias Poirier as the one responsible for bringing this good work about, thereby causing the priest to be angry with everyone. He also informed Dominic that Monsieur le Curé had made parish visits for the first time in thirteen years, but that he did not give him a cent because the priest had stolen twenty-one dollars from him previously. He further informed Dominic that Joseph Corriveau and Mathias Poirier had met with His Excellency Bishop Rhéaume in Amos to acquaint him with Michaud's unacceptable behaviour, resulting in the priest acting less foolish on Sundays. He closed his letter by expressing a wish that Dominic could return to live among them to teach them more about agriculture.

It was touching to learn that Mathias Poirier, one of the two guards who had conducted Dominic to Mastaï on November 23, 1934, was now playing such an active role towards bringing more honesty to St. Marc de Figuery!

That letter was followed shortly by another one from the same neighbour. It was dated December 30, and conveyed the information that Monsieur le Curé was asking for money nearly every Sunday and hardly anyone was giving him any because they wanted to get rid of him. He also mentioned that Royal Renaud had lost his job at the Land Office and that it was still an infernal clique. He again expressed his anger at Monsieur le Curé because of the twenty-one dollars the priest had allegedly stolen from him. He mentioned that if there was any justice they would return the Raina land. He expressed regret that he was not more educated so that he could write every week to give the news, but that it took him three whole evenings to write the present letter, and that he would rather talk to Dominic personally.

With the coming of the new year of 1939, Dominic applied to Gloucester Township for relief work. He was told that that type of employment was reserved for those people who had resided in the township prior to 1935.

Dominic had now written over one hundred letters to religious and civil authorities with regard to his case. While none of the letters had been written for pleasure, perhaps the most painful one he ever wrote, as a devout Catholic, was addressed to Reverend Father Louis Lee, the parish priest at Billings Bridge. It was dated January 15, 1939, and it read:

> "With the present, as one of your parishioners, I humbly submit the following for your serious consideration. After long and careful thought I have decided that beginning with the first Sunday in February I will quit from attending church services if an Ecclesiastical Tribunal is not accorded me in the very near future. The Honourable R.B. Bennet said the church failed. I, speaking only as a farmer, would rather say that the church did not fail, but rather that the clergy did fail the church, but if what was done to me is any criterion then the clergy are the first to break God's law and to make mockery of what they are preaching us.

> I do realize it is not fair to judge the church by the doings of a bad priest, but today I must say that all the dirty work done to self and family by Jules Michaud, priest at Figuery near Amos, P.Q., has been done to me by the highest religious authorities in Canada because Jules Michaud received full backing from them. Not long ago, his superior, Bishop Rhéaume, went as far as to tell you that Jules Michaud is one of the best priests in his diocese. If knowing my case, you consider that I do commit a sin in deciding to quit from going to church I beg you to tell me so in writing and I promise you that your instructions will be followed to the best of my capacity. I do hate hypocrisy and certainly it is high time for Bishop Rhéaume to accord me the Tribunal that he had promised long ago and that I have the right to have."

"You are Peter, and upon this rock I shall build my church, and the powers of hell shall not prevail against it".

Dominic believed firmly in that biblical passage, and he was convinced that the church would survive the ages regardless of the weaknesses of some of its hierarchy. He considered his Catholic religion to be necessary to the life of his soul, as was his blood to the life of his body. While he would never forsake his church, he was convinced that only through visible protests by the faithful against the increasing shortcomings of its clergy could there be hope of rejuvenation. Dominic explained his decision to his children, assuring them that he did not intend to interfere with their attendance at church services.

Mary was gratified at those assurances. Not only did she look upon her church as the place from which she drew strength, but it was also one of the few social outings she could afford. She especially enjoyed the beautiful gregorian chant, introduced in the parish by Father Louis Lee and sung each evening during the May devotions. She also enjoyed the latin part of the liturgy and would often muse: "I could travel anywhere in the world, among foreign languages, yet I could understand the language of the church because it is universal".

In late February, Dominic received a letter from Father Lee in which he transmitted correspondence he had received from the Apostolic Delegate. In it, the Apostolic Delegate commented on the letter he had received from Dominic and Elizabeth in which they had complained "in agitated terms" about the ecclesiastical authorities. He stated that his delegation was interested, not only in the ecclesiastical authorities helping the family, but in the Department of Colonization of Quebec assuming responsibility. He added that, according to a report he had received from the Bishop of Haileybury, he was under the impression that the church was not in the wrong.

Because His Excellency Bishop Rhéaume of Haileybury had always displayed a great interest in protecting Monsieur le Curé Jules Michaud and in avoiding an Ecclesiastical Tribunal with regard to the Raina case, it was not surprising to Dominic and Elizabeth to learn that the report he had transmitted to the Apostolic Delegate was not in their favour.

Elizabeth attempted, once more, to bring the true facts of the case to the attention of the Apostolic Delegate. She wrote to him again, on February 25, 1939, pointing out that she was not "agitated", but bitterly disappointed, over the actions of the clergy towards her family. She continued:

> "Below are some questions to which I believe I have a right to an answer in writing from the Clergy:
> a) By whom was Jules Michaud, Priest of Figuery, P.Q., sent to our house on Lot 39, R. III, Figuery, on November 23, 1934, and what was his purpose?

b) Why did Jules Michaud constantly refuse to let myself and the Council of Figuery see what he asked me to sign on November 23, 1934?

c) Why were all human rights refused to my husband while detained in jail in Amos on November 23, 1934?

d) Why, when Michaud called at my house on November 23, 1934, upon being asked by me if I could not see my husband, he answered that he did not know and at the same time he told me I could send working clothes for my husband?

e) Why was I told that my husband was being sent to a good hospital to be treated for his ulcers of the stomach, while they were sending him to an asylum?

f) By whom were Normand Bourque and Mathias Poirier hired to escort my husband to Quebec?

g) Since it had been proven conclusively that my husband was unjustly and against my wishes and knowledge sent to an asylum, in order to be a good Catholic wife and mother must I pay for the expenses of my husband's kidnapping and suffering?

h) Why, for over two years after I obtained the release of my husband, did Jules Michaud continually try to send my husband back to the asylum, causing me untold worries?

i) Did I do wrong to have confidence in a priest?

I insist on a written answer to the above questions. If I do not know my duties as a Catholic, please send me a good missionary. I am not residing in Africa, but just about three miles south of the Apostolic Delegation, Ottawa, where I made several trips on foot for nothing.''

During that worrisome period, Dominic and Elizabeth received another letter from Elzéar Laroche. He again assured them that he was always ready to defend their rights the same as he had done in the past. He again expressed hope that the family would return some day to St. Marc de Figuery. Dominic and Elizabeth were deeply touched by the sincerity and warmth of that communication.

On the morning of April 10, Dominic was summoned to the rectory at Billings Bridge by Reverend Father Louis Lee. The priest read him a letter which the Honourable Ernest Laforce, Minister of Colonization of Quebec, had written to the Apostolic Delegate, stating that Lot 39, R. III, Figuery, had been sold on March 7, 1935, because of debts Dominic owed to the Department of Colonization.

Such a distortion of the truth prompted Dominic to write to the Honourable Ernest Laforce, in an attempt to clarify some of the man's obvious misconceptions with regard to the sale of his land. He pointed out that he possessed written evidence, dated 1935, from the Honourable Hector Authier, ex-Minister of Colonization, to the effect that the sale of Lot 39, R. III, Figuery, was illegal.

A prompt reply to Dominic's letter was received from the Honourable Ernest Laforce. In it, he pointed out that in accordance with Canadian law, at least in the Province of Quebec, when a property, farm or house is sold for unpaid municipal taxes, he who was the owner had two years in which to remit the taxes to he who bought the property, plus an interest of six percent. He also pointed out that if the taxes were not paid at the end of two years, he who bought the property, even if he paid only ten dollars and said property was worth two thousand dollars, he would still be the owner.

It was evident that the Honourable Ernest Laforce was either deliberately missing the point, or was unable to grasp a matter of so deep and complicated a nature as the illegal sale of a property.

Again, Dominic wrote to the man, endeavouring to present the pertinent facts of the case in as clear and simple a language as possible. His letter, dated April 21, 1939, read in part:

"Yours of the 19th instant, in answer to mine of the 10th instant received and contents duly noted. I am sorry you misunderstood mine written in French so I try my luck with this in English . . .

. . . You are giving me a lesson in Canadian law that, though only a farmer, I already know. Please permit me to exchange our knowledge. In Canada, the Province of Quebec included, even the worst criminal is supposed to have a right to a trial, to be free to choose his defence . . .

. . . Now, still talking simply as a farmer, or rather as a man from whom his farm, his home, etc., was stolen . . . I always understood that Canada was a democratic country, that is, a country with a Government of the people, by the people, and for the people. I found it was so in Alberta, but if what was done to me in Quebec is any criterion, we must admit that, while there are many good people in Quebec, the law of the jungle is still in force.

. . . Father Lee of Billings Bridge told me about a nice proposition you have to settle us comfortably. Please write it down clearly in what your proposition consists and I would be glad to consider it carefully.''

In his next communication, the Honourable Ernest Laforce reprimanded Dominic for what he considered to be his lack of respect for the people of Quebec. He also discussed a property in the Temiscouata region of Quebec, which they were considering offering to him as a replacement for the one at St. Marc.

Dominic took strong exception to the Honourable Laforce's accusations, and what he took to be a deliberate misreading of his letters.

In a return reply to the man, dated May 5, he clarified his opinion of the people of Quebec in the following words:

"When in 1935, Royal Renaud, Inspector of the Department of Colonization and Jules Michaud, priest, with the full backing of civil and religious authorities told us that they were going to starve us, several kind people of Figuery stepped in and we did not starve.

The names of the kind people of Quebec who helped us . . . are written in our hearts, and you should be more than convinced that Dominic Raina never did accuse indiscriminately as thieves and bandits all the people in the fair Province of Quebec. You should know also that my kidnapper Michaud stole our home against the wishes of the good people of Figuery.''

With regard to Ernest Laforce's suggestion that the Raina family accept a property in the Temiscouata, Dominic continued: "*La commission du retour à la terre* is offering me a property of doubtful value on the apparent condition that I renounce forever Lot 39, R. III, Figuery''.

While Dominic continued his course of protest from Ottawa, in Quebec City the Department of Colonization penned an official letter, dated May 15, 1939, inviting him back into the province. The letter, bearing the signature of the Honourable Ernest Laforce, was mailed to the Apostolic Delegate, who transmitted it to Reverend Father Louis Lee with the request that he acquaint Dominic with its contents. In his communication, the Honourable Ernest Laforce informed the Apostolic Delegate that he had discussed Mr. Raina's case with His Excellency Bishop Courchêne of Rimouski. As a result of the discussion, the bishop was going to ask Monsieur le Curé Desbiens of Rivière Bleue to kindly receive Mr. Raina, and to take the necessary steps to befriend him and to help him by every means at his disposal. He stated that instructions had been issued to *La commission du retour à la terre* to help Mr. Raina, in a special manner, should he decide to re-establish himself on the place they had chosen for him. The Honourable Ernest Laforce assured the Apostolic Delegate that Mr. Raina would be given a good property to improve.

Dominic recognized, in that offer of a new home by Quebec authorities, an indirect admission of culpability. While he appreciated that small attempt at restitution, he felt that he could not consider such an offer because of the unsavoury strings attached. He did not wish to forego his rights as a Canadian citizen to settle where he wished. He felt that if his former home was returned to him he would be able to sell it, and to exercise those rights. Furthermore, he did not intend to repeat the mistake of settling in the Province of Quebec.

That spring of 1939 was a time of much activity in the Raina family. Extensive correspondence was being exchanged with the Department of Colonization of Quebec, and with various other authorities. A letter received from the Honourable René Pelletier provided amusement. Written on formal House of Commons stationery, it answered a question posed earlier by Dominic, in which he wanted to know whether or not he was entitled to beg in the parliament buildings. The Honourable Pelletier informed him that he had written to the Minister of Labour asking his opinion concerning the matter, and would advise him as soon as he received a reply. Dominic was gratified to learn that his inquiry was receiving such profound consideration!

A second, and far more disheartening, letter was received from the Honourable Réné Pelletier, when he officially bowed out of the case in a final communication received on May 3, 1939. He informed Dominic and Elizabeth that everything that he had been able to do concerning their case had been done, and expressed regret that his efforts had not been successful. He pointed out that, until the federal authorities admitted that the principle of relief and unemployment was a matter of national concern, such cases of injustice as the Rainas had suffered would continue to exist. He concluded by saying that there was nothing else that he could do.

Although the Honourable Pelletier's summation of their case was discouraging, an even greater blow was to follow. Dominic and Elizabeth had been told by Father Louis Lee that the long-awaited Ecclesiastical Tribunal was finally to be accorded them, and that Reverend Father Tessier (a lawyer from the seminary) had been assigned to represent them. But the Reverend Father Tessier was totally ignorant of the fact that he had supposedly been appointed to act on their behalf, when Dominic and Elizabeth went to meet him. They returned home feeling thoroughly defeated.

They learned later, through a communication which they received from Bishop Charbonneau, dated June 22, that an Apostolic Tribunal had never been seriously considered. The bishop's letter informed them that, as a result of the recommendation of their devoted pastor Father Lee, he had indeed prepared an interview for them with Father Tessier. However, later on, when he tried to get some information, both from Haileybury and from the parish in which they had gone through such dire trials, everyone was willing to shift the responsibility for what occurred on other people. He added that he did not know how to proceed because, being at such a distance from the place, he could not ascertain any fact; and he had no authority over any of those implicated in the matter, some of whom no longer resided there. He expressed genuine regret at their hopeless plight, and extended his sympathy to them and to their children. He advised them to keep in touch with Father Lee, in whom he perceived a great love for the Raina children, and whom he felt convinced would give them a helping hand. He counselled them to be faithful to God; and God would find a way to punish the wicked and reward those who put their trust in him.

Dominic and Elizabeth were aware of the truth of the bishop's statement that Father Louis Lee was the man who was willing to give them a helping hand. The priest had often proven his sincerity at attempting to solve their problems with the clergy, and had spared no efforts towards that end. He had also displayed his fondness and concern for the welfare of the Raina children on many occasions.

Since the Raina family had first become acquainted with Reverend Father Louis Lee, the priest had become afflicted with rapidly-deteriorating eyesight. He could no longer read, without great difficulty, the latin text during daily Mass. He had elected eleven-year-old Louis Raina, a daily altar boy, to select and read the required text for him during church services. His family was proud, yet mystified, at Louis' immediate grasp of latin, and the ease with which he read it.

Dominic spent endless days searching for employment during that time of the Great Depression. Johnny and Mary generously brought their small earnings home, and the family depended upon their help. Because the children always enjoyed a close companionship, and had so many things to talk about among themselves when they were together, they watched eagerly at the window for Johnny's return each evening. In the Raina family, each small triumph or disappointment of an individual member became the triumph or disappointment of all.

Elizabeth also watched at the window for Johnny each evening. The children noticed their mother shudder when she heard his loud and incessant coughs precede him across the fields. The persistence of the cough frightened her, although repeated appointments with doctors had failed to provide any significant diagnosis. Elizabeth knew with a mother's intuition that her son was too ill to perform the hard manual labour required of him. She had, on several occasions, shared her fears for Johnny with both religious and civil authorities, and had pleaded that justice be given the family so that all of her children might stand a chance to survive the relentless hardships.

One day, during the spring of 1939, Ralph became very ill. Elizabeth reported the matter to Father Louis Lee, who generously gave the family a cash donation of six dollars and sent a doctor to Ralph's bedside. Upon examination of the patient, the doctor suspected that Ralph had scarlet fever. The tentative diagnosis was reported to the local Health Officer, who called at the house that evening to verify the fact. A quarantine was immediately placed upon the house.

With the exception of Dominic and Johnny, who were exempt so that they might earn wages, the family was not permitted off the premises for four weeks. Fruit juices were seldom available to the patient as he fought the disease, although his mother had been instructed by the Health Officer that he be given a plentiful supply of liquids to combat the fever. In order to prevent a spread of the disease among other family members, Elizabeth was cautioned to keep the rest of the children away from Ralph as much as possible. Ralph spent many hours sitting on the top step of the stairs so that he could talk to his siblings, who took turns sitting on the bottom step.

After the end of four weeks, on his first visit to the house since he had diagnosed the illness, the Health Officer removed the quarantine sign from the door. He gave Elizabeth a verbal pat on the back by remarking, "Well, we did very well to avoid contamination among the rest of the children."

After Ralph's recovery and the lifting of the quarantine, the children rushed out to earn wages by again picking berries for the local farmers. Once again, they were able to eat reasonably satisfying meals.

In late July, Dominic wrote a letter to Reverend Father Louis Lee, in which he commented:

"Slow Starvation Overtaking Some Quebec Colonists."

"Those are not the words of a lunatic, but big front head-lines in *The Standard* of Montreal of Saturday, July 22, 1939. I am an ex-colonist from Quebec and slow starvation amongst settlers was going on there in 1934.

. . . The Department of Colonization is offering us a second home in Temiscouata, P.Q. The truth of the thing is that they are ready to give us a parcel of land that with several years of pioneering may be turned into a home, with the understanding that I put my life and soul, the life and soul of our family of ten, completely into their hands, and giving them the right to steal said second home when ready, if they feel like doing so.''

Dominic's decision not to subject his family to the arduous task of carving out a new future in the Temiscouata proved to be a wise one!

CHAPTER XV
THE KILLER DISEASE

"Great grief is a divine and terrible radiance which transfigures the wretched." Victor Hugo.

Merciless in its destruction, the ravaging disease of tuberculosis struck at the Raina family to claim therefrom some victims.

On August 1, 1939, in accordance with instructions received from a kind Ottawa doctor, Johnny reported for an x-ray to the Royal Ottawa Sanatorium. The Royal Ottawa Sanatorium was a hospital run exclusively for the treatment of tuberculosis. There, the searching eyes of the x-ray revealed lungs that were polluted with the much-dreaded disease. Johnny was instructed to remain isolated in a bedroom at home pending admission to the hospital.

The Health Officer called regularly to see the patient, and he reminded Dominic and Elizabeth repeatedly of the seriousness of his condition.

While fighting to conquer tuberculosis, Johnny's condition was further weakened when red measles swept through the family.

Elizabeth looked sorrowfully at her eight children, all of whom were ill, and several of whom lay on mattresses upon the floor. While some furniture had been donated by charitable organizations, the family still lacked several beds.

Elizabeth knew that unless excellent care and nourishment were given to her children immediately they would all fall victim to tuberculosis. Tearfully, she contacted the kind doctor who had first suspected tuberculosis in Johnny. He reported the situation to the Department of Health.

The red measles played havoc on the rundown condition of the children, and some of them developed pleurisy. Powerless to relieve the discomfort of her children, Elizabeth prayed for their recovery.

Religious authorities were notified of that latest development in the family.

"We will pray for you," repeatedly assured the priests of the Holy Catholic Church, when Dominic and Elizabeth begged that something constructive be done for the welfare of their children.

"We will try to make room for Johnny at the sanatorium as soon as possible," assured the local Health Officer, when he visited the patient in August.

On August 20, Dominic wrote to Reverend John A. MacDonald of the Ottawa Catholic Welfare Bureau, who was well acquainted with the facts of the Raina case, informing him that:

"Today is the eighteenth birthday of our oldest son. You did see him in bed when you called on us with our Pastor Father Lee on the 9th instant. He is still in bed and far from improving. The Sanatorium is full and we were unable to get a place for him so far. At home we are far from having the means to give the poor boy all the care needed. What are the authorities doing? . . . Shall I be forced to witness in silence the murder of all my children?"

Eventually, on September 4, a car was sent to drive Johnny to the Royal Ottawa Sanatorium.

With the admission of that first victim into isolation began years of a battle, on a new front, for the Raina family — a battle against tuberculosis. It marked the beginning of endless years of trips back and forth to the sanatorium by those who were well to visit those who were ill.

In accordance with instructions issued by health authorities, the Raina children all reported to the Royal Ottawa Sanatorium to submit to x-rays and examinations. Once again, the x-rays were cruel in their revelations. Ralph and Clara were admitted to the preventorium — the section of the Royal Ottawa Sanatorium reserved for children. George was confined to bed at home.

The rules of the sanatorium required that, in order to qualify for visiting rights, the visitor must have attained the age of sixteen years. Dominic, Elizabeth, and Mary were the only members of the family left at home who fell into that category. Ralph and Clara, under the required age, were permitted to visit Johnny on one occasion. That exception was made because they were already inflicted with tuberculosis and confined to the sanatorium. But the children were determined to keep in touch with one another, and Johnny, Ralph, and Clara exchanged letters constantly.

In one letter to Ralph and Clara, when he was very ill, Johnny wrote:

"I am not so sleepy tonight. How are you both? I still have a terrible temperature but I have no pains or aches and I feel real good. Do not think my writing is shaky because I am sick. It is because I usually put my pad on a book and I could not get up to get the book. Thank you for the Mass and for praying for me. I hope you can come and see me soon. I will try to write again soon.''

It was important to Johnny that he make every effort possible to conceal the seriousness of his illness from other members of the family, as he did not wish them to worry over him.

Patients at the sanatorium were permitted visitors twice a week, on Tuesday evenings and on Sunday afternoons. The highlight of those dark days for Mary was that on each Sunday afternoon it was her turn to visit the patients. An added pleasure, in addition to seeing her brothers and sister, was watching for a particular shoe store as the streetcar clanged down Somerset Street. It had been years since Mary had been able to choose a pair of shoes. All she had worn were second-hand, ill-fitting ones donated by charitable organizations. She considered her footwear to be most unattractive, and her feet always seemed to hurt. When the shoe store came into view, and while the streetcar stopped to let off or to pick up passengers, Mary would look with great interest at the display of shoes in the window of the shop. In her mind's eye, she selected the ones she hoped some day to buy. Just thinking about it was a source of excitement and satisfaction.

Because he was so ill, and because Ralph and Clara had each other, Mary spent most of the visiting hour with Johnny. He told Mary of all the things he would do once he was better. His greatest ambition was to buy beautiful things for their mother. Johnny reminded Mary each time she visited him of how much their mother had suffered, and how she had always been so good to them. He pointed out that, in return, they would always have to be very good to her. Johnny was still interested in airplanes. If one could be heard flying overhead when a visitor was with him, he would ask to be raised from his pillow so that he could get a better view of the sky and, hopefully, catch a glimpse of the plane. Johnny told Mary that he planned to be a pilot when he was better.

Ralph and Clara were allowed to continue their studies by attending classes at the preventorium. They passed much of their time in doing lessons, and in writing to Johnny and to their friends from school. Ralph had learned to do leather work, and he made several purses. Some he gave away as gifts, and others he raffled off in order to get money to buy leather to make more purses.

When Clara was not writing letters, she prayed. And prayed. And prayed. She had great stacks of prayers and novenas piled upon her bedside table. Each day, she methodically prayed through them, one by one, then neatly stacked them up again in readiness for the next time.

Although temporarily diverted by their battle against tuberculosis, Dominic and Elizabeth did not neglect their pursuit of justice. Responsible authorities were promptly notified of the rampant disease that was sweeping through the family — a direct consequence of the denial of their rights as Canadian citizens and of the resultant poverty in which they had been forced to live.

On one of her many trips to the sanatorium to visit the three patients, Mary was told by a nurse that her brother Johnny was a very sick boy, and that the doctors had given up on him. She instructed Mary to tell her parents that they could visit him whenever they wished. She cautioned Mary not to betray to the patient, on her entry to the sickroom, the seriousness of his condition. Mary followed her instructions, that day learning a valuable lesson: she learned how to smile on the outside and weep on the inside at one and the same time.

Mary delayed her return home as long as possible that day because she dreaded having to tell her parents the sad news about Johnny. At home, that evening, the remaining family members wept and prayed together for Johnny.

On October 9, Elizabeth notified Monsieur le Curé Jules Michaud, in the following words, of the tragedy that had befallen her family:

> "In case you would like to know the results of the persecution which you put my family through since November 23, 1934, they are as follows: John, aged eighteen, is a patient in the Royal Ottawa Sanatorium since September 4, 1939, with very little hope of recovery . . . Ralph, aged fourteen is also a patient there accompanied by his sister Clara, aged thirteen. George, aged seven, is in bed at home and will most likely follow the rest to the sanatorium . . . Authorities are astonished that we are still Catholics after such an injustice imposed on us by members of the clergy. At least we hope that our sufferings will help to clean up the Province of Quebec for others."

Elizabeth was expecting another child in January, and she had not been well throughout the pregnancy. She had been cautioned by her doctor to get plenty of rest, as he feared that she might miscarry.

On October 15, on her way to visit her slowly-dying son, Elizabeth became so ill that it was necessary for her to be hospitalized. She was kept there for four days, until the danger of a miscarriage had passed.

Mary had noticed on her recent trips to the hospital that Johnny appeared much weaker. He no longer talked about all the wonderful things he would do for their mother when he got better. Instead, he urged Mary to always be good to her, and to continue to help her as much as she could. He no longer talked about his ambition to be a pilot. Aware that Johnny knew he was going to die, Mary wished, desperately, that there could be a way for her to ward off her brother's death. He was her best friend, and the closest companion of her youth.

Ralph and Clara were gradually improving, and they were gaining weight. They were enjoying more nourishing meals than they had had for months, resulting in a transformation in their appearance that was most becoming. They accepted their confinement with resignation, confident in their eventual recovery. They prayed together constantly that Johnny might recover too.

As Johnny became daily weaker, Elizabeth spent much of her time with him. A bed was made available for her use at the sanatorium, so that she might remain there overnight if she wished.

In the peace of his religion, with his mother at his side, Johnny died at two o'clock a.m. on December 13, 1939, at the age of eighteen years.

At four o'clock in the morning, Mary awoke to the sound of a taxi driving into the yard. She rushed downstairs and unlocked the door. Her mother's anguished face told her, more effectively than words could convey, that her dear brother Johnny had passed away.

Closely united in their tragedy, the family attended Johnny's Funeral Mass, at St. Thomas Aquinas Church, Billings Bridge, Ontario, on December 15. They witnessed his interment, at the expense of Gloucester Township, in a free plot for the poor in the St. Thomas Aquinas Cemetery.

Alhough this waste of a human life served to awaken pity in the hearts of many individuals, it did not move responsible authorities to action.

That year, the Province of Quebec acquired a new Premier, in the person of the Honourable Adélard Godbout. Dominic wrote to the man, as he had so often written to his predecessors, to protest the injustices rendered his family in the Province of Quebec. He acquainted him with the troubles they had experienced under the Taschereau administration, and with the neglect of the Duplessis administration to deal with the situation.

In his letter, Dominic wrote: "My congratulations on your success against the traitor Maurice. Along with your great honour comes the responsibility of bringing peace and justice to the beautiful Province of Quebec."

Since the Raina family's departure from the Abitibi, the town of Amos had grown in religious significance, and now boasted an Episcopal See under the guidance of His Excellency Bishop J.A. Desmarais.

Shortly after Johnny's death, Dominic wrote a letter to the bishop informing him: "The present is to bring you news of the death of my eldest son, John Peter Raina, aged eighteen years, as a result of the wretched persecution that we received from Jules Michaud, priest at Figuery."

Early in the New Year of 1940, Dominic and Elizabeth received news from St. Marc de Figuery in the form of a letter written by Madame Elzéar Laroche. In it, she told them that she always remembered Dominic saying that Michaud would become either honest or more crooked. She commented that he was becoming more crooked, and that several of the men from St. Marc had gone to see Bishop Desmarais. His Emminence told them that St. Marc had done very well to keep Michaud so long, and that they were not the first ones to complain about him and that he would be replaced before long. She told Dominic that her husband Elzéar wanted a copy of a letter that he had written to the bishop so that he could read it to the mayor and to the others who were on their side.

On January 17, 1940, William Paul Raina was born. Little Billy was a happy smiling baby, and won the hearts of all the family. Elizabeth was comforted by the arrival of another son, who occupied much of her time and who helped, in a small way, to ease the sorrow of the loved one she had so recently lost.

During that winter, Dominic was able to do considerable relief work for Gloucester Township. Mary had advertised her services for the cleaning of homes in the local newspaper. She had several customers in Ottawa South, and each day went off to that work she hated so.

There was very little that seventeen-year-old Mary liked about that winter. She did not like the fact that Johnny had died, and she found it difficult to come to terms with his death. She did not like the fact that she was denied Ralph and Clara's companionship while they were confined in the sanatorium. She did not like walking through the Village of Billings Bridge on her way to work, where she met the other girls her age talking and laughing on their way to school. She longed so much to be one of them. She did not like missing parties because she did not have decent clothes to wear. She did not respond when the local boys hinted at taking her out on a date. She was convinced that they would reject her anyway when they found out about all the tuberculosis in the family. She felt that she may as well be walking around with a sign around her neck reading, "Walking Germ." She did not like being told by her parents that she must be an example to the younger children. And most of all, she did not like hearing about the case. She was fed up to the teeth with the case.

Mary longed for the return of the days before the family left Alberta to settle in Quebec, when everything seemed to be so normal. She went to the Ottawa Union Station one day to enquire how much a return ticket to Alberta would cost. She planned to save up enough money to return at some future time to visit the friends she had left behind there, and with whom she still corresponded. That night, while her father was working on his ledgers, she sat down and estimated how long it would take her to save up enough money for the fare if she squirreled away a quarter a month. She estimated that it would take her about a hundred years. There was no escape!

To help ease her despondency, Mary did what she had always been taught, as a good Catholic girl, to do. She stopped in at the Church of St. Thomas Aquinas each morning on her way to work. In the peace of her surroundings, she prayed for Johnny, and she asked God to help her get through the day. She repeated that procedure again on her way home each afternoon, except this time she asked God to help her get through the lonely evening.

One evening, she decided to write a story for George because that was something she really enjoyed doing. She chose to write it for her little brother because he was sick at home, and she thought that he must get lonely too. She called the story, "Gypsy Woman." George was very possessive of his book, and read it over and over, keeping it right beside him at all times so that the other children could not touch it.

Mary was so pleased at her little brother's reaction to her story that she decided to write another one. In fact, she thought that she would write a really long book. As she contemplated the subject matter she would choose her thoughts turned to the case. Where else could she find drama to compare to the drama she was living? She decided to write her family's story. She would vindicate the shame bestowed upon her father! She would vindicate the tears shed by her mother! She would vindicate Johnny's death, and the illness of her brothers and sister! Finally, she would vindicate the theft of her youth!

Mary knew that she would have to get all her facts completely straight. There could be no room for error in a story of that nature, because she could not trivialize the seriousness of the case by turning it into fiction. She questioned her parents endlessly, so that she could fill in any parts of which she was unsure. Dominic and Elizabeth spent hours, often far into the night, cooperating with their daughter's efforts. Mary caught them casting puzzled and resigned glances at each other from time to time. Nevertheless, she knew that they were impressed with her perseverence, and with the methodical way in which she ascertained the truth of everything she wrote. They neither encouraged nor discouraged her in her project. When her father asked to read the voluminous notes she had written, he could find nothing to criticize. Mary rolled the notes all up, tied a string around them, and stashed them away in a secret place.

The days were getting longer, and winter was coming to an end. Ralph and Clara were coming home. There was great excitement in the family when they were discharged from the sanatorium on March 2, 1940. With their return came an end to Mary's loneliness.

As the days grew warmer, and the fields dried up, Mary raced to a nearby hill that offered an unobstructed view of the surrounding countryside. She enjoyed standing on that hill because, from that vantage point, she could see in the far horizons a bright and shining future. She was filled with joy and optimism, and the sadness of the winter faded away.

Although Dominic and Mary were both working, and although the family was no longer as wholly dependent upon the generosity of sympathetic individuals, many of the necessities of life were still lacking.

For that reason, Dominic and Elizabeth had mixed feelings when Ralph and Clara were discharged from the sanatorium. They feared that if the children were again deprived of nourishing food, and removed from the warm comfort of the sanatorium to be plunged into a cold and draughty house, they would be in danger of a relapse.

With those adverse possibilities in mind, Dominic wrote to Reverend Father John MacDonald of the Catholic Welfare Bureau. His letter read in part:

>"It is a week since Ralph and Clara are at home. Before leaving the sanatorium they had about two quarts of milk each day to drink. Since they are at home they had none. It is almost the same for other parts of the diet. My home was stolen upon orders of religious authorities and not yet returned. I must report to the Department of Health, Toronto, about my children. The sooner the job I had before my kidnapping by the Abitibi's branch of the Laurentian Gestapo is returned to me, the better. I always did provide meat, butter, milk, eggs, etc. aplenty to my family until Jules Michaud and Company, with the full blessings of his bishop and the silence of the Cardinal Villeneuve had everything stolen from me.''

When Clara reported to the sanatorium for a routine examination on May 20, she already showed a nine-pound loss in weight since her discharge from that institution less than three months earlier.

Johnny and Ralph Raina. Taken on August 20, 1939, on Johnny's eighteenth birthday - four months prior to his death, at Billings Bridge, Ontario.

CHAPTER XVI

MOVING AHEAD

"The spirit of self-help is the root of all genuine growth in the individual; and, exhibited in the lives of many, it constitutes the true source of national vigor and strength. Help from without is often unfeeling in its effects, but help from within invariably invigorates." Samuel Smiles.

The Raina children had lived through years of shattered hopes and misplaced trust, growing up in the shadow of the case. They did not have reason to believe in the people who should have proven to them their ability to direct their church and to lead their country. Had those people not, by their protection of those guilty in the case, approved their dire situation? With a firm reliance only on their own capabilities, the children were united in their vow to rise high above their present circumstances!

In September, to the great satisfaction and pride of the entire family, Ralph was enrolled in St. Patrick's College at Ottawa. He became the first of the Raina children given an opportunity to attend high school.

In November, Dominic wrote once more to the Honourable Maurice Duplessis, the former Premier of Quebec. His letter read in part:

> "I read in *The Ottawa Citizen* of last evening your attacks on Godbout. I am not out to praise him but you should be the very last to criticize the present Premier of Quebec.
>
> . . . As Premier and Attorney General of Quebec, you did give full protection to the gangsters who massacred me and stole everything from self and family.
>
> . . . The Clergy? They trespassed into Caesar's field, and if Godbout does nothing worse than to force them back into their own ground, he will get the approval of all the freedom-loving Canadian people.

Laurier? Gouin? The unbelievable atrocities done to some poor settlers of the Abitibi is enough to awaken those great figures from their graves.

Godbout has smeared and dirtied the reputation of the province. When we try to raise from the mud and filth, when we come out and openly confirm ourselves our blunders and mistakes, that any person with eyes can see, that is a sign of greatness, and embodies hopes of regeneration.

If you have at heart the honour of Quebec, I hope you will use some of your talent to see so, even at this late hour, that justice be given to my sorely tried family.''

One evening, as Mary was walking past the Township Hall at Billings Bridge on her return home from work, she was invited by Mr. Carman Guest, the Town Clerk, to come into his office. He had taken a great interest in the Raina children, and that afternoon told Mary that he felt there was a better future in store for her than the one offered by doing menial cleaning jobs. He suggested that she take a business course, offering to personally enroll her in a business college and to advance the fees for her tuition and books. He explained that he would expect her to repay every cent of the advance, in reasonable monthly instalments, as soon as she completed the course and had found work as a stenographer. Mary was advised to discuss the matter with her father that evening, and to report the outcome of the conversation to him the following morning.

Mary left Mr. Guest's office in a state of great excitement. She hardly dared to hope, until she had spoken to her father. Her father was a proud man, and Mary knew that it would pain him greatly to have others plan for the education of his children when he had always hoped to do that himself. Before racing home, Mary stopped to pray at the Church of St. Thomas Aquinas. She begged God to influence her father to let her take the course, promising Him all kinds of impossible things if He would cooperate with her.

When Mary approached her father that evening, his answer was not quickly forthcoming. He sat down and added and subtracted columns of figures. Finally, he asked Mary to be seated, and he pointed out to her the conditions under which she could take the course.

1. She could not get the shoes that she had been promised she could have at the end of the week. The only footwear Mary owned was a pair of leaky overshoes. Her father explained that they would have to serve for both outdoor and indoor wear until the completion of the course.
2. Even though it was a ten-month course, Mary would have to complete it in three months.

3. Mary would have to walk the three miles to and from the business college each day, since there was no money available for streetcar fare.

Mary was overjoyed! She hugged her father and promised to meet all the conditions.

The following day, Mr. Carman Guest enrolled her in Gowlings' Business College, located above a drugstore at the corner of Somerset and Bank streets. He asked the Principal of the college to allow Mary to work at her own speed, explaining that she had only three months in which to finish the course.

Good fortune seemed finally to have come to Mary. A kind friend of the family rented a typewriter for her use, so that she could practice typing at home. A thoughtful neighbour, who she frequently met as she walked through Billings Bridge, invited her to be his guest on the streetcar on many occasions.

Desperation drove Mary to successfully finish the course in three months, as she had promised her father. She passed the government examinations, and was hired shortly afterwards to work as a stenographer with the Department of National Defence, Naval Services.

On receiving her first pay cheque, Mary gave ten dollars to Mr. Carman Guest — her first instalment towards repaying the kindness and understanding of the man who had so generously helped her take this giant step towards a better future.

Tuberculosis again invaded the family home when, in late May, Clara's latest x-ray revealed a lung that bore the shadow of that stubborn disease. She was instructed to remain in bed at home pending a re-examination in July. She was told that if she failed to improve during that trial period, it would be necessary for her to return to the sanatorium.

Due to the war and the shortage of manpower, money flowed more freely and the family lived more comfortably. But, unfortunately, it was too late to repair the damage to the children's health, caused by years of deprivation.

On July 5, 1941, Clara was readmitted to the sanatorium. A model patient, she cooperated fully with the doctors and nurses in the treatment of her disease, but her resistance to its progress appeared to be non-existent. Meanwhile, the doctors pointed out to each member of the family the danger to all of them after months of exposure to the tuberculosis germs. They solemnly urged careful and continued vigilance.

During the summer holidays of 1941 Ralph decided to forego further education at St. Patrick's College in order to join the ranks of civil servants. He wished to be self-supporting, and to be able to assist the family financially.

During August of that year, Dominic wrote another letter to the Apostolic Delegate, knowing that that venerated dignitary of his church was undoubtedly becoming weary of his letters. However, he was becoming even more weary at being forced, through circumstances, to write them. Where else could he turn for help in the settling of his grievances, if not to the highest authority of the Holy Roman Catholic Church in Canada, when those grievances had originated with the persecution of the family by a member of the clergy of that church?

Realizing that the likelihood of the long-promised Ecclesiastical Tribunal was remote, Dominic and Elizabeth wrote again to the Apostolic Delegate, during March of 1942, asking that they be granted a Conciliation Board for the settling of their case. In view of the reluctance of Bishop Rhéaume to enforce an Ecclesiastical Tribunal, because of the high expenses involved in such a procedure, they felt that a Conciliation Board could be conducted at less cost. Their letter read in part:

> "Since the objection was raised by His Excellency Bishop Rhéaume, about the cost of said (Ecclesiastical) Tribunal, we did ask and are asking now for a Conciliation Board, composed of not less than three English-speaking priests. We ask to have Jules Michaud, as the one we accused the most, present at the sitting of said Board with us. Said Conciliation Board to be considered as a preliminary to the Ecclesiastical Tribunal, in case a conciliation is not reached between the two opposing parties at said Board.
>
> The fact that our statements do not agree with statements that this Delegation has from other souces, proves conclusively that an Ecclesiastical Tribunal is needed. If our statements did fully agree with the Clergy's or others' statements, then certainly, neither Conciliation Board, nor Ecclesiastical Tribunal would be required.
>
> As matters stand now, the longer the Ecclesiastical Tribunal is denied or delayed, that much longer our poor innocent children will be made to suffer."

A reply to their letter, bearing the seal of the Apostolic Delegate, reached Dominic and Elizabeth shortly afterwards via the medium of Reverend Father Louis Lee, to whom it was written. The contents were discouraging. In it, Father Lee was informed that in view of the actual standing of the Raina case, and after having considered the particular request they wished to advance, it was not to the competence of the Apostolic Delegation to settle their problem. He stated that the file on record showed clearly that the Apostolic Delegate had done his utmost to find a happy solution to the case in question, but that circumstances beyond his control seemed to have impeded it. It was the conclusion of the delegation that their complaints should be made to the local ecclesiastical authorities.

Dominic hastened to explain to the Apostolic Delegate, by return letter, that he had attempted to obtain redress through the local ecclesiastical authorities on numerous occasions, but without success. Nevertheless, he followed the instructions and wrote, once again, to His Excellency Bishop Desmarais of Amos. His letter, dated March 30, 1942, read:

> "Enclosed please find copy of correspondence we received from His Excellency the Apostolic Delegate.
>
> We still insist that the right to bring Jules Michaud, priest at Figuery, before an Ecclesiastical Tribunal be accorded us in order to settle matters of a most serious nature. We humbly beg of you to explain us the steps we should take."

In early May, Dominic wrote to the Apostolic Delegate informing him that he had followed his instructions and written to Bishop Desmarais of Amos. In his letter, he wrote:

> "By registered mail, on 30th March, we wrote to His Excellency Bishop Desmarais of Amos, P.Q. No reply as yet. . . . My home, stolen under orders of the clergy, is still in the hands of the Gestapo of Quebec. The clergy of Quebec stole my right to an Ecclesiastical Tribunal. The clergy of Quebec do not wish to confess, nor do they wish me to confess. I shall make my confession before the people, and by the people the clergy of Quebec will be made to confess. The clergy of Quebec sowed a storm and they will harvest a hurricane.
>
> With Lieut. Colonel Réné de Salaberry I say: May God have pity on the French Canadians."

Since the war between nations, World War No. 2, had shaken and terrified the country, many Canadians had enlisted. Dominic tried, but unsuccessfully, to join the ranks.

In the spring of 1942 he passed the postal clerk examinations with an average of ninety-two percent. He was subsequently given employment at the Base Post Office, Ottawa.

During that same spring, Dominic and Elizabeth met the fiery Conservative Member from Lake Centre, the Honourable J.C. Diefenbaker.

Dominic was greatly impressed by the intelligence and enthusiasm of the man, and it was with renewed hope that he acquainted him with the troubles he had encountered in the Province of Quebec. The future Prime Minister of Canada assured them, with conviction, that he would look into the case, and asked them to submit a full account of their grievances in writing.

When Dominic eventually heard from the Honourable Diefenbaker, in a letter dated June 12, 1942, he was given the disappointing news that because the matters referred to were so long past, and having been originally in the hands of the police, they no longer gave cause for action.

Dominic felt it to be ironic that the injustices which he had never ceased to protest had occurred too long in the past to warrant restitution!

At the beginning of the new year of 1943, Dominic and Elizabeth learned, through a letter from a former neighbour of St. Marc de Figuery, that Monsieur le Curé Michaud was still at St. Marc and it appeared that he would remain there indefinitely. She mentioned two letters she had written to them which she believed they had not received. Because she feared that they had been intercepted, she addressed the present one to Mary, with the hope that it would reach its destination.

That letter served to strengthen Dominic's suspicions that mail to and from his old neighbours was not always getting through, as he had not received the letters referred to.

In February, the family received another letter from a former neighbour of St. Marc de Figuery, in which he reported that things were the same at St. Marc, although the priest no longer had his hands in the council. Dominic was gratified to learn that since Joseph Corriveau had become mayor things were going better in the council.

Dominic, Mary, and Ralph were now steadily employed, and the family's financial situation had improved greatly. Dominic began to repay some of the people who had helped when the family was destitute.

In a letter to the Apostolic Delegate, dated March 1, 1943, he wrote:

"Enclosed please find with my most sincere thanks a money order for twenty dollars as refund for charity that I received from you. Very likely you were not expecting it, and I had not promised any refund. I am not rich now, but since, for the present, my poor children have plenty to eat, I cannot forget those who gave bread to my children at the time that the Gestapo was determined to destroy myself and all my family. Your Eminence is not the first, and with God's help, I hope not the last that I hope to refund."

The improvement in the Raina family's financial situation was short-lived. It appeared that for every step the family moved ahead, two steps back were sure to follow.

At the beginning of April, Mary and Ralph reported to the sanatorium for routine x-rays, where it was discovered that they were both afflicted with tuberculosis. They were instructed to report for admission to the sanatorium. Fortunately, they were able to obtain a leave of absence from their positions in the Civil Service. On a beautiful morning in spring, their mother accompanied them to catch a streetcar en route to the sanatorium.

Dominic wrote immediately to Reverend John A. MacDonald of the Catholic Family Welfare Bureau to acquaint him of this latest setback. His letter read in part:

"With the present I must give you the unpleasant news that both Ralph and Mary had to give up their jobs (we hope temporarily) to enter the Royal Ottawa Sanatorium. Clara is there for about two years now, with no improvement in sight. Both self and wife accept humbly those hard crosses from the hands of God, but those human beings guilty of imposing those crosses on us will have some terrible accounts to give some day to the Divine Justice."

During the long years that Clara had been confined to the sanatorium she wrote lengthy letters to her family, and she was visited regularly by her parents and by those of her siblings who had attained the age required for visiting privileges. She was an optimistic patient and had great faith in an eventual recovery. The greatest tribulation of her years in the sanatorium was at being denied the joy of companionship with her older sister and brother, and in not being able to watch the younger ones develop and grow.

Clara had been permitted to spend a day at home on only two or three occasions since her admission to the sanatorium. The only time she was able to enjoy her younger brothers was on the rare occasions when they were brought to the grounds of the sanatorium by the older members of the family. They were permitted to stand on the grounds beneath Clara's window, and she was able to lean over the sill to laugh and talk with them, and to observe how much they had grown since she had last seen them.

On one occasion, Clara mailed her little brother Billy an Easter card because she had been his sponsor at Baptism and he held a special spot in her heart. When she arrived home for the Easter holiday, Billy ran to show the "visiting lady" the Easter card. He told her, with pride, that he had got it from his big sister who was in the hospital. Clara was swept with feelings of joy, mingled with feelings of sorrow. Delighted to know that Billy was so pleased with the card, she was shattered to realize that he did not recognize her as the beloved sister who had sent it. The tuberculosis, and the consequent segregation from her family, had robbed Clara of a very important part of family life that could never be regained.

Clara always presented a happy face to the world, and she never let her mother know of her longings to be better. The children remained united in their resolve never to worry their mother. Clara's greatest hope, and one for which she prayed constantly, was that none of her brothers or sister would ever again succomb to tuberculosis and need to be hospitalized. She was saddened to learn that Mary and Ralph had contracted the disease and were scheduled to be admitted to the sanatorium.

The condition of Clara's lungs had slowly deteriorated in spite of all the doctors' efforts to restore her to health. In an effort to control the further spread of the disease, Clara had undergone a thoracoplasty, in which three ribs had been shortened. Such an operation was used in order to effect a permanent collapse of the diseased portion of the lung. It was performed in those cases where the patient, because of adhesions, was unable to be given pneumotherapy — a less drastic, and temporary, collapse of the lung.

During that summer, a member of the Royal Canadian Mounted Police called on Dominic and Elizabeth in an unofficial capacity. He was interested in the welfare of their family, and wondered how they were getting along. He expressed amazement at the fact that they had continued to be practicing Catholics, and commented that they must indeed be crazy to remain faithful to their church. Elizabeth replied that God had been generous in many ways, and had given all family members the strength to bear the trials they had encountered. But the policeman replied that he was not convinced that even God had been good to them.

During the late fall of 1943, Mary was permitted to return home, on the understanding that she would continue "the cure" there, by remaining in bed upstairs. The shadow on her lung appeared to be remaining stationary, but several additional months of bed rest were prescribed as a precautionary measure before she could be permitted to return to work.

On December 3, 1943, Elizabeth gave birth to Margaret Anne, the last of the Raina children. Anne was a delightful little girl, and a welcome change in the family, preceded as she was by five brothers. Her father was enabled, by means of the thrifty saving of a small portion of his salary, to pay the expenses of her birth.

Disaster struck another member of the family during the winter of 1943-44. Four-year-old Billy appeared to be listless and unwell. Whereas he had always been an energetic child, and had spent many happy hours playing outdoors in the snow with his six-year-old brother Jimmy, he now wanted to spend most of his time sleeping. During Mary's bed rest at home upstairs, Billy was permitted to take the daily paper up to her each evening, and to stay for a brief visit. On one particular clear winter evening, as he looked out into the night from the window of Mary's room, he asked her what the stars were for. Mary explained that they were little lanterns that God lit up each evening and hung in the sky. Billy said that he wanted to go up to heaven, so that he could help God to light all the little lanterns. As Mary looked at her little brother's smiling face, she experienced a strange feeling of foreboding.

Billy's listlessness appeared to become more pronounced, and he started to complain of pain in the back of his neck. Elizabeth took him to the doctor on several occasions. After repeated failures to diagnose an illness, the doctor admitted Billy to the hospital for more thorough testing. The tests failed to reveal a problem, and Billy was discharged. Elizabeth was advised to ignore her little son's complaints, with the explanation that they were probably caused by a bid for attention in view of the recent arrival of a new baby into the home. Elizabeth continued to worry. She felt that she had enough experience to know when a child was ill or merely spoiled. Her fears proved to be justified. One spring morning Billy lapsed into unconsciousness and was rushed to the hospital. Too late, he was diagnosed as having tuberculosis meningitis.

On May 19, 1944, dearly-loved William Paul (Billy) Raina passed away. As six-year-old Jimmy studied the body of his little brother and playmate laid out in his coffin at home, he experienced his first conscious awareness of death, accompanied by pain such as he had never known before.

Billy's remains were laid to rest near those of his brother Johnny in the cemetery of St. Thomas Aquinas at Billings Bridge, Ontario.

During the summer of 1944, Ralph was discharged from the sanatorium, and Mary was permitted to discontinue bed rest at home. After routine examinations at the sanatorium, both the patients were recorded as having arrested cases of pulmonary tuberculosis and were permitted to return to their jobs in the government.

No sooner had Ralph and Mary settled back into a working routine, when George again became affected with a recurrence of tuberculosis. Once again, he was confined to bed at home.

Dominic mailed a letter to Monsieur le Curé Jules Michaud informing him of Billy's death, and the continued illness of members of the family. The letter was ignored.

On November 23, 1944, Dominic wrote, once again, to His Eminence Cardinal Villeneuve. His letter read, in part:

"Lest we forget:

Today is the tenth anniversary of my kidnapping by the Laurentian Gestapo. Though ten years old, the whole affair is of yesterday. The reactionary forces, on their last legs, are still trying to prevent a new and better Social Order to become a fact.

. . . Repeating all my former statements on this, the tenth anniversary of my kidnapping, I would like to repeat also that I consider myself and family simply "Mister Average Canadian Citizen;" no more, no less, with full right to be protected against criminals, etc., even if said criminals happen to be members of the Catholic Clergy of Quebec."

Clara Raina enjoying her young brothers on a day's leave from the Royal Ottawa Sanatorium, 1943. Back Row - Nicky, George, Clara, Louis. Front Row - Billy, Jimmy. Taken at Billings Bridge, Ontario.

Summmer 1946 - Billings Bridge, Ontario. Back Row - Nicky, Mary, Clara, Jimmy. Front Row - Elizabeth, Anne, Dominic.

CHAPTER XVII

VISITS TO ST. MARC

"Far better it is to dare mighty things, to win glorious triumphs, even though checkered by failure, than to take rank with those poor spirits who neither enjoy much nor suffer much, because they live in the grey twilight that knows neither victory nor defeat." Theodore Roosevelt.

Although Dominic and Elizabeth had acquainted His Excellency Bishop Desmarais of Amos, by means of numerous letters, with the wrongs inflicted on their family by Monsieur le Curé Jules Michaud, His Excellency had failed to respond.

Suspecting that the true facts of the case had been misrepresented to His Excellency by both civil and religious authorities of Amos, Dominic and Elizabeth felt that a personal visit to the bishop was indicated.

The matter was thoroughly discussed within the family circle. Ultimately, it was decided that Elizabeth and Mary would return to the Village of St. Marc de Figuery.

They left Ottawa by bus on the morning of August 26, 1945, with feelings of eagerness mixed with feelings of trepidation. Elizabeth decided that it might be prudent not to notify Monsieur le Curé Jules Michaud of her presence at St. Marc, at least until after the authorities in Amos had been approached.

In the late twilight of that day the bus came to a stop in front of the old familiar store of Napoléon Doucet of St. Marc de Figuery. Eagerly, Elizabeth and Mary arose from their seats to peer into the dusky evening. Faintly visible were the outlines of passengers preparing to enter the bus. Hoping to meet some of their old friends among them, Elizabeth and Mary grabbed their bags and walked down the aisle, to come face to face with Monsieur le Curé himself, who was boarding the bus.

"Madame Raina! Mary?" exclaimed and questioned the priest, staring at them in obvious incredulity. Elizabeth and Mary did not respond. They stepped from the bus and looked about them to note the changes time had wrought in the Village of St. Marc. Other than the favourable additions of a co-operative store and better roads, the changes were few.

Throughout their visit at St. Marc, Elizabeth and Mary were guests of the Laroche family. They were among the friends who had remained their loyal allies throughout the passing years, and who had kept them informed of activities at the council meetings after their departure.

On Tuesday, August 28, Elizabeth and Mary went into the Town of Amos. They walked along the streets where, as beggars, they had so often walked before. The Church of Ste. Thérèse still appeared as great and as impressive as in the days gone by, and the evidences of Catholicism were very marked within the town.

Elizabeth had surprisingly little difficulty in obtaining an audience with His Excellency Bishop Desmarais of Amos. Unfortunately, she soon suspected, by the Bishop's reaction to her visit, that he was far more interested in the concealment of the case than he was in its exposition.

As she became aware of that fact, Elizabeth firmly refused to leave the palace without first being permitted to present her case in the presence of Monsieur le Curé Jules Michaud. What a strange coincidence! After considerable evasion, the bishop reluctantly withdrew to beckon in the priest, who was in a nearby room and readily available.

Nervously, in a final attempt to hide his guilt under the pretense of ignorance, Monsieur le Curé asked Elizabeth whether the family had received the money for the property they had owned at St. Marc. He informed her that there were at least five hundred dollars intended for them.

"No!" replied Elizabeth. She strongly suspected that the priest was, himself, responsible for the retention of the money. She knew, also, that if the money had been transmitted to Dominic when the family was destitute, it might have done much toward preventing tuberculosis and death from invading the home.

Sheepishly, as he realized the weakness of denials and contrary to his usual custom, the priest admitted the charges laid against him. He accepted the numerous accusations!

His Excellency Bishop Desmarais could no longer deny the truth of Elizabeth's statements. As he became aware of the magnitude of the wrongs committed by the priest, he rose in the mightiness of his power to defend Monsieur le Curé Michaud. With the protest that the priest's acknowledged acts had been committed in his capacity as man, and not in his capacity as priest, the bishop dismissed the whole affair, explaining that it did not come under his jurisdiction.

On hearing the words raised in his defence, Monsieur le Curé confirmed that he had, indeed, done everything in the name of Alphonse Boutin of the school board.

The bishop asked Elizabeth whether she and Dominic would be willing to return to St. Marc de Figuery in the event that their property should be returned to them. Elizabeth replied that it would be impossible for her to bring her children back on stretchers, but that if the property was returned they would sell it and settle where they wished.

Elizabeth next visited Dr. Marcel Sarazin, in an endeavour to ascertain under whose orders he had so unceremoniously presented himself at the jail of Amos on November 23, 1934, to declare Dominic one hundred percent insane.

The doctor protested that it had happened so long ago that he could no longer remember. Since the Raina case had attained notoriety around Amos, it was surprising that the doctor could forget the role he had played.

Elizabeth and Mary returned to the Village of St. Marc with the intention of calling on Napoléon Doucet, the ex-mayor. Unfortunately, the man was absent from home at the time, but they were able to have a visit with Madame Doucet. In the course of their conversation, Madame Doucet asked whether the family had received the money for their property, explaining that the money had been put aside for them, and expressing surprise on learning that they had not received it.

Elizabeth and Mary paid a final official visit at St. Marc de Figuery, by calling at the presbytery of Monsieur le Curé.

Agitatedly, the priest dashed for his code book. Emphatically, Elizabeth refused to look at that volume, now much used and worn with age. Because of the priest's unwillingness to discuss sensibly the matter of their case, the visit proved to be brief. As Elizabeth and Mary walked out of the door, Mary turned and said to the priest, "Father, I promise that some day I will publish a book on our case and you shall be the most important person in it!"

"You write a book!" jeered the priest. With his mocking laughter ringing in their ears, Elizabeth and Mary walked away from the leader of St. Marc.

Before leaving the Abitibi, Elizabeth and Mary were invited by Antoine Lantagne, who had bought their property from the Municipality of St. Marc, to re-enter the house where they had passed such unforgettable years. Although the house had been moved and almost totally rebuilt since it had been vacated by the Raina family, Elizabeth and Mary were touched to note that their favourite crucifix hung on the wall where the family had placed it so many years ago.

They returned to Billings Bridge on September 4, to report all that had transpired to their interested family.

As Dominic learned of the futility of their visit to St. Marc, he decided to himself present his case before the haughty Bishop of Amos. Because he was uncomfortably aware of the possible dangers of this course of action, he took Ralph along as a witness to anything that might transpire. They left together for St. Marc de Figuery on September 14.

At approximately eleven-thirty o'clock a.m. on the following day, encourged by the voluntary presence of Ralph and several former neighbours of St. Marc, Dominic visited His Excellency, the unsuspecting Bishop Desmarais of Amos.

As Bishop Desmarais listened with reluctance to Dominic's charges, he raised his voice to a menacing pitch and threatened, "They got you once and they can get you again!"

Years rolled away as Dominic remembered the nearby jail of Amos and the abuse at the asylum at Mastaï. He knew that he stood in grave danger of a repetition of those experiences. He lost his composure and prepared to withdraw into the corridor.

At that crucial moment, Ralph arose to angrily assure the threatening Bishop of Amos that merely because the so-called "they" had succeeeded in abducting his father once, there was no reason to believe that "they" could do so again. He pointed out to the bishop that "they" would now have to contend with him and his brothers and sisters, all of whom were growing up.

Met with that rebuff, His Excellency calmed down and reluctantly displayed a certain willingness to listen to suggestions. Dominic expressed a wish that a public meeting of the Municipal Council of St. Marc de Figuery be called for the following Monday. He asked that a delegation of three priests be in attendance there. After considering Dominic's suggestions for a few minutes, His Excellency replied, "We will go."

Dominic and Ralph returned to St. Marc de Figuery with renewed hope. Dominic was confident that, if honestly conducted, the meeting could result in the settlement of a long and wearisome battle and the clearance of his name from the unjust stigma of insanity.

On the afternoon of September 17, while resting in an upstairs bedroom at Elzéar Laroche's home, Dominic was awakened from his nap by his host. He was informed that Monsieur le Curé Jules Michaud had called and wished to see him. Dominic responded with feelings of suspicion mixed with feelings of incredulity. It had always been Dominic who had approached the priest. The roles now appeared to be reversed.

"We are going to the meeting," answered Monsieur le Curé when the two men came face to face. The priest noted, with unconcealed disapproval, Ralph's presence in the room and his intention to accompany his father.

Dominic was gratified that the bishop had kept his promise. He expected to be driven to the Village of St. Marc, where he assumed that His Excellency and the councillors were already gathered. He became uneasy when Monsieur le Curé took the road that led to Amos. No explanation as to their destination could Dominic derive from the uncommunicative chauffeur!

Dominic rode in tense silence, until the journey terminated at the door of the bishop's residence.

With that air of secretiveness and confident authority which Dominic had come to recognize in certain members of the clergy, he was conducted to a room in the building. Four men garbed in clerical robes, and all personally unknown to him, were assembled there. The atmosphere was solemn. One man was seated at a desk, and appeared prepared to record any statements.

In the tenseness of the atmosphere, and without a word of explanation, Dominic was motioned to be seated on a single vacant chair before that assembled group of clergy. Reluctantly, after a reassuring glance from Ralph who was instructed to remain out in the hall, he acquiesced.

Dominic was put under oath. He promised to tell the truth, the whole truth, and nothing but the truth. Though taken unprepared, he was able to reply to the countless questions that were hurled at him for approximately thirty minutes. The solemn system of interrogation having been carried out to their satisfaction, the clergy then instructed the defendent to leave the room so that the procedure might be repeated on Ralph. Monsieur le Curé Jules Michaud was the third, and last, man to be heard in the strange courtroom.

The trio then drove back to the Village of St. Marc de Figuery.

Was this unconventional system of interrogation the long-awaited Ecclesiastical Tribunal? If so, the verdict was never revealed to the Raina family.

On Dominic's return to Billings Bridge, he and Elizabeth rediscussed the case and all the efforts they had made over the years to obtain justice. Together, they agreed that in the continued battle of the pen lay their only hope of redress. Although the letters they had written now numbered several hundred, both the civil and religious authorities still counselled, "Why don't you go home and write us the facts?"

In accordance with those repeated instructions, Dominic dispatched a letter, dated September 22, to His Excellency Bishop Desmarais of Amos. He summarized, in the following words, the visit they had had together the previous week:

"On Monday, September 17, 1945, at four o'clock p.m. while staying at Elzéar Laroche at Figuery, I was called and taken by surprise to appear before a board of members of the clergy at your residence in Amos, P.Q. No chance was given me to take along any advisor. There, I was put under oath and I had to answer questions. While I can produce full and complete evidence to corroborate my statements, when asked to give my specific charges against le Curé Jules Michaud of Figuery, I was not prepared to completely answer the questions.

Now returned home, and after consulting with my wife, co-partner in my sufferings, I am sending you my charges. Please incorporate them with my other statements given under oath before the Board of Clergy at your residence on Monday, September 17th, 1945.

Here are my charges:

I charge le Curé Jules Michaud, Parish Priest at Figuery near Amos, P.Q.

a) For badly deceiving my wife in obtaining her signature on November 23rd, 1934, at our home, to papers of a most serious nature, without giving her any explanation whatever about the nature of the contents.

b) For using all his influence amongst his parishioners to send me to the asylum at Mastaï near Quebec City as 100 percent insane.

c) For trying to keep me there, and doing his best to send me back after my discharge from said institution.

d) For using his influence with the ratepayers to take away and prevent the return to self and family of the home and property.

e) For causing untold physical and mental sufferings to self and family and badly impairing the family's health, I ask the sum of fifty thousand ($50,000) of lawful Canadian money, simply as part reparation, since all this world's money cannot repay in full the harm done to self and family.

Copy of the present will be sent by me to His Excellency the Apostolic Delegate and to His Eminence the Cardinal Villeneuve. With the hope that Your Excellency will act promptly, helping in so doing to alleviate my family's present sufferings.''

Dominic's reiteration of the facts fell on deaf ears and, once again, the bishop did not reply to his letter. Elizabeth resolved to join her husband in his charges, and mailed a letter to His Excellency as well, reminding the bishop of what he could not have failed to notice: Michaud had admitted to most of her charges in the August 28 interview. She said:

"Now about the weak defence of Father Michaud claiming of having done those things in the name of Alphonse Boutin. I believe I can prove to you the contrary, but supposing I was unable to do that, could any person do entirely illegal and criminal actions and get away with the pretext that those things were done under the order of a third party?''

On October 20, Dominic acquainted the new Prime Minister of Canada, the Honourable Louis St. Laurent, with the facts of his case. He emphasized to him the tragedies which had befallen his children as a result of the injustices they had suffered in the Province of Quebec.

On November 23, Dominic mailed a letter to His Holiness, Pope Pius XII in Rome. He had been advised to take that route by a provincial detective at Amos as far back as 1935, but he had hoped that such drastic measures would never be necessary. While an acknowledgement of his letter was received from the Postal Department, Vatican City, it did not result in action.

As time went on, Elizabeth's frustration at the bishop's reaction to her visit mounted. She again communicated with him through the mail, emphasizing that:

''. . . It not only shocked me, but it also gave me great sorrow, when my son, Ralph, after his return from Amos told me that Your Excellency intimidated my husband, reminding him that they got him once and they could get him again. Apparently you know then and you approve of this cruelty. Most certainly I do not approve that my son, Ralph, now twenty years of age, but only nine years old when those terrible things happened, was asked to take an oath of happenings while he was only nine years old. I was always anxious and still am ready for any kind of trial, but I want to take it upon myself to relate what took place.

Your Excellency excused himself that the reason he did not answer our letters was that you thought my husband was insane. Apparently you think the same of me since you do not answer me either. Now, if in your conscience you really believe my husband insane, it would be very wrong for anyone to ask an insane person to take an oath. I cannot understand why our clergy are so anxious to throw to the four winds all this filth which took place in a Catholic province and in which all guilty parties were priests or Catholics. I cannot understand why they make me write letters like this and waste my time, while they laugh at me, because for ten years they have kept what they stole.''

So that his position might be filled by a veteran of the Armed Forces, Dominic was honourably discharged from the staff at the Base Post Office in Ottawa at the end of December 1945. On his departure he received the very best of references, which read:

"To Whom it May Concern:

The bearer, Mr. D.A. Raina, has been an employee of this office since April, 1942, but unfortunately for him he has had no overseas service in the Armed Forces, and under the circumstances we are obliged to release him to provide a position for a returned soldier.

During his employment here Mr. Raina's services have been very satisfactory in every respect, and I have no hesitation in recommending him for any position of trust or responsibility to which he may be assigned''.

While there was nothing unusual about the wording of the reference, it was probably the first of its kind issued by a government department to a Canadian citizen previously declared one hundred percent insane.

During the winter of 1945-46, Dominic approached several lawyers, in both Ontario and Quebec. He hoped to locate one who could be persuaded to handle his case, even though he could not assure payment unless he was accorded redress.

Quite understandably, the uncertainty of Dominic's financial situation made them reluctant to spend the great amount of time that would be required to handle a case of such magnitude. Dominic kept His Excellency Bishop Desmarais informed of what was happening in the family. In a letter to the bishop during May of 1946, he stated:

"This week my three children of school age came home bringing the report of their Easter examinations to be signed by their parents. Before signing I read: Jimmy Raina, Grade Two, first in a class of eleven pupils. Dominic Raina, Grade Seven, first in a class of seven pupils. Louis Raina, Grade Eleven, at St. Patrick's College, Ottawa, first in a class of thirty-six pupils. It was the same story with my older children, not only at Ottawa but also at Figuery, near Amos, P.Q. With that I am not a braggart but if Your Excellency was in my shoes for a few days probably you could understand why my blood at times is not at the exact temperature that Your Excellency would like it to be . . .''

It was Dominic's firm belief that all children, not only his own, should be given the opportunity to develop their full potential. His inability to make this opportunity financially available to his children was a constant source of frustration to him, especially since they showed great promise, and since he had been unjustly deprived of the assets which might have ensured further intellectual development.

On May 9, 1946, Dominic received a discouraging letter from the Honourable John Diefenbaker, whom he had again approached with the hope of getting constructive advice. In it, he informed them, as he had done in the past when Dominic and Elizabeth had first approached him, that the time element was against them.

While time had worked to their disadvantage and their troubles were not over, Dominic and Elizabeth took note of the joys and blessings. They gratefully remembered those who had been helpful when they were in such dire straits. Through incessant struggle, and the co-operation of their children, they had been enabled to reimburse many of the people who had so generously contributed to their survival during their early days in Ottawa. They were also grateful to the priests who had sincerely wished to assist them in their attempts to obtain redress, but who were unable to carry out those wishes due to the restraining hands of their superiors.

Dominic and Anne Raina. Taken at Kemptville, Ontario, during the summer of 1947.

CHAPTER XVIII

DOMINIC'S LAST DAYS

"In one sense there is no death. The life of a soul on earth lasts beyond its departure. You will always feel that life touching yours, that voice speaking to you, that spirit looking out of other eyes, talking to you in the familiar things he touched, worked with, loved as familiar friends. He lives on in your life and in the lives of all others that knew him." Angelo Patri.

During the spring of 1947, Dominic and Elizabeth realized one of their fondest hopes — that of once again owning a home of their own. By means of parting with the last of their hard-earned savings they were enabled to pay the final instalment due on a farm which they had contracted to buy at Kemptville, Ontario.

Even though they once again owned a home, they never ceased to protest the loss of their other home at St. Marc de Figuery.

When the Raina family moved to Kemptville, Mary remained in Ottawa to continue working as a secretary for the federal government. She took up residence at Laurentian Terrace on Sussex Street. Laurentian Terrace was a hostel that had been built to accommodate the many young women flocking into Ottawa from all over the country during the war, to work for the Federal Government. It provided cheap accommodation, freedom of responsibility, and a great deal of fun, as new and lasting friendships were formed.

Mary enjoyed her new life. She also enjoyed going home to Kemptville on the weekends to be with her family. Like homing pigeons, the Raina children were always drawn back to the family roof. Perhaps it was because of the comfortable feelings of assurance that home was a place where they were always enveloped in love. Or, perhaps it was because home was such a stimulating place to be. Whatever the reason, it was from their parents and siblings that the children drew their strength.

A special joy to Mary, when she disembarked from the bus at the end of the laneway leading to the house, was to see that Jimmy and Anne were happily awaiting her arrival.

Dominic and Elizabeth had now explored all possible sources of law enforcement in Canada. They were appalled at the necessity of admitting that there was no justice to be found for their family anywhere in their supposedly democratic country. They questioned the effectiveness of a system of government where it was possible for such crimes to be perpetrated with impunity. They feared that unless there were vast improvements in the judicial system such wrongs could be repeated on other unsuspecting Canadian citizens. So that their trying experiences might not have been in vain, they resolved to throw the case wide open to the general public.

In order to accomplish that goal, Dominic wrote to Mr. John McLean, Editor of *The Ottawa Citizen,* on February 3, 1949. He gave him some of the details of his case and asked him to give it publicity.

A reply from Mr. McLean, dated February 8, 1949, reached him promptly. In it, Mr. McLean stated that he had never set eyes on such a weird case as that contained in the copies of Dominic's letters. He informed Dominic that he had written to His Excellency Bishop Desmarais of Amos, demanding that he challenge the accusations. He added that he was prepared to expose the case if it had merit, and asked for further evidence of Dominic's charges.

Any feelings of optimism that Dominic and Elizabeth might have felt on receipt of that letter were bitterly squelched on the transmission to them, by Mr. John McLean, of a copy of the bishop's reply to the letter he had written to him asking for information on the case. In flattering words, the bishop thanked Mr. McLean for his beautiful loyalty in contacting him, and congratulated him on his prudence. He went on to tell Mr. McLean that when he had arrived in Amos as its first bishop, in 1939, he received correspondence from Mr. Raina. He said that he had been advised by all those who knew him, both clergy and laity, to ignore him because he was an old boarder of the asylum at Mastaï, where he had been placed for just reasons and, once released, did not recover his sanity. He went on to inform Mr. McLean that he had organized an Ecclesiastical Tribunal for Mr. Raina two years previously, which he had attended with one of his sons. The conclusion of the tribunal was that they had nothing to do with his case.

The bishop ended his letter by saying that he had decided to ignore Mr. Raina's letters as being the wisest thing to do, and suggested that Mr. McLean reach his own conclusions.

Such blatant misrepresentation of the facts provoked Dominic to write a scathing missive to the Bishop of Amos, under date of March 7, 1949. In it, he emphasized that, "Your Excellency and myself stand as far apart in our views as the north from the south pole, and for that reason we should agree on one point: put our case before the eyes of the public."

Dominic felt that Bishop Desmarais' letter represented an attempt by the clergy to deal a death-blow to his integrity and good reputation. He was swept with feelings of hopelessness and impotence as he saw the evidence of power, so much greater than his own, wielded by dignitaries of the church. Dominic was aware that his many letters to authorities were not always kindly received. Yet, what alternatives were given him to speak in his defence when there was not a court in the whole Dominion of Canada prepared to give him a fair and open trial?

One of Dominic's last official letters in connection with his case was mailed to His Excellency Archbishop Roy of Quebec City. It was dated May 10, 1950, and read:

"I humbly beg to be excused if, for causes beyond my control, I am compelled to address the present as an open letter to Your Excellency. I understand that the Diocese of Amos is in the Ecclesiastical Province of the Archdiocese of Quebec and that Your Excellency is in charge of that jurisdiction. On February 12, 1949, the Bishop of Amos wrote a letter to the Editor of *The Ottawa Citizen* re myself. Copy of said letter goes with the present and that is a genuine sample of the references that the clergy of Quebec did spread about me during the past fifteen years without giving me the slightest chance to defend myself.

The bulk of contents of said letter of the Bishop of Amos is a complete distortion of facts and malicious to the extreme. Apparently said bishop is taking full advantage of the fact that a varnished lie from the lips of a bishop is more easily believed than the naked truth coming from the mouth of a poor man. I may humbly point out that almost three years ago, I did appeal to Your Excellency for a measure of justice. My pleas were completely ignored. If Your Excellency had acted then, probably the devilish letter from the hands of the Bishop of Amos would not have been written. Cardinal Villeneuve plainly stated that rich and poor alike have the right to the Ecclesiastical Tribunal. I asked for said tribunal for a period of fifteen years. Many times it was promised to me but never granted. I am still asking for it now and to be held well in the open, with the chance given to a representative of *The Ottawa Citizen* to be present. My farm of eighty-two acres, home and shelter for my family, lot thirty-nine, range three, Figuery, near Amos, stolen from me under the instructions of Father Jules Michaud in 1935, has not been returned so far. I have no objections if Your Excellency will mail a copy of this to *The Ottawa Citizen*."

A reply to the above letter, dated June 2, 1950, reached Dominic shortly afterwards. In it, he was advised that the competent tribunal to hear his petitions and discuss them would be the Tribunal of Amos or a Roman Dua, the Roman Rota. It was pointed out that the Tribunal of Quebec had no competence over people who did not belong to the Diocese of Quebec, but that recourse to Rome could be established through the Apostolic Delegate, if necessary.

Dominic was disappointed to learn that conditions had not improved at the asylum of Mastaï since he had been a patient in that institution. This was evidenced by an editorial which had appeared in *The Ottawa Citizen* of April 24, 1950. It read:

"Quebec Mental Hospitals"

The Quebec Minister of Health, Mr. Paquette, can scarcely leave the question of investigating the death of a patient of a mental hospital at Quebec City where his statement has put it. The patient, Arthur Paré, has died as a result of a shocking incident in which, according to evidence given in court, two members of the staff assaulted him in a brutal and revolting manner. Since the two guards are facing manslaughter charges, there will be no disposition to prejudge the case. The evidence, as Judge Achille Pettigrew, who presided at the preliminary hearing has said, is "formidable", and the case will go to the criminal assizes.

Mr. Paquette, meanwhile, has launched an inquiry into the incident, adding that it will be concerned only with the death of the patient and "not with the administration and conditions at the hospital." Mr. Paquette appears to have matters twisted. The question of responsibility for the death of the patient is now a matter of court decision and the crime (if any) will be punished properly. But according to the autopsy the patient died of injuries which included a fractured nose, fractured ribs and breastbone, and many other fractures and injuries. In other words, the patient was beaten to death.

Mr. Paquette's concern should be solely with the question how such a terrible thing could happen in an institution under his control and direction. It may be wise for the Quebec government to await the outcome of the trial of the two attendants before conducting its own enquiry, to avoid the risk of prejudicing the trial. But the least M. Paquette can do is to start looking into the conditions in which such a revolting incident as that reported from Quebec City is allowed to take place.''

The spectre of tuberculosis had continued to haunt the Raina family through the late 'forties. Clara had suffered through a second thoracoplasty, and Ralph had been readmitted to the sanatorium. George had again become infected, and this time a home cure would not suffice, so he had been admitted as well. But, when the family received word that Dominic, himself, had fallen prey to the dreaded disease they were incredulous. Dominic was informed of his illness on July 13, 1950, after a routine chest x-ray at the Royal Ottawa Sanatorium.

To witness a person of great strength and presence fall into decline, whether that person be a statesman, teacher or parent, produces a profound emotional reaction in those most closely involved with that person.

After her initial natural reluctance to accept that latest blow, Elizabeth mustered all her strength to comfort her husband, and to reassure her children that all was not yet lost.

In early September, Dominic was admitted to the Kingston Sanatorium, on the understanding that as soon as a bed became available at the overcrowded Ottawa Sanatorium, he would be transferred there so that he might be with those of his children who were patients in the hospital.

When the promised transfer took place, on October 13, Ralph, Clara, and George welcomed their father to the Royal Ottawa Sanatorium with compassion and encouragement. Dominic was gratified to learn that he would be sharing a room with his son George.

The presence of his father in his room occurred at a providential time for George. Although George had had three thoracoplasties since his admission to the sanatorium, in an attempt to halt the relentless progress of his disease, he was scheduled for a fourth one on November 2. This particular operation brought the total number of ribs involved to twelve. It was a comfort to George that his father could be with him during that crucial period.

George had no sooner recovered from his operation, when Ralph was scheduled for a similar one. He now had a successful thoracoplasty on one lung, and an established pneumothorax on the other.

Even as the ravaging disease was playing havoc with their bodies, both boys were preparing diligently for the day when they would leave the sanatorium and need to be self-supporting.

George was given an opportunity to learn the watch repair trade, to which he applied himself with great enthusiasm and at which he became highly skilled.

Ralph was doing leatherwork. He hoped to go into business for himself after his recovery, and had already saved a tidy nest egg from the profits he had made from the sale of attractively tooled purses and wallets. He was also studying the pros and cons of various businesses. What Ralph lacked in capital, he planned to make up in hard work and sacrifice. He had so very much to prove, both to himself and to the world, but...it was a time of self-made men!

Between visiting the members of the family who were ill in the hospital, and filling the role of both mother and father to the young children at home, Elizabeth had little time to dwell on the reverses in the family. With her husband and three of her children in the sanatorium, and Mary living in Ottawa, the changes in the atmosphere of the house were palpable. For the sakes of all those who depended on her, Elizabeth presented a brave and cheerful front. There was no other choice! She could not afford the luxury of feeling sorry for herself!

At the beginning of 1951, Ralph and George were both discharged from the sanatorium as cases of arrested tuberculosis. The two boys proceeded to carve out their futures. Ralph pursued his dream by venturing into the retail clothing business. Using the family home at Kemptville as his base of operation, he began the long and rocky road to success by peddling, from door to door, work clothes to local farmers. George obtained employment as a watch repairman at a prominent Ottawa jewellery store.

At around that same time, twenty-year-old Louis, and sixteen-year-old Nick enlisted in the Royal Canadian Air Force and left home to report to their respective bases.

Because Dominic's condition was not improving at the sanatorium, he begged to be given an opportunity to try the rest cure at home. He was granted that privilege on July 28, 1951. Elizabeth transformed the living-room into a bedroom for her patient, so that he could more readily enjoy the family than would have been possible were he segregated away upstairs. It also gave the two youngest members, Jimmy and Anne, an opportunity to visit their father more often, and to store up treasured memories for the day when they would no longer have him.

Jimmy felt that the period preceding his father's death was a time of beautiful family unity. To witness the gradual and peaceful dying process taking place within his home, and the courage with which his father faced his last days, convinced Jimmy that death, like life, had a singular beauty and that it was a natural process not to be feared.

Anne was sensitive to the interaction of the various older members of the family towards her father's illness. Their calm acceptance of what was happening reassured her. From her dying father she learned that death can be faced with courage, peace, and a radiant smile. She learned the meaning of compassion and sensitivity in the humble home of her childhood.

With Dominic and Clara suffering from tuberculosis, Mary considered herself fortunate that she had not experienced any further recurrence of the disease. She had been working for several years as an executive secretary for a senior official of the federal government and was confident that she had conquered tuberculosis for all time, and that her life would continue on an even keel. Her optimism proved to be premature.

On a January evening in 1952, as Mary was leaving the apartment of a friend, she laughed at a humorous remark made by her hostess. With her laughter came a frightening gush of blood. Mary was rushed to the Ottawa Civic Hospital with a massive lung hemorrhage.

The nurse in charge at the hospital asked Mary for a phone number at which her next-of-kin could be notified of her condition. Elizabeth's health was already being overtaxed caring for Dominic, whose health was rapidly deteriorating. Mary felt that her mother did not need an added worry, and begged that the news of her situation be kept from her mother until the following day when her condition had stabilized. But, contrary to Mary's expressed wish, her mother was notified that evening of her daughter's admission to the hospital. Elizabeth arrived early the next morning to accompany Mary on her transfer to the Royal Ottawa Sanatorium.

Raised in the school of hard knocks, Mary accepted that, no matter where she went, she could never escape the tentacles of the ubiquitous case. Tuberculosis, which had invaded the family home during the period when the children had been forced to live in a continued state of semi-starvation, and had no resources with which to combat it, had never been sucessfully eradicated. It appeared that, even after the family's financial situation had improved, the aftermath of that period resulted in continued reinfection among members of the family through contact with each other.

Mary determinedly set about to regain her health, helped and encouraged by assurances that her job in the federal government would be awaiting her return. Mary was fortunate in that the use of a new wonder drug, streptomycin, had only recently been implemented in the battle against tuberculosis. Its impact on her health was remarkable.

No doubt the hardest hit of all had been Clara. She had now been in the sanatorium for eleven consecutive years, in addition to an earlier confinement there and nearly a year of bed rest at home. Thirteen years of Clara's youth had been lost to tuberculosis. Her condition had gradually deteriorated over the years, but her faith in an eventual recovery had never been diminished. After all other treatments had been tried, and failed, injections of streptomycin proved to be her salvation. Confined to bed in separate buildings of the sanatorium, the two sisters kept in touch by a constant transmission of letters and notes back and forth.

Although the Raina children had faced many tragedies together, they had also shared much laughter and companionship. They were the very best of friends. While they might not have chosen some of the circumstances of their childhood, not having been given a choice in the matter of their fate, they had come to consider many other lives dull in comparison to their own. That was the silver lining in the cloud.

Dominic suspected that he might not recover from his illness. He was concerned about the welfare of his younger dependent children at home. He regretted that thirteen-year-old Jimmy, his youngest son, might be fatherless at an age when he would most need paternal guidance. He was determined to enjoy his wife and children to the utmost while he was still around. He was a most gentle and co-operative patient, and an atmosphere of peace was to be felt throughout the home.

As Dominic's conditon gradually worsened, Ralph and Elizabeth shared the burden of his care. He was given round-the-clock attention because of his frequent hemorrhages. It was to Ralph's great credit that, due to his kind and expert assistance in the care of the patient and at great risk to his own health, his father was able to spend his final days at home.

There came a time when Dominic's condition appeared to be critical, and his absent children were summoned home. Louis and Nick were granted compassionate leave from their respective stations in the Royal Canadian Air Force. George arrived from Ottawa. Mary and Clara were granted a two-day pass from the sanatorium.

Unfortunately, when Ralph arrived at the sanatorium to collect his two sisters, Mary was flat on her back in bed and her patient pass had been cancelled. Mary had started spitting blood that morning and, fearing that she was a candidate for another hemorrhage, the doctor on duty ordered her to remain in bed. Clara was driven home to see her father, while Mary was detained in the hospital.

Mary was determined to visit her father before he died. She knew that she would find a way to do so! Her roommate promised that she would arrange to have her husband drive Mary to Kemptville, should she find a way to leave the hospital. Mary had a plan. While she was normally a co-operative patient, this was quite literally a matter of life and death. Mary sneaked out of bed and donned her street clothes under her night-gown, so that she would be prepared for a quick getaway. She then crawled back under the covers. When the evening staff arrived to replace those who had been on day duty, Mary asked the oncoming doctor for permission to visit her dying father. Unaware of her threatened hemor-rhage, because he had not yet had an opportunity to familiarize himself with what had transpired on the ward during the day, the doctor granted his permission.

Mary rushed to her room, grabbed her coat and hat, met her waiting chauffeur downstairs at the door, and was driven to Kemptville, some fifty kilometres away. When she entered the doorway of her home, wearing a "Well, here I am" look upon her face, the stunned reaction of all the members of her family was gratifying.

Even more gratifying, was the joy with which her father received the visit of his eldest daughter, and the last of the children to arrive at his bedside.

During Mary's last visit alone with her father, he told her that he was bequeathing to her all his correspondence on the case, noting that it did not obligate her to anything, and that she was free to either retain, or dispose of it as she wished. Mary assured her father that it would always be her most treasured possession.

Mary understood that her father's greatest hope had always been to lavish the good things of life upon his family, and that his inability to fulfil that wish had pained him greatly. Through his life he had demon-strated his conviction that persons or things must be sacrificed for the common good of society as a whole, if a situation warranted such a sacrifice. As Mary said her last good-bye to her father she was convinced that she was in the presence of greatness.

On March 27, 1952, Dominic knew that time was running out for him. He asked for stationery on which to draw up a brief will. With shaky fingers, and in handwriting that contrasted sharply with the bold firm strokes of healthier and happier days, he wrote:

"I hereby appoint my wife, Mrs. Elizabeth Raina, to be the sole administratrix of my estate, with the exception of my correspondence and records which are to be turned over to my oldest daughter, Mary Elizabeth Raina".

During his final days, Dominic told Elizabeth that he continued to believe in God and justice, and that he was prepared to forgive those who had so greatly wronged him. He assured her that his beliefs in the principles of the Holy Catholic Church remained strong. He counselled her not to worry unduly over the children, because he felt confident that they would all turn out alright. He expressed deep gratitude for her unfailing support throughout their years together, and at the care she had so lovingly bestowed on him during his illness. He promised to ask God to bring health and prosperity to his family.

Dominic Raina passed away on April 20, 1952, after having received the Last Rites of the Holy Catholic Church. Thus, the curtain fell on a strong and forceful man, whose refusal to compromise his principles led to such incredible repercussions.

As his children stood around his coffin, they remembered the words their father had so often spoken to them when they were all together:

"Remember always, my children, you may be robbed of your home, your honour, and your country, but the things you have learned can never be stolen."

EPILOGUE

Monsieur le Curé Jules Michaud of St. Marc de Figuery, in the Province of Quebec, eventually met with a violent death in an automobile accident.

James Raina was admitted to the Royal Ottawa Sanatorium with minimal tuberculosis shortly after his father's death. Mary and Clara Raina were both discharged from the sanatorium in November of 1952 with cases of arrested tuberculosis. James was discharged within a year's time of his admission. Never again, did tuberculosis afflict any members of the Raina family.

The years passed.

All the children married and had families of their own.

As they had vowed in their childhood, the Raina children had all risen, by their own efforts, high above their early circumstances and had attained success.

Mary continued at her job in the Federal Government until she started her family, when she elected to stay at home with her children. She became active in the local Parent-Teachers' Association and the Social Action Committee of her church. She realized her life-long dream, when she knew that her book "We Have Written," written as a tribute to her parents, was prepared to roll off the press.

Ralph became a successful businessman in Kemptville, where he served as mayor for three terms. He was also active, on a volunteer basis, in provincial and federal politics.

Clara became an industrious housewife, unhindered by the thirteen years she had spent in bed as a victim of tuberculosis. She was a positive contribution to her husband and son.

On October 2, 1953, Louis won the Honour Scroll in his class upon his graduation from the Officers' Navigation Course with the Royal Canadian Air Force. He was awarded the centennial medal for community services to Canada during Canada's centennial year.

George established a watch repair trade, utilizing skills he had first acquired while a patient in the sanatorium. He died a tragic death through drowning in 1986.

Dominic, Junior, retired from the the Royal Canadian Air Force at an early age. He became a successful salesman for a company which sold aluminum doors and windows, eventually establishing his own business.

James owns a successful drapery business in Ottawa. He is an active member of the Rotary Club. His great love of sports, encouraged by his father when he was alive, has continued through the years.

Anne works in Management and Planning for National and International organizations. She is public-spirited and instructs on a volunteer basis for the Christopher Leadership Course – a course in leadership through effective speaking.

In the twilight of her years, Elizabeth lived in comfort in Kemptville, Ontario.

That wonderful mother, who gave so much to her husband and children, and who was such a positive inspiration to all those who had the good fortune to know her, enjoyed her many grandchildren as much as she had enjoyed her children before them. She passed away suddenly with a massive coronary on October 31, 1979.

As the Raina family paid their final respects to a wonderful mother and a great lady, they were overwhelmed by the enormity of their personal loss.

The Raina family never did receive redress of any kind for the injustices rendered them in the Province of Quebec.

While the children never became reconciled to the fact that justice had been denied their family, or that their parents had never been accorded a fair trial and the consequent opportunity to defend their case, they were able to look back on it more objectively. They realized that many of the people to whom their parents had gone for help in obtaining redress were indeed powerless to help them. They understood that their parents had had to grab at any straw, when those whose responsibility it was to obtain justice for them refused to become involved.

A great factor responsible for the case attaining such magnitude was due to the unrestrained power of one single individual, Monsieur le Curé Jules Michaud, parish priest at St. Marc de Figuery, and because of Dominic Raina's refusal to submit to such dictatorship. The failure of the priest's superiors to curb that power, or to even acknowledge that a problem existed, was directly responsible for the persecution of the

Raina family. The hierarchy of the Holy Catholic Church must bear the lion's share of the guilt for the part it played in the cover-up of the case.

But it must be recognized that the denial of justice to the family can also be blamed on those political leaders in Quebec who condoned and protected the actions of the clergy of the province, and refused to recognize a distinction between church and state. Finally, blame can also be placed on the Canadian judicial system, which did not authorize the federal authorities to interfere in the maladministration of justice in the Province of Quebec.

With the exception of Louis Raina, who settled in Red Deer, Alberta, on his retirement from the Air Force, the Raina children all live in the Ottawa area.

They continue to enjoy each other as much today as they did during the days of their childhood, when all they had was each other, and when such unbreakable bonds were forged among them.

Surviving Family Members – Taken in 1985. Back Row: From left to right – Mary, Clara, Louis, Dominic Jr., James. Front Row: Ralph, George, Anne.